D0934773

EPIRUS

ON THE LAKE AT IOANNINA

by the same author

The Ionian Islands . Majorca . Ibiza and Minorca

EPIRUS

Arthur Foss

LONDON **Faber** BOSTON

FOR

Kenneth Johnstone and Ian Scott-Kilvert

First published in 1978
by Faber and Faber Limited
3 Queen Square London WC1
Printed in Great Britain by
Latimer Trend & Company Ltd
Plymouth
All rights reserved
© 1978 Arthur Foss

*British Library Cataloguing
in Publication Data*
Foss, Arthur
  Epirus
  1. Epirus – Description and
    Travel   I. Title
914.95'3'047   DF901.E6
ISBN 0-571-10488-6

Contents

Illustrations

Maps

Introduction

Epirus lies east of Corfu between the Ionian Sea and the high Pindus, the rugged central backbone of mainland Greece. The province, 3,553 square miles (8,698 square kilometres) in size, is as large as Kent, Surrey and Sussex. It is a land of limestone mountain ranges, rushing rivers, gorges and upland valleys, of Greek and Roman antiquities, Byzantine churches and ruined mosques and minarets. Because of its remoteness from the main lines of communication, it has been the home of much which before the 1939–45 war was most traditional in the Greek countryside.

The splendours and rigours of Epirus with its rich diversity of peoples were first introduced to the sophisticated world in Canto the Second of *Childe Harold's Pilgrimage*, published in 1812, in which Lord Byron described his journey through Epirus from Preveza to Albanian Tepeleni, where Ali Pasha and his court were then in residence. A number of adventurous and literate travellers quickly followed in the poet's wake, at a time when the normal itinerary of the Grand Tour had become impossible on account of the Napoleonic Wars, and in due course wrote lively accounts of their experiences. They included, among others, Dr, later Sir Henry Holland, who became a physician-inordinary to Queen Victoria, the Rev. Thomas Smart Hughes, a good classical scholar, and C. R. Cockerell, later a Royal Academician. Other published accounts included those by John Cam Hobhouse, who had been Byron's travelling companion in 1809, and by Lt-Colonel W. R. Leake, who was British Resident in Ioannina when Byron and Hobhouse rode through and whose *Travels in Northern Greece*, published in 1835, still contains some of the best descriptions yet written of the peoples, monuments

11

and landscapes of Epirus. These travellers were nearly all well versed in the classics and took obvious pleasure in trying to identify the whereabouts of Dodona, the most ancient of the Greek oracles, and in reconciling what they saw with the descriptions of Strabo, Polybius and other ancient geographers and poets. Even Disraeli and Gladstone were visitors—a rare distinction for so remote a corner of the Mediterranean.

Before the Peloponnesian Wars, Epirus merely meant 'the mainland', a little-known area inhabited by barbarians who were outside the Hellenic pale, although they probably spoke a Greek dialect. By the time that Olympias, a princess of the Molossian tribe of Epirus, had given birth to the boy who became Alexander the Great, Epirus and Macedon, with the kingdoms and communities they embraced, were accepted as Greek.

The western boundary of Epirus has always been the Ionian, with the Ambracian Gulf, also called the Gulf of Arta, and the Pindus range forming its southern and eastern limits respectively. Its northern frontier, however, has varied according to political circumstances. Only in 1913, at the end of the First Balkan War, was Epirus incorporated into the modern Greek state. Its frontier with Albania was afterwards delineated in 1923; it starts on the coast opposite Ipsos in Corfu and runs circuitously north-east to Mount Grammos and the Macedonian border. Unfortunately it left many Greeks in Albania and Albanians in Greece, with serious consequences for both groups after the Second World War. During the thirteenth century, however, Epirus, under the Byzantine Despotate, consisted not only of its present area but stretched as far north as Valona and even for a time to Durazzo. Approximately the same area was ruled from about 1780 until 1821 by Ali Pasha, the 'Diamond of Ioannina', when it was known as Albania and thus described by Byron in the stanza in *Childe Harold's Pilgrimage* which begins:

> Morn dawns; and with it stern Albania's hills,
> Dark Souli's rocks, and Pindus' inland peak . . .

It was in Epirus that I first set foot on Greek soil; this was in Lakkasouli, some twenty miles south of Ioannina, at the beginning of August 1944, under a full golden moon. Ian Scott-Kilvert and I had been posted here by Kenneth Johnstone, then our commanding officer, with a wide brief which included the dissemination of news, the gathering of regional information, propaganda to and subversion of the enemy; this book is dedicated affectionately to them both. In Epirus Ian and I came under the command of the Allied Military Mission to the Greek Resistance forces, and were attached to that part of Force 133 which worked with EDES, the guerilla force commanded by the late General Napoleon Zervas; both organizations then had their headquarters in Derviziana, the valley's principal village. Ian went to Athens on its liberation, but I remained in Epirus, with headquarters in Ioannina, and in the Ionian Islands until December 1945. It was not until 1973 that I was again able to spend more than a few days in Epirus, on that occasion with this book in mind.

But this is not an account of wartime Greece, except in so far as conditions and incidents during that period help to illustrate the character of Epirus and its peoples. The Resistance in Greece has been well covered, especially in the works of C. M. Woodhouse, then universally known in mountain Greece as Colonel Chris, who succeeded Brigadier Myers as commander of the Allied Military Mission late in 1943.

Here, then, is an account of Epirus past and present. In it I have quoted from previous British travellers, whose works are listed in the Bibliography, as life in 1944–5 had not changed altogether from that of the early years of the nineteenth century and their observations were at least the equal of mine. In 1973, however, profound changes were radically altering the life of the province. The standardized materialism of the second half of the twentieth century had already broken down the traditions, old in the days of Pyrrhus, of the migrant shepherd communities which until some twelve years ago had existed since time immemorial. The population, given in the 1971 census as 311,000, was appreciably smaller than it had been in 1961, due to the flight of people from the land to work in Greek cities or abroad, or to emigrate. This book is also about these circumstances.

I have had much help and encouragement from friends at Faber's, especially from Charles Monteith, Michael Wright, Tony Kitzinger and Helen Paniguian.

First, however, I must thank Elli Kirk-Deftereou, now

living in Kalamata, for helping as organizer and interpreter during my 1973 Epirot travels, and her husband, Bill Kirk, for allowing her to come. Elli did splendid work for Anglo-Greek understanding in 1944–6 as a member of our staff in Ioannina, where she was born and brought up. Her standing there is such that every door flew open at our approach as we journeyed to different parts of Epirus, using Ioannina as a base. I hope she will find that this book reflects something of her energy and enthusiasm.

I am most grateful to Professor Sotiris Dakaris, the distinguished Epirot archaeologist, for giving so much of his time and knowledge of different parts of Epirus. I would also like to thank M. Evangelos Averof-Tositsas for his kindness to us in Metsovo and M. Constantine Frontzos, founder and Chairman of the Society for Epirot Studies, a remarkable achievement in itself, for advice on our itinerary and other help. I am grateful to Kenneth and Pauline Johnstone for their guidance on a number of points, to the late Robin Fedden for very useful maps and to M. Karatzenis for information about the Venetians in Arta. I must also record the help I gained from the works of Professor N. G. L. Hammond, of Professor D. M. Nicol and from those of Professor Dakaris as well. Any mistakes are entirely of my own making. Last but not least I must acknowledge once again how much I owe to Clare, my wife, for her patience and work in preparing this book for publication.

Finally a word about pronunciation and spelling. Epirus is pronounced with emphasis on the first syllable as in 'evening', although in my schooldays it used to be pronounced in the same way as 'expiring'. There are several spelling versions of the capital of Epirus, including Janina, Yanina and Yannina; I have used 'Ioannina' throughout as this is the official Greek version. The emphasis comes on the first 'a'. The emphasis (or accent) usually comes, when there are three or more syllables, on the second syllable before the end, as in Epirus and Ioannina. In words of only two syllables, the emphasis should be given to the first, as in Arta, pronounced in the same way as 'martyr'. There are, however, many variations; Igoumenitsa has the accent on the penultimate syllable and Paramythia on the final one.

1

From Corfu to Ioannina

The first impressions of Igoumenitsa from the Ionian Sea on that late May morning were deceptive. As the grey ferry-boat from Corfu entered the long bay, its opening partly screened by islets, the town, standing at its eastern end, gave momentarily the impression of some great sea city portrayed by Claude or Turner in the light of the morning sun. By the time the ferry, after its hour-and-a-half journey, had lowered its ramp on to the quay and the lorries started to roll off, the disillusionment was complete. Here, hemmed in by hills, was a humdrum, dusty little town, newly built, and whose bustling peasant population was reminiscent of a scene by a fifteenth-century Flemish painter. Was this a true reflection of Epirus which Aristotle had regarded as the cradle of the Hellenic race?

My Corfiot friends, when they heard that I intended to visit what they call *i steria* or the continent, were surprised that I should prefer this to remaining on their enchanted island. They themselves have little interest in or knowledge of the mainland opposite. Robert Curzon, the author of *A Visit to the Monasteries of the Levant*, experienced a similar state of affairs in 1834. 'I found I could get no information respecting Albania at Corfu, though the high mountains of Epirus seemed almost to overhang the island.'

From Venetian Corfu with its covered arcades, its sun-drenched Baroque churches and its statues to imperturbable Ionian and British worthies, the soaring mountains of Epirus looked green, empty and enigmatic, without sign of life or habitation. The blue sea, too, was empty. No dolphins escorted us out of the harbour as they had done in 1944 and 1945, before increased shipping had driven them to remoter stretches of

15

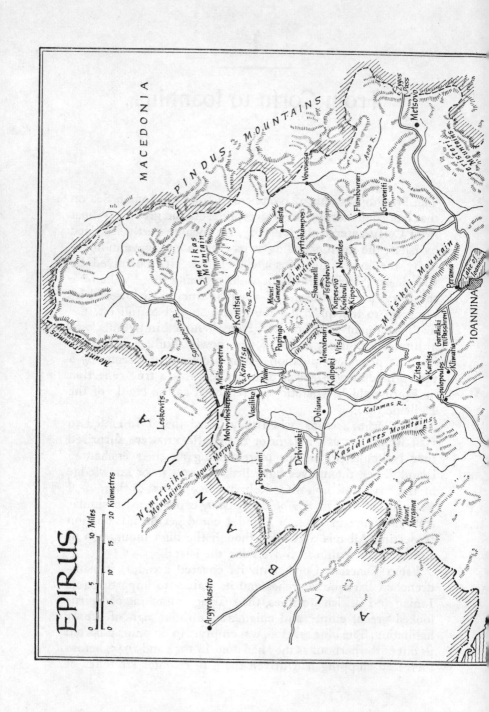

the Mediterranean. The innumerable lines of green hills and mountains rose ever higher the further inland they went, graceful lines which met and mingled and marched together until their final distant ramparts in central Epirus sealed the eastern and south-eastern horizon. To the north, the brooding Acroceraunian range stood guard over Albania. In winter and spring these snow-embellished peaks and ridges glitter like jewels on clear, sunny days. As we approached Igoumenitsa, the Epirot coast further north seemed to merge into that of Corfu, so close are they brought by the narrowness of the Corfu channel, but to the south there was a widening glimpse of the open sea where, out of sight, the Ionian Islands of the Paxoi, Levkas (Santa Mavra), Ithaka, Cephalonia and Zakynthos extend southwards towards the final outpost of Kythera between the Peloponnese and Crete.

Igoumenitsa before 1936 was an insignificant place. It had in any case only become a port after the division of Epirus between Greece and Albania. Even after 1923 and until the Italian seizure of Albania in 1939, travellers from Corfu to Ioannina found it easier to sail to the little Albanian port of Ayii Saranda (the forty saints) opposite the north-east tip of Corfu, because there was as yet no good road from Igoumenitsa to the Epirot capital. Ayii Saranda was opened to shipping in 1878; before then, the main landing-place in this area had been Sayiadhes, just south of the present frontier; severely damaged in 1940–1, it has since been rebuilt. Henry Holland, who was twenty-four when he toured through Greece and Albania in 1812–13, described it as a large town. Certainly it was much used during the British occupation of the Ionian Islands between 1814 and 1864 by travellers going to Turkey in Europe.

In 1936 Igoumenitsa became the headquarters of the *nome* (or prefecture) of Threspotia, one of the four administrative divisions of Epirus, the others being those of Ioannina, Arta and Preveza. Today, its population largely comes from nearby villages, attracted here by its recent development into an important centre of communications; in addition to the Corfu service, large international ferries call here en route between Brindisi and Patras. There are, moreover, excellent bus services from here which connect with the rest of Greece.

18

Accommodation, however, is limited, for the town has no pretensions as a tourist resort. Nor does it boast of ancient associations; no signs of a Greek or Roman settlement have yet been found.

A sturdy, talkative, middle-aged porter helped me with my luggage to the bus station. 'Yes,' he replied to a question about Igoumenitsa's growth, 'more and more people come here. It's a better life than in the villages. I came here in 1945, having been an *andarte* (guerilla) with General Zervas, not that it did me any good. There he is,' he added, pointing to a white pedestal, supporting the bust of a bearded man, standing amid flowering bushes on the sea front. 'He was no better than the lot we've got now,' referring to the 'Colonels' Regime'.

There was time for a meal before the bus departed for Ioannina, two hours and more away. The little restaurant I entered served only *kokoretsia*, or sheep's intestines, cooked on a machine-turned spit over an open fire. In the past the spit would have been turned manually with immense patience for several hours; today it is wound up and set like an alarm clock to cook for a given period. Even such evident signs of progress did not improve the somewhat greasy taste.

Igoumenitsa has a makeshift, unfinished air. The inhabitants live in conditions almost as simple as in their former villages. There is little comfort in the western European sense, perhaps because of an inbred uncertainty about the future. Life has nearly always been at risk hereabouts on account, in turn, of warring city states, Illyrian arrogance and Roman vengeance, of the destructive urge of Bulgars and Slavs, the greed of Crusaders, Angevins and of the sea-born republics of Genoa and Venice and the indifference to the lives of others of Turk and Albanian. Then in 1940 came the Italian invasion, followed by the Germans. When the latter retreated, there arrived the *andartes*, some of them with old scores to pay off, especially against the Muslim villagers who had supported the invaders, and afterwards the Communists who attempted to seize power in 1944–5. But there is a cheerful air about the little town, emphasized by the harmless simpletons who roam the streets, gaily shouting at the passers-by, who accept them as part of their heritage.

The Ioannina bus, which had been steadily filling up for

19

Page 19, Line 12. *For* he was no better *read* he was better some twenty minutes before departure time, nosed its way punctually into the main street and turned left. After passing a narrow stretch of beach, it turned inland to climb over the ridge separating Igoumenitsa from the river Kalamas, which reaches the sea some two kilometres south of Sayiadhes. An earlier outlet once terminated on the northern approaches to Igoumenitsa Bay.

The passengers except for myself were Epirots. Laden with innumerable parcels, including a large hen in a shopping basket, which was thrust into a locker under the bus, they were obviously returning from a visit to relatives or from conducting some business. Thirty years ago the men would have worn black or navy-blue suits of home-woven cloth, sometimes in breeches instead of trousers, their feet shod in thick slippers or boots. Now they were dressed in standard lightweight slacks and terylene shirts. This style was not only more comfortable in summer but welcomed because it placed the wearer on the same sartorial level as men in Athens, New York, Cairo, Singapore and Valparaiso. Only the older women still wore long black peasant dresses, their hair covered with a scarf, a traditional sign of modesty.

It was a relaxed journey. The bus bowled sedately along the excellent road, typical of the trunk roads of contemporary Greece. The bus radio was turned on, but not noisily. We passed places I had known in the past, including the once prosperous Muslim Cham villages which were destroyed because of their Axis support in autumn 1944 by the avenging Greek *andartes*. Then, after a bend in the road, there suddenly appeared the great limestone mountain ridge, towering above the Kalamas river, which stood between us and Ioannina. At first sight it seemed insurmountable but it was just possible to make out a distant vehicle following the road towards the summit of the pass in the far north-east, well over 3,000 feet high, beyond which lay Vrousina. It was a magnificent sight. I know of no entry into Greece which is more dramatic.

The geography of Epirus and much of Albania is very similar. Four great limestone ranges, often with little or no vegetation, run from north-north-west to south-south-east, rising to heights approaching 6,000 feet and more. In between these limestone formations are three Flysch zones which unlike the limestone, retain the rains near the surface to give fertile valleys and woodlands. Here and there rivers have broken through these limestone structures; the Kalamas, for example, whose source is on Mount Merope (Nemertsika) on the distant Albanian frontier, first cuts through such a range near Zitsa, locally renowned for its monastery and its wines, and then through the ridge west of Vrousina before finding its way to the Ionian. This difficult, remote country with its precipitous mountains, inscrutable forests and tumbling rivers is ideal for the deployment of small armed bands for resisting an invader or living off the inhabitants.

The first time I travelled along this road was in late October 1944, after the withdrawal of the Germans north-westwards from Epirus into Albania. It was a time of heightening political tension, leading up to the first attempt by the Greek Communists to seize power in December 1944; their aim was to disengage themselves and Greece from what they considered to be an attempt by the Western Allies, especially Britain, to impose on the country a Royalist regime once more. King George II of the Hellenes was unpopular because he was widely associated with the military dictatorship of General Metaxas, who had been in power when the Italians invaded Greece, and with the Greek defeat in 1941.

After the Axis triumph over Greece that year, the ever-resilient Greeks were soon organizing Resistance movements, which reflected the many different political colours of the Greek scene. By far the best organized of these movements was EAM, of which ELAS was the military wing; EAM represented the left-wing radical republicans but was Communist inspired and dominated. In the course of 1942–3, EAM came to dominate most of Greece by its ideological appeal and by the ruthless elimination of its rivals. Its aim was to take control of the country before the Allies' return; they would find that a Communist regime was a *fait accompli*. The one Resistance group it failed to overthrow was EDES, although it had tried to do so in the autumn and winter of 1943–4 by military action. EDES stood for the initials of the National Republican Greek League, originally formed in Athens in September 1941; its guerilla army was commanded by General Napoleon Zervas, himself an Epirot, who had been persuaded by British agents to undertake its formation, which he did in the Tzourmerka mountains in July 1942.

After ELAS's failure to destroy Zervas, who had received much-needed supplies, dropped by the RAF at the critical moment, the Allied Military Mission, commanded with distinction by Colonel C. M. Woodhouse, had with difficulty achieved agreement with EDES and ELAS at the Plaka bridge on the Arakhthos that they would continue to serve under the Allied Commander-in-Chief. The enmity between the two organizations continued short of fighting until the German retreat started in September 1944. Then ELAS seized Preveza a few hours before the arrival of EDES; this resulted in shooting which was ended on the instructions of the Allied Commander-in-Chief, General Maitland-Wilson, at Caserta whither Zervas and General Sarafis, the ELAS commander, had been summoned to receive their instructions regarding the next phase in Greece. EDES was allotted the Epirot towns of Preveza, Arta and Ioannina, the last of which it entered in mid-October after driving in a German rearguard. There was immediately a general move from the surrounding countryside to the Epirot capital to find out how friends were faring, to assess the opportunities of reverting to a peaceful life and to find out about the political difficulties ahead. Because the Allied Military Mission, whose personnel was virtually entirely British, had also moved into Ioannina, I decided to hasten there from Corfu, where I joined an official Greek party also going in that direction.

We arrived at Igoumenitsa early one mid-October evening in pelting rain to be told that we could not reach Ioannina by motor transport because a vital bridge had been destroyed and because there was insufficient petrol. The situation was extremely vague. The Greek official party decided to continue by caique to Cephalonia. A Polish officer, who had been attempting to contact the many Poles impressed into the Nazi forces, and I decided to go in the one serviceable truck to Paramythia, where, we were told, further petrol supplies might be available. Our fuel ran out several miles before reaching Paramythia so we trudged the rest of the way on foot, only to find that there was no petrol there. We put up for the night and hoped for better things on the morrow.

Next morning we decided to continue to Ioannina on foot, in spite of the bleak wet weather, because of our room's leaking roof and the bugs which had welcomed us all too warmly. We covered the sixty-two miles in two and a half days over a road in extremely poor condition. At Plakoti, where we spent the first night, we were asked for our passes by the villagers who at first took us for stray Germans; fortunately we were quickly able to convince them otherwise. On the second day we continued through Vrousina and Butsara and reached Soulopoulo, twenty-five miles further on, by nightfall to find the village completely burnt down by the Germans and the bridge across a tributary of the Kalamas destroyed. As the Monastery of the Panaghia (the Holy Virgin), where we hoped to spend the night, was on the opposite side of the swirling, muddy river, we waded across in the dark. The abbot, the monastery's only occupant, quickly had a fire blazing for us; he spoke a little English, having lived for some years in Ohio. Wearing an old jacket over his black gown and a greasy cap over his ecclesiastical bun, he produced some *tsípouro* while we shared with him what food we had. *Tsípouro* is a rustic spirit of potency and charm, made in a still from the skins of grapes to which a little 'must', or unfermented grape juice, has been added; if the spirit is distilled twice, a much stronger brew emerges, from which comes the expression *raki metavgalméni* which is applied to someone considered very sharp or clever.

On the following morning, the abbot conducted us to the next village along the road, where lived a crony of his who had also worked in America. Here we were well received. The constant demand was for news; nobody knew what was happening. Fortified with coffee, we then made excellent time for the remainder of the journey through hilly, stony country to arrive at our destination in mid-afternoon.

The long grey bus, in which I travelled to Ioannina in 1973, swung round Gardhiki hill near Zitsa and crested the rise before coasting down towards Ioannina. From here the view of the Epirot capital, some 1,500 feet above sea-level, is unforgettable. There before us was the well-remembered valley with the still lake, shaped like a long shield under the great shoulder of Mitzikeli rising steeply to the east, and the fortified promontory with its citadel and two minarets jutting out into the green waters. Beyond in the distant south-east rose the massifs of Peristeri and Tzoumerka.

Trudging down this road in October 1944, the view indeed impressed, but we were more concerned at what we might find in the town. Was the Mission already established there, had fighting broken out between the rival factions? We too had heard no news, merely rumours for the preceding few days. Our foreboding was heightened by the suspicious expressions on the faces of the villagers, probably from EAM dominated areas, who were also loping long in the same direction. It was with relief that we found a peaceful, orderly town where the presence of the Mission was taken for granted.

2

Ioannina's History

The long valley which now holds the lake of Ioannina must have been an important centre of communications since man first arrived here. For thousands of years there must have been tracks climbing eastwards to the high Pindus through Zagori or winding up the long barren slopes to the Zygos Pass above Metsovo and on into Thessaly; other tracks running southwards over the Ioannina plateau down through the gorges of the Louros river, between the Xerovouni mountains and Lakkasouli, and into the plain around Arta to continue south towards Acarnania or to the south-western extremity of Epirus, where Preveza stands today with the towering shoulder of Levkas beyond; westwards towards Paramythia and the distant Ionian; north-westwards to Albania and north-eastwards into Macedonia. The earliest pastoral peoples would have used these trails when taking their livestock from the high summer pastures of Zagori and Pindus down to the winter grazing by the Ambracian Gulf and the Ionian. Later they were trodden by the armies of the Molossians and the other Epirot tribes, by the heavily-armed infantry phalanxes of Macedon and the legions of Rome as they in turn marched and counter-marched through central Epirus during the Classical and Hellenistic centuries until Rome imposed the peace of desolation on the province in 167 B.C.

There was then, however, no settlement on the present site of Ioannina, which gains much of its importance from its fortified promontory, surrounded on three sides by water, because in those days the lake did not exist. For a long period the waters coming down into this basin from the surrounding mountains were easily drained away through underground channels or drains, known as *katavothres*. Then, perhaps as

25

the result of an earthquake, these *katavothres* became partly blocked, as a result of which the present lake has formed; its surplus waters are even today drained away in this way.

The earliest history of Ioannina is extremely sketchy. Procopius described how Justinian in the sixth century A.D. resettled the inhabitants of Eurhoea on the promontory which he fortified and which is now called the *kastro* or *frourion*— both words mean a fort or fortress. A church dedicated to St John the Baptist (*Prodromos* in Greek, meaning 'forerunner') was erected on its north-east corner, close to or actually on the site where the Aslan Pasha mosque now stands, and it is thought that Ioannina was named after the saint. The church no longer exists but the fishermen still describe the lake thereabouts as 'St John's waters'. Nothing now remains of Justinian's fort. In 673, there is mention of the bishopric of Ioannina coming under the Metropolitan (senior bishop) of Navpaktos on the Gulf of Corinth. In 879, 'Zacharius Bishop of Ioannina' is reported to have attended a synod at Constantinople. By the tenth and eleventh centuries, the see of Ioannina appears to have been transferred to the Metropolis of Okhrid, where today the frontiers of Yugoslavia and Albania meet.

Since the beginning of the crusading movement and its increasing contact with Byzantium, as successive expeditions made their way through Eastern Europe and Asia Minor on their way to the Holy Land, there had been a growing interest in the wealth and the apparent weaknesses of the Greek Orthodox Empire. The Normans, under the restless, boundless energy of Robert Guiscard, the greatest Norman warrior of his generation, were particularly anxious to profit from its decline. Guiscard besieged Durazzo in 1081 and trounced an Imperial army under the Emperor Alexios Komnenos coming to its aid; in the following year the town surrendered. Bohemund of Taranto, Guiscard's son, in the meanwhile advanced far into the interior of Epirus to harry the Emperor's forces and to seize Ioannina.

Anna Komnena, Alexios's daughter, relates in the *Alexiad*, her account of her father's reign, how Bohemund first ordered trenches to be dug in the vineyards outside the town. Having sited his troops around it, he set up his tent inside the walls. He then made a survey of the defences, and finding those in the *kastro* in a dangerous condition, not only restored but added to them at strategic points. He also sent out raiding parties to plunder the surrounding countryside.

From this account there was already a town of some size outside the *kastro* walls on the lower slopes of St George's Hill which climb gently westwards from the lake to where today stand pine woods, among which fireflies glimmer in early June; it was here that the vineyards were planted. Such was the importance of Ioannina that the Emperor Alexios hastened to contest its control. Only too aware of the skill and bravery of the Normans he tried to get Bohemund to reveal the size of his forces by sending a picked body of light infantry against them. How effective this opening gambit was is not related.

Alexios then seized on the idea of building light wagons with four poles fixed to each of them, to be used by the heavy infantry to break the Latins' cavalry charge. Bohemund seems to have guessed their purpose. He therefore divided his army into two divisions, each of which was ordered to attack one of the Byzantine flanks; in this way he avoided the wagon trap. A stiff fight followed in which Alexios performed prodigies of valour, but it was Bohemund who triumphed and the Emperor only escaped with difficulty over the mountains to Okhrid. The Normans then advanced over the Pindus into Thessaly and posed a threat to Constantinople. Some months later, however, Bohemund was defeated by the Imperial troops at Larissa and returned to Italy in 1084. It was Alexios who eventually triumphed over the Norman prince who surrendered to him outside Durrazo in 1108: Bohemund then retired discredited to Apulia where he died three years later.

The Normans invaded Greece again both in 1146 and 1185; on the first occasion they sacked Thebes and Corinth and on the second devastated Salonika. At this time Ioannina formed part of the *theme*, or administrative region, of Nikopolis, the city originally built by Octavius Caesar immediately to the north of Preveza. Mainland Greece was divided by the Emperor Leo the Isaurian in the eighth century into four *themes*; that of Nikopolis included all western Greece down to the Gulf of Corinth, namely Aetolia, Acarnania and

Southern Epirus or approximately that part of Epirus which is Greek today.

The Fourth Crusade in 1204 was cleverly manoeuvred by the Venetians to attack the Byzantine capital before proceeding to the Holy Land. The Italian city states, especially Venice and her rival, Genoa, were more concerned with commerce than Christianity. When the Eastern Empire was apportioned out among the Crusaders, Venice acquired Nikopolis and the territory of Arta, the Ionian Islands and the best harbours and markets in the Levant. Genoa was later able to obtain a share of the Aegean trade by supporting the Byzantines against the Venetians, who were never forgiven their role in the 'crusade against the Christians'.

Although Constantinople was lost in 1204 to the Latins, the Byzantines remained vigorously alive, nowhere more so than at Nicaea in Asia Minor where the Greek empire was now established, at Trebizond at the eastern end of the Black Sea, and in Epirus, where Michael Angelos Komnenos Doukas created the Despotate of Epirus. Of illegitimate birth, he was descended through his paternal grandmother from the Emperor Alexios I. His father had been for a time governor of Epirus and Thessaly. Michael Angelos himself, brilliant and unscrupulous, for a time served Boniface, Marquis of Montferrat, one of the crusaders who had been awarded the Kingdom of Salonika. Finding that Greeks could hope for little advantage from the Franks, he slipped away over the Pindus to Ioannina, which became briefly the capital of his Despotate before he moved it to Arta. Soon his power stretched from the Gulf of Corinth to as far north as Durazzo, together with Corfu, Levkas and a part of Thessaly. Michael, who made and broke promises as it suited him, was assassinated in 1215.

The collapse of Byzantine Constantinople brought numerous refugees from there into Epirus, a majority of whom seemed to have settled in Ioannina, thus bringing it into prominence. For this reason the Despot made it the administrative centre of his northern territory. He fortified the most important places in his care; he built the castle of San Angelo above Palaiokastritza in Corfu and expanded and strengthened the fortifications of Ioannina. Professor Nicol refers in his

Despotate of Epiros to a document which mentions Michael as 'the founder, protector and saviour of Ioannina'.

The history of the Despotate was a stormy one, in keeping with the intense ambition of the Despots themselves. As the might of the Latin Empire of Constantinople steadily waned, so the strength of both the Nicaean Empire and the Epirot Despotate waxed and became increasingly involved in an outright struggle between themselves for leadership over the Greek Orthodox world.

Michael I was succeeded by his even more unscrupulous half-brother, Theodore, who seized Peter of Courtenay in Albania while on his way to inherit the Latin Empire of Romania. Later he captured Salonika in 1222, when he assumed the Imperial title and put on the purple mantle and red sandals. He then overstretched himself by perfidiously attacking the Bulgars by whom he was defeated, captured and blinded, only to carry on with his intrigues for a further generation.

In 1236, Michael II Angelos, illegitimate son of Michael I, succeeded to the Despotate, but not to Salonika. He married Theodora, a daughter of the distinguished Norman-Italian family of Petraliphas, which had settled in Thrace long before the Latin Conquest. Her saintliness was such that she was later canonized by the Orthodox Church. In spite of his wife's attempts to reconcile the Despotate with Nicaea, Michael II, encouraged by his Uncle Theodore, spent the 'fifties in building up allies against the Nicaean Empire. He gained support from William de Villehardouin, Prince of Achaia, his son-in-law, who rallied the flower of the Latin chivalry of the Peloponnese to his side, and a strong contingent was sent him by Manfred of Sicily, who had married another of Michael's daughters. The culminating clash came at Pelagonia, in what is now Serbian Macedonia, in 1259. The Imperial forces, led by the Sebastocrator John, brother of Michael VIII Palaiologos who had recently made himself Emperor, were the victors; for Michael II, dispirited by the sudden desertion of his bastard son, John, fled the scene without warning, leaving the Prince of Achaia and Manfred's troops in the lurch. After the action, part of the victorious Nicaean army was sent over the Pindus into Epirus under General Alexios Strategopoulos,

29

who detached part of his forces to besiege Ioannina while he continued to Arta which he easily occupied.

The Despot's defeat was not, however, final. After a few months he regained his capital, raised the siege of Ioannina and continued to rule until his death in 1271. Before this, however, he reached a compromise with the Emperor Michael VIII, who had in 1261 regained Constantinople from the Latins and had put an Imperial garrison into Ioannina.

The death of Michael II Angelos marked the end of the great period of the Despotate. He was succeeded by several Despots whose tortuous efforts to maintain their independence found them weaker at the end than at the beginning of their reigns. Nikephoros, Michael's son, was unable to prevent the French House of Anjou, which had been given the Kingdom of Naples by the Papacy in return for support against Byzantium, from occupying Corfu and part of the Epirot coast. However, thanks to the machinations of Michael VIII Palaiologos with King Peter III of Aragon, the invasion of the Eastern Roman Empire by Charles of Anjou was finally frustrated by the Sicilian Vespers in 1282, by which the French were ejected from the great island in favour of the Aragonese. Nikephoros was later to drive the Imperial forces from Ioannina by his alliance with the Frankish nobility of the Morea and with Count Richard Orsini of Cephalonia. The *Chronicle of Morea* gives a clear picture of Ioannina's fortifications when describing how in 1293 Nikephoros and his allies 'arrived in Yannina before the splendid castle; there they encamped in siege of it. The Castle is formidable and stands in a lake, for Great Ozeros [another name for the lake was Pambotis] is all around the castle. The inhabitants enter the castle by a bridge; they bring the supplies into the castle by skiffs. The whole world considers that the castle of Yannina cannot be taken by assault, so long as it has supplies.'

In 1318, the feeble Despot Thomas, the last of the Angelos Doukas dynasty, was assassinated by his nephew, Count Nicholas of Cephalonia, who was in turn murdered in 1323 by his brother John who assumed the title of Despot. John was poisoned by his wife in 1335, and was succeeded as ruler by Byzantines, Serbs, the Florentine Esau Buondelmonti (1386–1408), Albanians and by the Tocco dynasty of Levkas and Cephalonia. Of all these, perhaps the most colourful and certainly the most disagreeable was Thomas Preljubovich who in 1367 succeeded Stephen Dushan, the Serbian tsar, whose brief empire had stretched from Arta to Belgrade. 'All wickedness is small', commented the *Chronicle of Epirus*, 'compared with the wickedness of Thomas.' Perhaps not unexpectedly he was killed by his own bodyguard in 1385.

Ioannina, throughout the period of the Despotate, appears to have enjoyed a reputation for beauty and prosperity. Early in the fourteenth century, soon after the murder of the last of the Angelos Despots, it was described as a populous and wealthy city, where Jews could make money and whose strong Hellenic sentiments were encouraged by the establishment of a metropolitan, transferred there from Navpaktos.

The Turks had first arrived at Ioannina towards the end of the fourteenth century, when the Turkish general, Gazi Eurenoz, is said to have built a military camp at Turkopalouko, close to the lakeside *kastro*; here many Turks established themselves. In the absence of their own womenfolk, their lives became so dreary that they took unto themselves a number of Ioanniniot maidens, married them and settled down in the area for good.

The Turks conquered Ioannina in 1430. From then until the end of the eighteenth century conditions were largely peaceful and, according to Dr Spon who was there in the middle of the seventeenth century, certainly prosperous. There was, however, a rebellion in 1585, instigated by Venice and led by Theodore Boua Grivas who, supported by two captains of irregular bands, Drakos and Makrinos, took Arta and marched on Ioannina; this revolt was easily suppressed. Greek nationalism was not, however, dead for in 1611 there was another uprising, led by one Dionysios, known as the 'skylosophist' or 'dog-sophist'; before being unfrocked for drunkenness and dabbling in astrology and black magic, he had been bishop of Trikkala. This strange, unbalanced ecclesiastic dreamt that he saw the Sultan himself rise up to receive him. And so it came to pass but in circumstances very different from those the 'skylosophist' had imagined. He led an unorganized body of Greeks against Ioannina, killing about a hundred Muslims, but this irruption was quickly crushed.

Dionysios managed to hide himself for some days but the Turks eventually caught, executed and flayed him. His skin was then stuffed with straw and sent to Constantinople for the edification of the 'Lord of the Lords of this World' who, hearing the cheering crowds, stood up to see the cause of the commotion—and made Dionysios's dream a reality. The result of this embroilment was that the Greeks of the city, by and large a sober and hardworking community as always, were seriously compromised and lost several valuable privileges, one of which was the right to live in the *kastro*. Their place was taken by the Turks and Jews. What was particularly sad was the punitive destruction at that time of the churches which had been erected in and around Ioannina during the Despotate, especially as those of the same period in Arta, several of which still stand, are among the most interesting in Greece.

Ioannina enjoyed great importance during the domination from 1788 until his violent death in 1822 of the Albanian Ali Pasha, one of the most powerful characters and certainly the most extraordinary in the history of Epirus. When Napoleon occupied the Dalmatian provinces in 1805, Ali, fearing a French advance into Albania, set about improving the town's defences. The Rev. Thomas Hughes, who was there in 1813, was told how everybody in the city was forced to work on the fortifications and in the deep entrenchments among the vineyards on St George's Hill. Lt-Colonel Leake heard a similar story. The only reward for the labourers was music from a band to cheer them on. Hughes wrote that Ali 'spared not even the primates, archons and priests of the Greeks, anymore than the beys and agas of the Turks; nay, he forced the archbishop and his own son Muchtar to work.'

The town also expanded up the hillside of St George. Henry Holland, also there in 1813, counted some sixteen mosques and seven or eight churches spread over the area. Facing the entrance to the *kastro*, which in Ali's day was protected by a large ditch, was the bazaar consisting of twelve or more streets, intersecting at irregular angles. The shops and stalls were low-built and sheltered by projecting roofs which shut out much of the daylight. Each trade had its own section and included jewellery, pelisses, Turkish shawls and other haberdashery, groceries, tobacco, pipes with amber mouthpieces, coloured leather and Turkish slippers, dried fruits and cotton goods. The bazaar was closed at night and protected by fierce watchdogs.

This area of Ioannina today retains something of the character of the old bazaar. Many of the houses are one-storeyed with corrugated iron roofs. Footwear and clothes shops, wine and ouzo merchants and those who sell knives and farm implements are inclined to concentrate in their own groups; scattered among them are little cafes and taverns catering mainly for rural visitors and spurned by the established citizens of Ioannina. There was also a shop which sold sheep-bells, which were of great importance to the shepherd. By the sound of these bells the *tséllingas* or owner of flocks could tell the whereabouts of his sheep and whether they were in danger. The leading ram would be given a deep-toned bell with which all the others harmonized. In the days of really large flocks, sometimes consisting of several thousand sheep, a *tséllingas* might have required as many as fifty bells.

Other kiosks today are used by barbers and by lawyers who, preferring to see and to be seen, sit in offices with large windows at street level, dispensing coffee and wisdom to their clients. Cakes, different sorts of yoghourt, some flavoured with garlic, and local cheeses are to be found there too. The crafts-men also keep together—wood carvers, jewellers and metal beaters. The antique shops, filled in 1973 with the rural handi-crafts of the Epirot shepherds, are likewise close to the old bazaar; the tourist souvenir shops are nearer to the *plateia* or main square of the city.

After Ali Pasha's death in 1822, Ioannina enjoyed a period of calm when the fortifications fell into disrepair. Visitors from Britain still came to the town. Disraeli arrived in 1830 from Corfu and was glad to be received in audience by Reshid Pasha, whom he described as 'an approved warrior, a con-summate politician, unrivalled as a dissembler'. 'I bowed', added the future prime minister, 'with all the nonchalance of St James's Street to a little, ferocious, shrivelled man, plainly dressed, with a brow covered with wrinkles and a countenance clouded with anxiety and thought.' Reshid, known to the Greeks as Kiutahi, and one of the more successful of the Turkish commanders, was an Orthodox Christian.

It was not until the First Balkan War in 1912-13 that Ioannina was again besieged and its defences put briefly to the test. Then the Greek army had advanced up from Arta as far as the southern end of the Ioannina plain, where the Turks were entrenched at Bisdouni, and where today a somewhat elaborate war memorial commemorates their defeat. The Hellenic commander, the Crown Prince Constantine, had built up its strength through the winter of 1912-13 until he was confident that it could take Ioannina. Other Greek units had been steadily advancing elsewhere in Epirus and the port of Ayii Saranda, now in Albania, was occupied on 3 March 1913.

Then on 4 March, the Turkish lines were overrun. On the following day, after strenuous fighting and a particularly successful bombardment by the Greek artillery, Essad Pasha, the defender of Ioannina, signified that he could no longer hold out. Constantine entered the town on 7 March and, as well as attending a Te Deum in the cathedral, went to a special service in the main synagogue to acknowledge the pro-Hellenic sentiments of the Jewish community. Twelve days later, news arrived that King George I of the Hellenes, brother of Queen Alexandra, then the widow of Edward VII, had been assassinated by a madman in Salonika. There is a plaque on the exterior wall of Dr Lappas's house on Dangli Street, close to Papazoglou Street, which states that the Crown Prince was given the tragic news close to this spot.

Ioannina's walls suffered little on this occasion, although the town was subjected to what must have been one of the first attempts at aerial bombardment. On 18 December 1912, *The Times* reported from Preveza that a Lt Moutousi of the Greek Engineers had flown from Nikopolis in a Maurice Farman biplane with a 70 h.p. Renault engine. 'He has just telegraphed', read the report, 'that he flew right over Yanina and dropped some bombs with good results.' His plane was pierced by Turkish bullets, but he returned safely to base after a round flight of over 100 miles. During the 1940-1 Italian campaign, the *kastro* walls served as air raid shelters against Italian bombers.

The frustrating problem for Greece of northern Epirus began with the end of the First Balkan War. After the fall of

Ioannina, Greek troops continued northwards until they had occupied that part of present Albania south of a line from Valona to Lake Okhrid. Here Greek expansion was blocked by Italian ambitions to control both sides of the Adriatic. Although this area was historically a part of Epirus, its population was fairly evenly divided between Greeks and Albanians, partly Christian and partly converted to Islam. Italy, supported by Austria, succeeded in November 1913 in having this area declared part of the newly created Albanian state.

During the First World War Greek opinion was divided between support for Venizelos, the liberal prime minister whose achievements made him the outstanding Greek statesman and politician of the first half of this century, and loyalty to King Constantine, who had captured Ioannina. Venizelos warmly supported the *Entente* and Serbia, but Constantine, married to the Kaiser's sister, favoured the Central Powers. In summer 1917, Italy took advantage of this situation by occupying not only northern Epirus but Ioannina as well on the pretext that Epirus, where some irregular bands had supported the King, was hostile to the *Entente*, which had established a front against Germany and Bulgaria in Macedonia. The Italians were soon persuaded to withdraw from Ioannina but not from northern Epirus. Hopes that northern Epirus could be incorporated into Greece rose again in 1944–5 but were finally frustrated by the Soviet bloc.

Today, Ioannina's *kastro* has changed little over the last thirty years except for the erection at the south-east corner of a pavilion, a sturdy reconstruction of part of the *serai*, originally Ali Pasha's residence, in which his vast harem was housed. It is now used only to accommodate important visitors. It stands close to the Fetiye mosque whose graceful minaret still rises above the lake; its interior is neglected. Close by, half hidden in shrubbery and long grass, is the grave of Ali Pasha where his body was buried, surrounded by a low stone wall from which the iron railings have long disappeared; his head, however, was sent in 1822 to Constantinople by Kurshid Pasha, the Sultan's commander, as proof that his campaign against Ali had been successfully accomplished.

The Fetiye mosque, the pavilion and Ali's grave are part of the inner citadel and under military control but visitors are

35

not discouraged. We wandered peacefully among scattered Turkish buildings—a hospital, a refectory, a kitchen, the interior walls covered with graffiti but the exteriors still retaining an oriental elegance.

Another fine minaret rises next to the Aslan Aga mosque in the north-east corner of the promontory, from which there are glorious views over Ioannina, the lake and surrounding mountains. This was the last mosque to be used by the faithful; it was closed in 1928. Designed in the shape of a hexagon within a square, it was converted into a museum. Nearby a dervish monastery or *tekké* was built in 1618 behind its own wall. To the west is the Islamic library, which in 1973 was being restored, and the *hammam* or Turkish baths. There is another military installation closeby but most of the space within the *kastro* walls is occupied by private houses. Motor transport has limited access inside this area so that one can stroll leisurely along the cobbled streets past the little houses, built during the Turkish ascendancy, some with wooden first-floor balconies and gardens, or pause in the shade of one of the giant plane trees which stand sentinel in the many open spaces.

3

Ali Pasha

Cruelty is perhaps the characteristic most often associated with Ali Pasha, who was at the peak of his power in the first two decades of the nineteenth century, when he ruled most of Greece and Albania from Ioannina, the city with which his name will always be associated. His instruments of torture were in constant use. Hughes wrote that in an open space between the bazaar and the *kastro* were enacted scenes of the greatest cruelty: 'Criminals have been roasted alive over a slow fire, impaled and skinned alive; others have had their extremities cut off and some have been left to perish with the skin of their face stripped over their necks.' Yet in spite of abundant evidence to support Hughes's report, Lord Broughton, who as John Cam Hobhouse accompanied Byron to Ioannina and Tepeleni in 1809–10, could many years later write thus about Ali: 'Mr Hughes gives a bad character to the Signior in his account of his visit, but we received nothing but civilities from him.' Perhaps the truth was that criminals and suspects then received much the same treatment everywhere throughout the Ottoman Empire.

Turkey, towards the end of the eighteenth century, presented a disordered picture, for the Sultan's power was often tenuous in the outlying parts of his dominions. Arabia was ruled by the Wahabites, the Mamelukes held Cairo, the Pasha of Vidin on the Danube had long ignored the Sultan's authority and the Russians, by the Treaty of Kutchuk Kainardji of 1774, had the right to champion the Ottoman Empire's Christian subjects.

Ali Pasha was born between 1740 and 1750 in Tepeleni, Albania. His father, Veli, became the vice-governor of the town and received the rank of Pasha of Two Tails; this was achieved as a result of trickery and murder. He did not survive for long because of his quarrelsome nature which his enemies reported to invoke the displeasure of the Sultan, who stripped him of office. Ali's mother was Khamco, who enjoyed considerably higher social status than his father. Her violent disposition, in which the characteristics of greed and vengeance were balanced by her fierce love for Ali and his sister, Shainitza, was immensely forceful; she maintained a powerful influence over her children throughout her life.

Albania was not a co-ordinated state. The pashas were appointed from Constantinople to govern important centres but other places were allowed to retain their independence on payment of tribute. The people of Albania consisted of a number of tribes; those in the north tended towards Christianity while those further south were mainly Muslim. In general they called themselves *Shqipetars* and their country *Shqiperia*, the land of the eagle. It was also the land of the vendetta. The Albanians who went south through Epirus in the fourteenth century, afterwards to settle widely in central and southern Greece, seemed to have been slightly more responsive to law and order. Those who remained in Albania were constantly involved in raids on rival villages and on rival pashas and beys, in which courage was matched by cruelty and endurance by treachery. There was obviously scope for the ambitious and ruthless.

Khamco was not left well provided for by her deceased husband, but such was her spirit that she discarded her woman's veil, rallied Veli's supporters and, accompanied by Ali, embarked on a career of robbery with violence. 'My son,' she is reported to have said, 'he who does not defend his patrimony deserves to lose it. Remember that the property of others belongs to them only by the right of the strongest and, if you wrest it from them, it becomes yours.' Ali, many years later, declared that he owed everything to his mother. She decided to retire from her vocation only after her capture by the people of Gardhiki and Khormovo, who had suffered much from her brigandage and who in turn subjected Khamco and her daughter to what Hughes described as their 'brutal passions' while they had them in their grasp.

Ali now had his own band and was able to move at will.

Soon his wide-ranging activities came to the attention of Kurd
Pasha of Berat, who was chief of police in southern Albania
and over large parts of western Greece. Kurd, who was
nicknamed 'the Wolf', rounded up Ali's gang and sentenced
them to be hanged. Ali, however, so impressed the Wolf that
he alone was spared and no doubt employed against the
Pasha's enemies. Almost without exception, the Turkish
pashas enjoyed a ferocious and bloodthirsty reputation; if
Ali in due course achieved the worst reputation of them all, it
was only a matter of degree. R. A. Davenport, who wrote the
first life of Ali Pasha in English in 1837, told how the Pasha
of Vidin, having defeated some rebels, ordered their severed
heads, the best possible proof of his success, to be put into a
sack and sent to the Sultan. By mistake the secretary in his
letter of explanation gave a greater number than the sack
contained. Rather than change the letter, the Pasha thought it
simpler to order his officers into the streets to collect the
requisite number of extra heads.

At the age of twenty-four Ali married Eminé, daughter of
Caplan Pasha of Delvino, but this did nothing to soften his
nature. In fact he was soon successfully intriguing with the
Porte to have his father-in-law executed in the hope of
inheriting his title; when, instead, Caplan's own son succeeded
to the dignity, Ali soon found a way of disposing of him.

The death of the Wolf of Berat gave Ali his real opportunity.
Kurd Pasha, as chief of police, had also been the chief in-
spector of roads and of public safety with the title of Dervendji Pasha. Ali successfully applied for this post and in
about 1783 gained the Pashalik of Trikkala as well. The road
to wealth and power was now open to him. Ali set out for
Trikkala with a company of *Shqipetars*. Here he found that
the population in the surrounding Thessalian plain had been
sucked dry by the greed of the Beys of Larissa, whose wealth
he quickly set about absorbing in his turn. At the same time
he ruthlessly attacked the Klephts and the Armatoles; the
former were part robbers and part heroes, not unlike Robin
Hood in resisting the Turks, and were often referred to as
Palikars or braves; the latter were Christians formed into a
gendarmerie to preserve order in rural areas, but who were
always ready to enrich themselves when they saw an oppor-

tunity. Ali's success in dealing with these bodies was such that on the outbreak of war with Russia in 1797 he was given a high appointment in the Turkish army which he joined with his *Shqipetars*.

When he eventually returned to Trikkala, he learned that the then Pasha of Ioannina was away from home. Ali had long cultivated his own party within Ioannina and now he suddenly appeared outside its walls. When the inhabitants showed signs of resistance, he neatly forged an Imperial decree, complete with crimson case, giving himself the pashalik. Ioannina was to remain his until his death.

For the next thirty years, Ali was intent on amassing ever more power, territory and wealth. For a time his realm embraced all Greece with the exceptions of Attica and Boeotia. His constant qualities were ruthlessness, deceit, meanness, treachery, cruelty and much charm when the situation required. His energies and appetites were enormous and to cater for these he maintained a harem of some five hundred women. In addition, according to Colonel Baron de Vaudoncourt, a French artillery officer sent to train Ali's army in the use of a battery given by Napoleon, there was a *seraglio* of youths, some of whom were in constant attendance, as his pleasures were rumoured to be mainly homosexual. His appearance rarely indicated his brutal and barbaric nature. His features were fair and round with quick blue eyes, which gave an impression of honesty and good humour. In height he was only about five feet five inches. He rode well, according to Hobhouse, and was so good a shot that he could kill a hare when at full gallop. He was, moreover, fearless. Hughes reported that 'he constantly rides through Ioannina on horseback attended by a single guard, and admits freely all persons into his presence, armed and unarmed, whether he may be alone or surrounded by his attendants. His very confidence seems to be his protection, and the multitude fancy that he bears a charmed life.'

Ali was responsible for much building in Epirus and Albania. According to David Urquhart, who served in the Greek navy under Lord Cochrane during the Greek War of Independence and later took an active interest in the frontiers of the new Hellenic state, Ali built a carriage road from

Preveza to Ioannina and scientifically drained the marshes to the north of Arta. His most grandiose construction was the Litharitza in Ioannina, still in use although in a ruined state some twelve years after his death, for Robert Curzon was received there by the then Vizier of Ioannina. Ali kept an elaborate household; its officers, according to Hughes, were many and included the Selictar-Aga who carried the sword of state; the Bairactar-Aga who carried the standard; the Capi-Baloukbashee who lodged in the palace and superintended the police guard; two Bouchurdan-Agas who perfumed him when he went to the mosque; and the Shamdan-Aga who preceded the wax candles into the apartment.

Ali's pursuit of territorial aggrandisement was not always immediately successful, but his perseverance, often bolstered by a burning desire to avenge some insult real or imaginary, usually gave him victory in the end. His vengeance, mainly against Albanians, struck at Khormovo, Gardhiki, Berat, Khimara, Delvino, Argyrokastro, Valona and other centres, usually ending in the bloodiest way. Shainitza, his sister, entered heartily into such schemes. So exacting was she in wreaking vengeance on the Gardhikiots that she tore open a pregnant woman with a razor when she discovered that the father was from Gardhiki. Ali's two elder sons, Muchtar and Veli, were true sons of their father. Muchtar, according to Hughes, was endowed with all his father's vices but with none of his virtues except for bravery. He was extremely avaricious and his lusts were so ungovernable that he had been known to rape women openly in the streets of Ioannina. Veli was more urbane and a better politician than his brother, but with fewer military accomplishments; sexually he was as grossly self-indulgent as his father and elder brother.

There was little love lost between Ali and his sons. When Veli, on returning from service with the Turkish army on the Danube, was unable to restore order in his pashalik of the Morea, which had grown unruly during his absence, he was transferred by the Porte, the Imperial administration, to Thessaly. Ali, furious at the loss of the Peloponnese, kept Veli's wife, Zobeidé, as a hostage in Ioannina as a guarantee of Veli's good behaviour. He then decided that it would be fun to rape her, which he did after the poor girl had been drugged.

Unfortunately she became pregnant and the services of the most distinguished local abortionist were necessary. In order to hush up this scandal, Ali arranged for the odalisques who had carried out the drugging to be sewn up in sacks and flung into the lake, then the standard way of disposing of loose women; the gypsies who deposited the sacks in those murky waters were then beheaded by a deaf and dumb negro.

Muchtar was also made to suffer. He fell passionately in love with an exceptionally beautiful Greek girl, called Euphrosyné who, although married, became his mistress. Pasho, Muchtar's wife, became exceedingly jealous when Euphrosyné tried to sell to a jeweller a magnificently distinctive ring which Muchtar had often worn himself before giving it to her. The jeweller in all innocence offered it to Pasho as one of the few people in Ioannina who could afford to buy it. Of course she recognized it at once. Having established how the ring came into the jeweller's possession, she went with the story to Ali. He at once decided to avenge the insult and went in person to Euphrosyné's home at night to arrest her; in despair she offered him all her jewellery which he accepted, but nevertheless sent her as prisoner to the *kastro*. She was soon joined there by fifteen of the loveliest girls in the city whom Pasho in her jealousy had denounced as loose women and objects of Muchtar's attentions. They too were thrust into sacks and thrown into the lake, their shrieks lost in the uproar of a thunderstorm.

The Napoleonic Wars brought Ali into contact with the principal contestants. The French in 1797 had concluded a peace with Austria at Campo Formio whereby Austria acquired Venice, and France the Ionian Islands which she occupied together with the former Venetian mainland coastal bases of Butrinto, Parga, Preveza and Vonitsa, all of which Ali had long coveted. The arrival of a Turkish-Russian expedition in the Ionian, to expel the French from the Ionian Islands after Nelson's victory at Aboukir Bay over the French, gave Ali the opportunity of seizing Preveza, Vonitsa and Butrinto. He was, however, denied their control, for these prizes passed into the hands of the Sultan, in spite of Ali's lavish bribery at Constantinople. Instead he was given as a consolation prize the title of Vizier.

For the Russians Ali had nothing but loathing as they frustrated his every attempt to gain a footing on the Ionian Islands. When, therefore, Napoleon gained control over Dalmatia after defeating the Austrians at Austerlitz in 1805, Ali, as well as strengthening Ioannina's defences in case the French came further south, also made friendly overtures to them. This suited Napoleon's policy at the time and a French consul was established in the Epirot capital.

François Pouqueville, who was given this post, was experienced in Turkish conditions as a result of having been imprisoned in the Peloponnese and in Constantinople when he had occupied his time by learning Greek. He was a man of courage, but he expected difficulties from the first, and arise they did in 1807 after Napoleon's agreement with Tsar Alexander I at Tilsit, whereby the Ionian Islands reverted to the French. Ali sent envoys to see General Berthier in Corfu and gain his agreement to Ali's proposed annexation of Parga, but the Parguinots got there first and opened the French general's eyes to the real state of affairs. Ali was furious and did everything possible to harass the French by closing his ports to their shipping and denying them supplies. The only local butt for his anger was the unfortunate Pouqueville who complained vigorously of his ill-treatment to the Porte, which in turn admonished Ali but to no avail. For Ali was beginning to weigh seriously the possibilities of making himself independent of the Sultan. Pouqueville was eventually to have his own back through his pungent descriptions of the Vizier of Ioannina in his lively and observant three-volume *Voyages dans La Grèce*.

With the French back in the Ionian Islands, Ali started to cultivate the British in earnest. He made contact with Admiral Collingwood who sent Colonel Leake in an English brig to a secret rendezvous off Preveza, where he was rowed ashore at night for a huddled conference with Ali on the beach. Ali promised all help to the British against the French and Leake remained to survey Albania and Epirus in case of British military intervention; afterwards he stayed on as British Resident in Ioannina where he met Byron and Hobhouse in 1809. That same year the British captured Zakynthos and sent Ali considerable supplies of artillery, including Congreve rockets for use against the French, but which Ali took into Albania against his enemies.

In 1810 Pouqueville reported the arrival in Ioannina of a British consul. George Foresti, a Greek with wide connections in the Ionian Islands, was a man of strong personality and considerable wisdom. He managed to gain the respect of Ali through his firmness and his constancy of character and was on several occasions able to make Ali adopt a more conciliatory attitude towards individuals and problems. Foresti was equally well regarded by the British authorities who consulted him about Levkas and Parga, both of which Ali wanted; Foresti's advice was taken over Levkas but darker counsels were eventually to prevail over Parga.

Levkas, a beautiful island, was part of the mainland until separated from it by the Corinthians who built a canal in 640 B.C. but which was of little material or strategic value. Ali wanted the island for self-aggrandisement. As far back as 1798, he had offered the French his support against the Russo-Turkish expedition in return for Levkas and the four former Venetian possessions on the mainland. During his second flirtation with Napoleon he again offered the French help against the abhorred Russians, then the sole power in the Ionian Islands, in exchange for Levkas, and prepared an expedition of four thousand under the command of his foster-brother, Yusuf Arab the Blood-drinker, whose deeds lived up to his reputation. Ali, between the departure of the Russians and the arrival of the French, tried to seize Levkas, but was repulsed by Greeks, commanded by Count John Capodistria, who later became foreign secretary to the Tsar and finally president of the embryonic Hellenic state which emerged at the end of the Greek War of Independence, only to be assassinated in 1839.

By 1810 the British, after taking Cephalonia and Ithaka, were ready under General Oswald to attack Levkas, but without Ali's troops, for Foresti had made it clear that Ali's presence on the island would be disastrous. Instead, General Oswald sent Ali twelve horses laden with silver, and a boatload of coffee and sugar. At this point, however, Ali was trying to get the French to allow him help man the Levkas defences, should the British attack, at the same time that he was entertaining the British commander in Preveza.

For the rest of his life Ali maintained friendly relations with the British who became the protecting power over the Ionian Islands at the end of the Napoleonic Wars. General Airey sent his wife together with the Resident of Zakynthos and his wife to Ioannina with wedding presents for Veli's daughters. It showed little understanding of Muslim custom for a woman to be given such a role, but the valuable jewellery and a large sum of money which accompanied it convinced Ali that the gesture was a well-intentioned one.

The closing years of Ali's life were crowned in 1819 by his brief occupation of Parga, but he lost it the following year to the Sultan who had by then decided to square his account with his rebellious subject. Ali was also saddened at the loss by fire of his palace at Tepeleni, his childhood home, though he was quick to devise a scheme to rebuild it without expense to himself. He invited contributions towards its reconstruction and fixed a day for their collection. When that day dawned, Ali was found sitting on a dirty, frayed rug with an old red cap in his hand, the picture of poverty. He had previously sent large sums of money to needy retainers, who early in the day returned them to him in full public view as their contribution. If a rich man gave too little, Ali pointed out how much more generous his own humble servants had been; he went on to explain that he would prefer his rich friend to keep his money as he so obviously needed it. This invariably produced a far more generous response.

Meanwhile, there had slowly but surely been growing a party in Constantinople dedicated to bringing about Ali's downfall. Ali was then close on eighty but as fierce and deceptive as ever. His decision in 1820 to send assassins to the Ottoman capital to murder a particularly relentless enemy, Ismail Pasha Bey, who had gained the ear of the Sultan, finally decided the latter to dismiss Ali and his sons from their positions.

The Sultan's expedition against Ali under the command of Ismail Pasha Bey, who had now been promoted to the rank of a Vizier of Three Tails, was slow to start. In the meanwhile Ali tried in every way possible to make his peace with his master. He wrote letters asking for forgiveness and distributed much largesse in quarters which in the past had proved useful—but not on this occasion. He invited Colonel Charles Napier, British Resident in Cephalonia, later the conqueror of Sind, to advise on his defences, advice which he then refused to take because of the expense. It was Ali's intense meanness, more perhaps than any other defect, that brought about his downfall. If he had followed Napier's advice, the Ottoman expedition would probably never have reached Ioannina. Ali flirted with the *Philiki Etairia* or Greek Friendly Society which he found meeting at Preveza in April 1820 to plot against the Sultan. Ali let loose the Armatoles on the country-side and then arranged for the Porte to be flooded with requests that he be ordered to bring them to heel, because he was the only man capable of doing so. The Sultan remained unmoved.

The Imperial army moved slowly and overwhelmed with their customary brutality the Vizier's outlying garrisons until only Ioannina remained. In the meanwhile, Ali's three sons, tempted by supposed offers of pashaliks in Anatolia, deserted their father in his hour of need, although not entirely to his surprise. His main army of fifteen thousand also went over to the Sultan, leaving him with only a few thousand men. Under these circumstances, all his courage and bravado came to the fore. Having first concentrated his remaining forces in the *kastro* and Litharitza, he set about destroying the town, to deny its shelter to his enemies, with his artillery, including the remaining Congreve rockets; the houses had already been looted by his followers.

The siege dragged on inconclusively throughout the autumn and winter of 1820 and into the new year. Ali, in spite of the odds against him, won a number of actions. 'Greater in misfortune than he had ever been in his glory,' declared Pouqueville, 'Ali seemed suddenly to be enjoying a second youth.' The Sultan, angry at the little progress made, dismissed Ismail Pasha Bey, who later lost not only his command but his head as well, and replaced him with Kurshid Pasha, formerly Grand Vizier and then Pasha of the Morea.

Unfortunately for Ali, his *Shqipetars* holding the Litharitza found numerous kinsmen in the ranks of some recent Ottoman reinforcements and deserted to them. Then arrived the news that Muchtar, Veli, Sali, who was Ali's youngest son, together with Veli's son, Mehmet, far from being granted pashaliks in Asia Minor, had instead been beheaded. Now Ali's garrison in the *kastro* began to slip away, largely because of his meanness over pay, and Ali himself, while still maintaining a cheerful demeanour, had shrunk to but a shadow of what he once had been.

Kurshid now tried to persuade Ali that the Sultan would pardon him and give him a senior position in Asia Minor in return for surrendering Ioannina. Ali eventually agreed to meet Kurshid on the island in the lake, whither he went himself. As a safeguard he left Selim Tchami, a devoted follower, on guard at the entrance to his magazine in the *kastro*, with a lighted match. If anyone tried to seize it, the match was to be applied at once to the gunpowder. Only if someone produced Ali's amber beads should Selim give up his post.

Ali remained in suspense while Kurshid's officers tried to persuade him to surrender the *kastro* with its powder magazine, a necessary move, they explained, if the Sultan's pardon was to become operative. At first he refused to discard his one remaining trick, but eventually he handed over the beads. Later on the same day a boat was seen approaching the island from the town. Ali stepped on to the verandah of the little monastery in order, as he expected, to receive the pardon, only to be greeted with bullets instead. He himself was fatally deceived as he had deceived so many others. After a short fight he was overpowered, having received an agonizing wound in the groin, and killed; his head was first shown to Kurshid and then sent on to Constantinople. After being publicly exhibited, it was interred near those of his sons. Ali's body was buried in the citadel of Ioannina. His only real mourner was Vasiliki, whom he had placed in his harem when she was only twelve and whom he later married in 1816. Such had been his great affection for her that she had been allowed to remain a Christian. Endowed with some property by Ali, she was offered marriage by many, but she refused them all. 'There's no man living', she would explain, 'for the widow of Ali Pasha.'

The Sultan's campaign against Ali denuded the Peloponnese of Turkish troops, a situation which helped to create the conditions for the successful raising of the Greek flag in 1821 against the Turks at Kalavryta in the northern Peloponnese. As these Ottoman troops marched up into Epirus, they left a trail of plundered, burnt-out villages and naked corpses behind them. As a result the *Philiki Etairia* enrolled more and more members in Greece. General Makriyannis gives an excited, tumultuous account in his *Memoirs* of the support which he and his associates elsewhere gave to Ali Pasha as the lesser of two evils, regarding his struggle against the Ottoman armies as theirs as well.

Ali was well served throughout his career by Greeks. The leading landowners in Epirus were probably descended from Byzantine proprietors who became apostates to Islam in order to retain their estates during the Turkish supremacy. They and the more substantial Greek merchants, in spite of Ali's extortions, valued the security, however arbitrary, imposed by him. Again, many Greeks who were prominent in the Greek War of Independence and afterwards in the Hellenic kingdom under King Otho, received their early training through employment with Ali. Odysseus Androutsos, for a time the commander of the Greek insurgents in Eastern Greece, had served in Ali's bodyguard; Trelawney, the friend of Shelley and Byron, married his half-sister. Gogos Bakolos, uncle of Karaiskakis and responsible through his temporary defection to the Turks for the decimation of the Regiment of the Philhellenes by the Turks at Peta in 1822, served Ali as an Armatole. Another member of Ali's bodyguard at one stage was Karaiskakis who commanded the insurgent forces in Central Greece. John Kolettis, who was born in Ioannina and studied medicine at Pisa became one of Ali's doctors; he was later to have a distinguished political and diplomatic career, ending as prime minister of Greece from 1844 to 1847. There were many others.

4

Ioannina: its Cultures and Peoples

In the mid-eighteenth century Gibbon wrote in *The Decline and Fall of the Roman Empire* of the contemporary Athenians that they 'walk with supine indifference among the glorious ruins of antiquity; and such is the debasement of their character that they are incapable of admiring the genius of their predecessors.' Gibbon never visited Greece. True, the Neo-classical Movement, which developed slowly over several centuries in the west through revived interest in the classical authors and ancient monuments, did not influence the Greeks until late in the eighteenth century. It was only then that some of the more educated among them began to see themselves as descendants of the ancient Hellenes and to show interest in the idea of a Hellenic state, based on the laws and precepts of Pericles and Aristotle, of which European scholars, travellers and poets wrote and dreamed. Nevertheless, if Gibbon had visited Ioannina during the last two decades of the eighteenth century, he would have gained a very different picture of Greek intelligence and initiative.

Ioannina under Ali Pasha, in spite of his treachery and extortions, became the most prosperous centre in the Balkans. Ali quickly saw the advantages his exchequer would gain from trade. For these benefits he depended upon the Greeks because of their great gift for commerce, which Islam despised. He encouraged the annual two-week trade fair, held in the plain south-east of Ioannina. Here were displayed goods not only from Epirus but from different parts of the Mediterranean and even from Britain. The sheep and goats were sold to the Ionian Islands, while olive oil, timber, corn and tobacco were exported, according to Hobhouse, to the Kingdom of Naples through the Adriatic ports. The stocks of guns and

49

pistols, when mounted in chased silver by Ioanniniot silver-smiths, were very highly prized. In addition, there was a two-way trade with Russia, Venice, Malta and Constantinople. Hughes noted that Ali's customs collected four percent *ad valorem* on all these items. From this commerce, the merchants prospered handsomely—and so did Ali. By visiting this fair, the Vizier gained a shrewd idea of who was prospering and from whom he could extract additional contributions for his exchequer. He made no bones about his extortionate methods. Leake remarked that Ali 'since he has become of political importance in Europe, shows some wish that foreigners should have a favourable opinion of him. Nevertheless, he has little scruple in alluding to those actions of his life which are the least likely to obtain such favour.'

The importance of Ioannina did not decline after Ali's death. David Urquhart arrived in Ioannina in 1833 to look for openings for British trade and declared that 'this is the Manchester and Paris of Roumeli'.

As well as the revenue derived from Ioannina's role as an important *entrepôt*, there was the wealth accruing to various Epirot families which had established themselves in the Danubian provinces of Wallachia and Moldavia, and beyond the Ottoman frontiers in Russia, Austria and elsewhere. Ali would never allow a family to emigrate completely; an important member was always compelled to reside in the Vizier's dominions as a hostage. The Zosimas brothers were a case in point; this generous family which maintained a school for the local Greek community which still flourishes, had brothers in Russia and Italy, but always one in Ioannina.

It was largely the successful Greek merchants in Europe and Russia who became caught up in western speculations about their ancient Hellenic ancestry. By establishing prosperous, well organized communities in the main cities of Europe, these merchants proved that their drive and intelligence were at least equal to those among whom they had settled. They were happy to support these Hellenic aspirations but were rarely prepared to go further. They did not, for example, join the *Philiki Etairia*, founded in Odessa in 1814 by three Greek merchants, two of whom were Epirots. This Society aimed at overthrowing the Turkish yoke and setting up an independent

Greek state. Those who supported the Society among the merchant class, which formed over fifty percent of its membership, were mainly those who had not yet successfully established themselves; many of them had been ruined by the trade depression which followed the end of the Napoleonic Wars. The Society grew rapidly outside the Turkish Empire but it was not until 1818 that it began its recruiting campaign inside Greece. Ali was early aware of its activities and gave it some encouragement as a further means of weakening the Porte at a time when the Sultan first started to consider taking action against him.

Because he was so dependent upon Greek skills, Ali not only tolerated but encouraged Greek education. This was at first in the hands of the Greek Orthodox Church. Evyenios Voulgaris, a Corfiot nobleman and an Orthodox prelate, taught Greek grammar in Ioannina in the 1750s at the school founded by the Marontsi brothers then settled in Venice; it closed in 1797. The Greeks looked primarily for leadership to the Orthodox Church which, after the collapse of the Byzantine Empire, had inherited the traditions and awe of the Christian Roman Empire, founded by the Emperor Constantine and which in turn had been the heir to the earlier learning and authority of Rome and Greece, but from which the pagan elements had been eliminated. The Turkish government acknowledged the Orthodox Patriarch as the head of the Greek *millet* or nation within the Ottoman Empire. While there were many disadvantages of tax and status, there was nevertheless a recognized system of law and order which, even if often abused, gave the Greeks an established standing in the Ottoman realm and enabled the most intelligent among them to achieve the highest distinction in the service of the Sultan, as witnessed by the wealth and honours harvested by the Phanariot Greeks of Constantinople in the eighteenth century.

From the middle of the eighteenth century in Ioannina, wealthy Greeks were also benefactors of Greek learning. Two secular schools, according to Leake, flourished in Ali's capital in the 1800s—the Zosimas school, already mentioned above, and that founded towards the end of the eighteenth century by a Greek merchant named Pikrozoi, who also built a hospital. The name of Pikrozoi is today unknown in Ioannina.

Athanasios Psallidas, who was headmaster of this school, again according to Leake, was Ioannina's leading scholar at that time; he became head of the Patriarchal School following his return home in 1797 after studying for a time in Europe. We can but assume that Pikrozoi, if that was his real name, was an important benefactor of the Patriarchal School. The actual founder of the Zosimas school was one Ghioni, a merchant, who had made a fortune in Wallachia, invested it in Venice and lost it when the French overthrew the Serene Republic in 1797. The Zosimas brothers then took over what Ghioni had founded; their funds allowed up to three hundred pupils to be taught under the inspiration, then at its height, of Adamantios Korais. Korais, who was born in Smyrna in 1748, later established himself in Paris; there he devoted his life to the revival of both the classical Greek language, a much purer tongue than the Romaic or popular language, and knowledge of ancient Greek literature.

Psallidas, who was cantankerous, opinionated and devoted to Ali Pasha, displayed much of the distrust entertained by many Orthodox Greeks towards the west, as Hughes discovered; this Byzantine suspicion remained until the foundation of the modern Greek kingdom brought with it a strong revival of Hellenism which enabled Greeks to regard the west with far more sympathy, for it was from there that Hellenism had emerged. The western record in the eyes of Psallidas and many of his contemporaries was besmirched by the catastrophe of the Fourth Crusade, the continuing enmity of the Papacy, the greed of the Italian traders, especially the Venetians, and by the contemporary despoilers of ancient Greek monuments, especially the British and the French, at a time when the more cultivated Greeks were at last becoming aware of their historic value. Ali Pasha was careful not to hinder this educational renaissance in Ioannina since his civil service, like that in Constantinople, was almost entirely drawn from his Greek subjects.

It is therefore not surprising that both Hughes and Leake remarked on the greater purity of the Greek language as then spoken in Ioannina than elsewhere in Greece, including Athens. Leake said that 'its phrases are more Hellenic, and its construction more grammatical. This is the natural consequence of the schools long established here.' Hughes added that the language 'is here much less mixed with oriental barbarisms, or exotic Frank and Italian terms'. It is therefore fitting that since 1945, Ioannina has had its own university, built on the southern edge of the town.

The position of the Greeks and their Church under the Turks can in Ioannina be summed up by the site and structure of its metropolis or cathedral, dedicated to St Athanasios. It stands inconspicuously between the Litharitza and the *kastro*. It was built in the 1820s on the site of an earlier, smaller church, and surrounded by a high wall, for it behoved Christians in the Sultan's dominions to be discreet in their devotions. The building is extremely restrained and the central lantern as seen from outside is low and humble. There is a paved courtyard on the north side and above it to the west stand the bishop's palace and a clock tower, obviously built after Epirus became part of Greece.

If the outside shape is in a minor key, the interior of the basilica with its great nave and supporting aisles is deeply impressive. Above, over the rich iconostasis, the screen between the nave and the sanctuary, rises the great dome with its lantern; there are smaller domes above the nave and aisles, hidden from outside view by the slope of the roof. In the glimmering candle-light the massive figures of saints, painted on the walls, can be seen standing in humility before the risen God in the sanctuary. Perhaps the greatest glory of the metropolis is its splendid carved iconostasis. The woodcarvers of Konitsa and Metsovo were invited to compete for the honour of creating it, so the former carved the metropolitan's throne and the latter the pulpit; an inspection of these two artifacts quickly reveals why it was the Konitsa craftsmen who made the iconostasis with its intricate detail of vineyards, fruit, labourers, birds and dragons.

One way into the cathedral is through the chapel of St George of Ioannina, whose marble tomb was raised there in 1858, twenty years after his martyrdom at the hands of the Turks. The brown mahogany paint in which the chapel is decorated is as depressing as the icon depicting the saint alive and the manner of his death by hanging. A simple, uneducated peasant, his only fault in the eyes of the Ottoman authorities,

who had him classified as a Muslim, was his steadfast Christian
faith, which was capped by his betrothal to a Christian girl.
Spurning the temptation of apostacy, he met his end on the
gallows, close to the main gateway into the *kastro*, where a
shrine to him now stands. His cult as a New Martyr spontane-
ously established itself and many tales are told of his powers.

There were, however, other peoples who were allowed to
exist, if not to flourish, during the reign of Ali Pasha. Ioannina,
according to Leake when Resident there in 1809, consisted of
about three thousand two hundred houses, of which about a
thousand were Muslim, two thousand Christian and some two
hundred Jewish. He noted that some of the Greek and Turkish
houses were among the best in European Turkey, but the
conditions under which the Jews lived were for the most part
appalling. Their ghetto stood close inside the west wall of the
kastro, where the Old Synagogue stands today, but their
houses, each of which accommodated from four to six
families, had usually only three walls and were often open on
the fourth during all weathers. Many Jewish families preferred
to live in this way, according to Hughes, for policy reasons.
Being mainly occupied with banking and money-lending, they
were anxious not to call Ali's attention to their wealth by over-
presumptuous living. Those not engaged in the money market
were dealers in the bazaar or employed as artisans in the
Vizier's *serai*.

The largest Jewish emigration into Ottoman territory
followed their expulsion from Spain in 1492 by Ferdinand and
Isabella, but Jews had settled in Epirus at a much earlier date,
certainly by the time that Nikopolis was founded in 31 B.C.
St Paul probably came there as shown in his Letter to Titus;
his visits were primarily to Jewish colonies where he preached
in the synagogue. Jews had very likely settled in Ioannina by
1160, when Benjamin of Tudela arrived there, and were of
some importance to the community at the beginning of the
fourteenth century when the Emperor Andronicus Palaiologos
granted them certain privileges.

The Jewish colony reached its zenith in the late nineteenth
and early twentieth centuries, when their numbers approached
six thousand. In Arta their colony was probably correspond-
ingly large. In those days in Ioannina there were four syna-

gogues; two large and two small. One of the four was built for the influx of refugees from Apulia because of Spanish and Papal persecution during the sixteenth century and was accordingly known as the Pules synagogue, as it was customary to name each place of worship after the community who built it; thus the second largest synagogue in Athens is known, so I was told, as the Ioanniniotiko, after the Jews from Ioannina who now live there.

Then early in this century there was a mass migration to the United States. Although the Greek Government recognized the Jews as a legal entity in 1920, the numbers in Ioannina continued to dwindle and, by 1940, only some two thousand remained. Then came the Axis occupation with the inevitable and catastrophic persecution. The Jews of Ioannina, like those of Corfu, were deported to concentration camps. Today, only about a hundred remain, many of them impoverished, having returned after the war to find their property destroyed or looted. Only the Old Synagogue still stands because it was used by the Nazis as a warehouse; it is an elegant building, dating from 1790, a previous building having been destroyed by fire. The earliest synagogue erected here was thought to date from the tenth century. The Jewish community is immensely grateful to the memory of the late Mr Vlachvlides, who was mayor of Ioannina for many years, including the war period. He hid the synagogue's treasures throughout the Axis occupation, later returning them to their rightful owners. A tablet in the Old Synagogue commemorates this act of kindness and compassion.

According to the head of the Jewish community of Ioannina, whom I met in a block of flats erected on the site of the New Synagogue, destroyed by the Nazis, numbers are still dwindling. Nor have the authorities always been as considerate as Mr Vlachvlides. The Greeks in general have shown some hostility at times to the Jews; this was certainly true during the last quarter of the nineteenth century when Valentine Chirol visited the city. The Turks were less biased, for the Muslim authorities have regarded both Christians and Jews as people of the Book, namely the Bible, which had contributed to the development of Islam; so long as they kept the peace and paid their taxes, they were not disturbed. The Turks have on occasion been known to protect the Jews from the Christians. Today, the smallness of the Jewish community creates no problem.

Another much larger community in Ioannina up until 1913 was that of the Muslims, who worshipped at as many as eighteen mosques. There were still seven thousand Muslims there with their own *mufti* and judge at the time of the disastrous Greek campaign in Asia Minor of 1921–2 which ended with the complete destruction of the Greek quarters in Smyrna. The population exchange between Greece and Turkey which followed removed all those of Turkish origin so that, by 1940, only some twenty Muslim families of Albanian origin were left. In 1973 only eight Muslims remained, living together in an ancient house in the centre of Ioannina. The local authorities, we were told, had refused to allow them to use one of the remaining mosques for worship, their estates remain sequestered and a long battle for what they regard as their rights has so far come to nothing. Although Albanian, they could hope for no sympathy from the present regime in Albania and there was nowhere else for them to go.

During the Ottoman Empire, Ioannina had been the administrative centre for the territory west of the Aoos from Valona to the Gulf of Arta. The Turkish governor, who resided here, was advised by committees which represented all interests. Muslims of good family, we learned, had lived here since the arrival of the Turks in 1430.

Until the First Balkan War, there was said to have been little religious or racial prejudice among the leading inhabitants, and respectable familes—whether Christian, Jewish or Muslim—had mixed freely. Muslim women of the better class wore Turkish costume in the streets, but dressed in European clothes at home. Christians as well as Muslims wore the fez when on official business. The Greek-Turkish conflict of 1921–2 had altered all this, and the bitterness of the Greek refugees from Asia Minor had since kept alive the antagonism between the Christians and Muslims. In the northern coastal areas of Epirus, a considerable number of villages had been inhabited by Muslim Albanians known as Chams, an abbreviation for Tshamides or Tzamourians, who had been unaffected by the 1924 exchange of population between

Greece and Turkey. During the Second World War, however, they became the dupes of Axis propaganda. Most of them had to be convoyed into Albania by the retreating Germans in 1944, only to fall into the hands of the Communist Albanians who no doubt regarded them as traitors; most of those who remained in Greece were massacred by the Greeks for the same reason. Even today there is little sympathy or compassion for the few who are left.

As Mrs Elli Kirk-Deftereou and I sat in a little café near the *kastro*, we chanced upon yet another people who inhabit Epirus. We were struck by the handsome dark features and the somewhat glamorous dress of three people talking at a nearby table, especially of a man wearing a smart black Homburg hat and a flowered waistcoat on which he sported a gold watch-chain. Elli was listening to them with intense interest, then suddenly leant across and asked what language they were speaking.

'We are speaking Tsakonian,' replied one of the men with dignity. 'It's a dialect spoken in the eastern Peloponnese,' he added in explanation. Tsakonia lies in the mountainous region east of Sparta, with Parnon at its centre, where a distinctive Dorian dialect is still spoken. But his explanation did not ring true. He then admitted that they had been speaking Romany for they were gypsies. They peddled smart city shirts and ties to the villages of Zagori, Tzoumerka, Pogoniani and elsewhere in Epirus, and their super-smart appearance was part of their stock in trade.

We spoke together for a while but they soon departed, a people who never feel really at ease except among themselves, who here in Greece look so much darker in complexion than their English cousins, so much nearer in every way to the land of their origin somewhere between Egypt and India.

5

Ioannina Today

Ioannina, which today has a population of at least forty thousand, twice what it was in 1939, is the place of residence of the Governor-General of Epirus, the seat of a metropolitan and a regional military headquarters. Its importance can be judged by the size of its long, irregular, spacious *plateia* (square). It was obviously not planned as such as in Agrinion or Argostoli, but seems to have come haphazardly into existence. The impression given is that as the rubble from Ali's bombardment of the town from the *kastro* was gradually cleared away, a long, narrow space was left where people could perambulate in comfort. Every evening from six until well after nine, the promenade or *volta* is in full swing, weather permitting. Up and down people go, the men clicking their amber beads, while clouds of aromatic tobacco smoke mingle with the evening air. The upper part of the *plateia*, named after Pyrrhus, is above the Hotel Acropol, while at the lower end is the military headquarters, from which an infantry platoon emerges at sundown to present arms as the national flag is lowered and a bugler sounds the retreat—the only time when conversation drops to a hush. Opposite the entrance to the barracks is the town hall, formerly a bank, with a stork's nest on its roof, one of the few left in Ioannina.

On the west side of the *plateia* are the cafés whose tables crowd across the pavement and into the road, and whose waiters also service those in the little public garden opposite. The occupants of these tables, eating sticky cakes and ice cream, appear even better dressed than the strollers, especially the children in elaborate, spotless attire. Traffic is diverted round the square's perimeter.

Between the public gardens and the barracks stand taxis

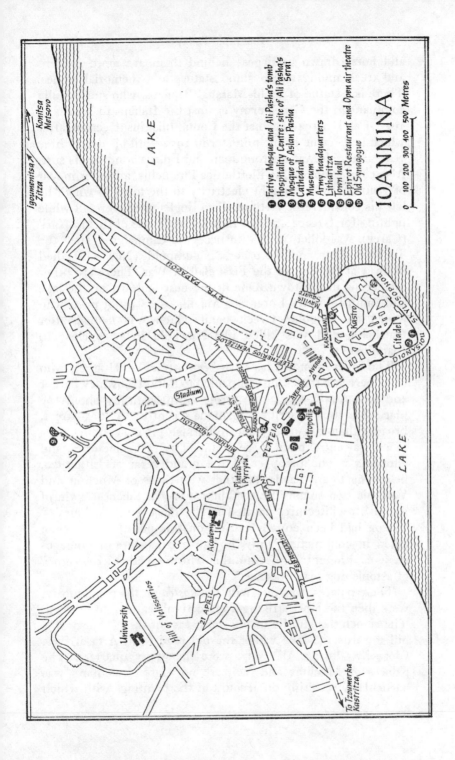

IOANNINA

1. Fetiye Mosque and Ali Pasha's tomb
2. Hospitality Centre: site of Ali Pasha's Serai
3. Mosque of Aslan Pasha
4. Cathedral
5. Museum
6. Army headquarters
7. Litharitza
8. Town hall
9. Epirot Restaurant and Open air theatre
10. Old Synagogue

0   100 200 300 400 500 Metres

LAKE

Konitsa
Metsovo

Igoumenitsa
Zitza

ELIA PAPAGOU

ELEFTHERIOS VENIZELOS

Stadium

KARAMANLI

MARKO BOTSARIS PANGOU

OKTOBER 28

MIKHAIL ANGELOU

NAPOLEON

AVEROF

AVEROF

AVEROF

NAVILLIS Square

Kastro

DIONYSIOU

SKYLOSOPHOU

Citadel

PLATEIA

BIZAN

Metropolis

Platria
Pyrrou

FESSOULION

Academy

21 APRIL

Hill of Velissarios

University

To Tzoumerka
Kastritsa

LAKE

and horse-drawn carriages; behind them are more gardens and trees among which stand statues and memorial stones. There is a statue of Field-Marshal Papagos, who successfully commanded the Greek army against the Italians in Epirus in 1940–1 and in 1949 against the Communist insurrection, after which he became prime minister in 1952 until his death three years later. He was a strong man and Epirus admires his sort. Also commemorated is Eleftherios Pirsinellis, a former mayor of Ioannina who brought electricity to the town to which he left his considerable fortune. Two Englishmen who fell while fighting for Greece are also remembered; one of them, 'Xari' (Carey), was killed in the unsuccessful campaign against the Turks in 1897 and the other, 'Nioumpold' (Newbold), died in 1913 at the end of the First Balkan War. There are other memorials in the town. One of the best is down by the lake and commemorates Lorentzos Mavilis, the Corfiot poet, who joined an irregular Greek band which was named after Garibaldi, and was killed like Newbold in 1913 close to Ioannina.

The town must always have been attractive. Hughes, who came here as a travelling companion to Robert Townley Parker and with C. R. Cockerell, wrote enthusiastically about the place. He thus described Ioannina's centre: 'A long street, broader than is usually seen in Turkish towns, conducted us to a large central open space occupied by vast cemeteries, and affording a fine prospect of the grand serai of Litharitza, belonging to Ali Pasha, together with those of Muchtar and Veli, his two sons. These edifices were in the best style of Turkish architecture, painted in the most gaudy colours'— (Byron had been equally critical on this point)—'and when taken in conjunction with the noble expanse and range of snow-capt mountains beyond them, form together a *coup d'oeil* of astonishing magnificence.'

These palaces, together with the *kastro* on the promontory, were then the most striking architectural features to be seen. The cemeteries still lie to the south-east of the *plateia* downhill towards the lake where the old road from Arta arrives. Close by, during Ali's day, were the gypsy quarters. The palaces of Muchtar and Veli are no more. Muchtar's was particularly revolting on account of the paintings with which some of the outside walls were embellished. One, over the main entrance, depicted the execution of two Greeks who were shown being tied to the same rope by the hangman. The Litharitza was being restored in 1973.

Ali built a number of kiosks in and around the town, where he could work or dally in seclusion; he would choose a different one each day, having arranged for the appropriate companion to be transported there. The most remarkable was among the trees on the slopes of St George's Hill; in its interior, according to Leake and others who saw it, was a marble basin of water. In its centre, wrote Leake, stood 'a rude model of a fortress mounted with cannon, which when the fountain is set at work spout forth water and are answered by a similar discharge from besieging cannon round the edge of the basin. If,' added Leake, 'instead of this silly bauble in the childish taste of the Turks, there had been some simple and more elegant fountain, the building would have been as perfect a work as can be conceived.' None remain today.

Ioannina in 1944–5, when I spent some months there, still retained much of the atmosphere of a Turkish provincial city. There were several more minarets than can be seen there today. The better houses in the residential area, which stretched away to the west of the *plateia*, were often stone mansions of two storeys with storage rooms in the basement. Inside the heavy front door, a small flight of steps led up to the ground floor, which was entered through a glass door. The dining and sitting rooms led off this hall, at one end of which was a solid wooden staircase leading to the first floor.

As Ioannina is surrounded by high mountains, the winters there are hard and cold, so every room usually contained stoves of coloured procelain, fitted inside with fireclay and designed to burn firewood gathered from the surrounding countryside. I am indebted to Elli, who was born and brought up in Ioannina in the 1920s and 1930s, for a picture of life in one of these houses. The best firewood was considered to be ilex or holm-oak, found in abundance in Lakkasouli. The peasants—wiry, toughly built men of middle height—would bring their loads on mules and donkeys into the cobbled yard which ran round the side and back of the house. Here the wood would be weighed and payment made amid altercation

and laughter, the braying of the donkeys and the barking of
the dogs, all to the children's delight. Later, woodcutters
came to chop the wood to the right length for use in the
kitchen and house stoves.

Piped water came to the town only a few years before the
recent war and Ioanniniot families depended upon their wells;
each house usually had one and sometimes two. The house
of Mr Vlachvlides, then mayor, had a fine well in his paved,
rose-embellished garden which was laid out between the house
and the separate kitchen building; kitchens were not often
part of the main house, perhaps as a fire precaution. Every
drop of water for whatever purpose had to be drawn from the
wells, which were always kept covered to prevent children
from falling in.

Every so often, these wells had to be cleaned. This was the
work of the *pigadides* or wellmen; *pigadas* still exists as a
family name although the profession has now disappeared.
The importance of keeping the wells clean went back to the
days before the introduction of electric refrigeration; food,
which might quickly perish in summer, was lowered halfway
down the well for coolness in large baskets secured by rope to
the well head. Electricity only reached Ioannina in 1928.

A large household bought seasonal produce in bulk and
preserved it for the winter. Freshly made cheese was pur-
chased in great rounds, then cut into large slices, salted and
packed into sealed tins. Olives and olive oil were bought once
a year from the groves of Threspotia. The olive oil arrived in
skins and was stored in a huge earthenware jar in the cellar.
The preserving of the olives was a complicated task. First
they were incised and placed daily in fresh water for ten days
to rid them of their bitter taste; afterwards they were put into
brine for ten more days and finally into vinegar, where they
were left until sufficient of the liquid had been absorbed by the
fruit to give them the desired taste. To test the water and salt
mixture, an unboiled egg was put into it; only if it floated at
the halfway mark was the solution of the right proportion.
The olives were then packed into earthenware jars and covered
with olive oil to which were added sprigs of origan and slices
of orange and lemon. Families made their own tomato paste
by boiling down and then crushing ripe tomatoes and leaving

what remained to dry for several days in the sun. All this produce together with the wine, which was also made at home, was locked away, before the arrival of electricity, in a great vaulted storeroom in the basement behind a heavy iron door.

Servants were in those days still obtainable. Elli told me that until 1940 her parents had a cook and two maids; the cook did the shopping and washing in addition to the cooking. He cooked extremely well, having worked in foreign consulates and big houses in Athens, and had learned French, Italian and Austrian cuisine. He had started work as a peasant boy from Lakkasouli in her great-grandmother's house and ended his days in her parents' after nearly thirty-five years of service. He stole moderately, drank heavily, spied on the maids with relish and entertained the children with the most unsuitable stories which, fortunately, they did not understand.

Life in provincial Ioannina was and still is quiet and rather formal. Families usually entertain at home only relatives and close friends. On one's nameday it is still usual for friends to call for some fifteen minutes to offer their congratulations, or long enough to consume without undue haste a sweet, consisting of fruit crystallized or preserved in a thick syrup, a glass of water and a small cup of Turkish coffee. A variety of fruits are used for these occasions, including tangerines, oranges, plums, quinces and walnuts. If a toast of 'many years' is proposed, it is drunk in water, never coffee because that would bring bad luck; coffee is the customary drink at funerals. Alcohol is rarely if ever produced at such times if only Greeks are present.

In summer, family entertainments consisted of excursions to the surrounding countryside and on the lake; these are still basically the only forms of entertainment available, except that the motorcar and the excellent bus services bring the remotest villages very much nearer. There is in addition the cinema and in winter an occasional touring company from Athens; before the war there was also the shadow theatre, now much less often seen. Finally there is radio and television.

Ioannina remained unsettled and crowded with refugees from remote villages until the Communist rebellion was finally put down in 1949. In 1946 the streets were full of peasants, often wearing dyed battle-dress, leading their mules along the cobbled streets. They would be seen in little cafés, sipping coffee and smoking home-grown tobacco, their faces stern, their hair clipped short, their moustaches full and their blue eyes staring into vacancy. They often knew people in town, relatives who had managed to find a job there or friends who might be able to help track down someone of influence to help over the question of a piece of land or grazing rights.

Then, after 1949, came peace and with it prosperity and plenty of work either locally or abroad. Because of the shortage of domestic labour—a postwar phenomenon—and the mounting cost of upkeep, the small grey stone mansions became increasingly difficult to maintain. People now wanted modern, easily run apartments, such as were springing up in Athens, but which did not yet exist in Ioannina. Then the local builders offered a very attractive plan. The owner surrendered his home and garden to the builder, whose responsibility it then became to demolish the old building and to erect in its place a four- or five-storeyed block of modern flats. The builder then returned in kind to the original owner that percentage of the block which the value of the site, regarded as building land, represented. This usually amounted to one, sometimes two of the flats, one of which the owner would make his new home, and the other he could sell or rent. Now there are few of the old stone houses left, but many apartment blocks which have inevitably changed the town's character.

Only a few ancient houses from the time of Ali Pasha now survive. One of these still stood in 1973 on a corner of Papazoglou Street. Thick stone walls, without apertures of any sort at street level, supported the structure up to the first floor; just below it was a row of several small openings, heavily protected by iron grilles, which allowed a little light into the stables and storerooms which occupied the ground floor. Above them larger windows at first-floor level opened out of the reception and bedrooms. This upper part was constructed of wood and plaster. Handsome heavy wooden doors, large enough to admit a carriage and horses, opened into a wide courtyard adjoining the house; beyond was the garden. In 1945, when the house was still occupied, storks had made their nest on the roof; in 1973 they had departed.

1. Fetiye mosque, Ioannina, with Ali Pasha's tomb on the left

2. Ali Pasha

3. Ruined house in
Koukouli, Zagori

4. Entrance to
monastery at
Monodendri,
Zagori, with
Vikos gorge

5. Turkish bridge
in Zagori

6. Village mansion,
Tsepelovo, Zagori

7. Entrance to monastery church of Vlachernae, near Arta

8. Carved oak door in the church of the Monastery of the Dormition, Molyvthoskepasto

9. Church of the Monastery of the Dormition, Molyvthoskepasto, with Mt. Merope behind

Although this house is an outstanding example of its kind, it may have to make way for an apartment block because of the cost of restoration. Another fine example is Dr Vassili Lappas's house; here, however, only the exterior has been preserved; the interior has been reorganized to provide a practical home and surgery. There are also some attractive houses, built with a simple elegance of design, close to Mavilis Square and the lakeside, which would be much in demand if in one of the more fashionable parts of London.

The storks, which were once a prominent feature of Ioannina, are now only occasionally seen. Thirty years ago, there was scarcely a roof of any size which did not have its stork nest, built usually on the chimney. On Mr Vlachvlides's house, now pulled down to make way for offices and show-rooms, there were, in addition to the stork family, a species of small falcon and clans of swallows and house martins, which nested under the eaves; these various birds lived harmoniously together as none encroached on the interests of the others. Every spring, the storks returned from the south to settle back in their old nests and to start the immemorial pattern of hatching their eggs and teaching the young to fly. By mid-June strengthening wing exercises had started for the youngsters in the nest; by early August they would start training flights for short, then for longer distances, until one day between the end of August and late September one would suddenly realize that the long grey column of wheeling birds had not returned from their morning flight, but had continued away over the mountains towards their winter home in Africa or Asia. Only a few elderly storks, too ill or feeble to venture on the journey, languished in the deserted nests before they too departed on their last flight into the hills to die.

The demolition of the old mansions and their replacement by blocks of flats has meant that there are now few suitable roofs and chimneys for storks' nests. Their nesting has been discouraged because twigs have been known to fall down the chimney and to cause damage when a fire is burning in the hearth below. Now the townspeople are beginning to miss the personality of this splendid bird; one or two were even planning their roofs, when building, in such a way as to encourage them to nest once more.

c

6

The Lake of Ioannina

Henry Holland, like Hughes, was enchanted by the loveliness
of Ioannina and its surroundings—'the lofty palaces of the
Vizier and his sons, the minarets of numerous mosques, each
surrounded by its groves of Cypresses . . . the singular inter-
mixture of houses and trees through every part of the city
together with the noble situation on the lake, and the magnificence of the surrounding mountains, are the features which
will most impress the stranger in approaching the capital of
Ali Pasha.' Ah, the lake, a magical sheet of water without
which much of Ioannina's charm would be lost.

What Holland expressed in prose was depicted in pencil by
a young French artist, Louis Dupré, a pupil of David. Dupré
arrived in Corfu in 1819. His drawings of some Souliots,
refugees in Corfu from Ali Pasha, came to the notice of Sir
Thomas Maitland, the first and least attractive of the British
Lord High Commissioners who from 1814 ruled the Ionian
Islands until 1864, when they were made over to Greece. Maitland invited Dupré to accompany him to a conference at
Butrinto with Ali Pasha when the fate of Parga was to be
discussed. While there, he was able to record the only known
likeness of the 'Diamond of Ioannina'.

Dupré drew several members of Ali's family and executed
a view of Ioannina from the island in the lake, where Ali met
his death; these illustrations were reproduced in his *Voyages
à Athènes*. This view is particularly fine, showing the east side
of the *kastro* with its low cliffs; today the waters of the lake
have fallen sufficiently to allow for a road, now shaded by vast
plane trees, round the *kastro*'s outer perimeter. At its northern
end stands the mosque of Aslan Pasha with its graceful minaret; nearby in Ali's time was a *tekké* or monastery of der-

vishes, established there behind its own wall in 1618. At the southern end is a complex of buildings, including the citadel, the *serai* and the Fetiye mosque; Ali's little kiosk, built for him at water level, is clearly visible with the covered staircase leading down to it from the *serai*. Beyond and to the rear the Litharitza is just visible against the outline of St George's Hill.

Edward Lear spent three days here in May 1849, and was enthralled. With his usual energy and industry, he made many sketches of Ioannina and its surroundings, especially of the lake, and described how he enjoyed the 'placid solemnity of the dark waters reflecting the great mosque and battlements of the citadel as in a mirror'. He took a boat to the island 'where that most wondrous man Ali Pasha met his death'. He recorded in his journal that he would have been very happy to have spent a summer there and that 'Yannina will always hold its place in memory as one of the first of interest of the many scenes I have known in many lands', which included most of Europe, Egypt, parts of Asia Minor and India.

The Lake of Ioannina is first mentioned as late as the twelfth century by Eustathius who called it Lake Pambotis. 'But', writes Hammond, 'the city of Ioannina is mentioned some centuries earlier as an important place, and the strength of its defences arises primarily from the existence of the Lake, into which its acropolis projects. We may therefore assume the Lake to have been there before c. 879, when "Zacharius, Bishop of Ioannina" attended a synod at Constantinople. If this form of the name was inspired by the like-named daughter of Belisaurius, then the city was founded, or at least so named, in the sixth century. But this is a matter of conjecture.'

The lake, which is about five miles long from Perama village in the north to the hill of Kastritza in the south-east, is roughly triangular in shape with Perama at the apex and the south-eastern shore as the base; Perama, incidently, has in recent years gained renown throughout Greece for its extensive and remarkable limestone caves, which attract many visitors. The level of the lake remains constant because the overflow is drained away by the *katavothres* under Kastritza, possibly emerging some distance away to join the Louros river which is born on Mount Olytsika to the south-west, or the

Arakhthos river at some point even as far off as Khanopulo at the southern end of the Xerovouni mountains near Arta. These *katavothres* exist on account of the karst formations in the limestone.

Professor Dakaris showed us a cave facing the lake at the foot of Kastritza, which had been used by Palaeolithic man; it had been discovered by archaeologists from Cambridge University. He pointed out the layers of deposits which went well below the level of the road close by. Three of these layers contained sand and the shells of freshwater oysters, thus indicating that the lake, now several hundred yards to the north, had filled the cave on three separate occasions during the Ice Ages, which separated Palaeolithic from Neolithic man. The rising of the lake waters would have been caused by the expansion of the ice. Below these three layers was evidence that Palaeolithic man had used the cave as long ago as 30,000 B.C., and that the game he hunted included not only various species of deer but rhinoceros as well.

After the end of the last Ice Age in about 9000 B.C., the cave was occupied by Neolithic man as shown by a much darker layer—darker because it contained carbon from wood fires. The cave was obviously situated close to the routes taken by the animals which were hunted as the herds moved higher up to the mountain pastures in summer and back to the warmer coastal lands for winter. In the deposit for this period we found several small razor-sharp implements.

In Leake's day there was another lake at the northern end of the same valley, but it has largely disappeared in recent years. This was Lake Lapsista whose surplus waters were drained by *katavothres* into a tributary of the River Kalamas at Veltsista, now called Klimatia, in the shape of a waterfall, which still plays. Today there is an artificial channel emptying these waters into the river; before the lake disappeared, a canal connected it with the lake of Ioannina. Elli remembers, when young, being taken through this waterway in a long narrow boat, called a *karavouli*, where leeches dropped on to her from the weeping willows along the banks and from the tall reeds growing at the water's edge.

The lake contains a large number of coarse fish, such as pike, tench, perch and carp, which are caught for the market;

they may be seen awash in their own blood in tanks on barrows near the *kastro*, especially during Lent. Eels are particularly popular and are prepared in various ways—grilled or baked with a pastry covering in the oven. There is also an abundance of water snakes living on the frogs which breed among the reed beds; these grow round much of the island and along the lake shore.

The lake attracted 'myriads of wildfowl of every species'—the words are Hughes'—and grand shooting parties were organized on behalf of Ali Pasha and especially of Muchtar, who was particularly addicted to this sport. Hughes and his companions were on several occasions invited to participate by Muchtar and members of prominent Ioanniniot families. At times more than a hundred boats were involved. These would slowly drive the waterfowl to one end of the lake and then encircle them. The shooting would start when the birds, finding themselves endangered, began to rise in clouds into the air. The reedbeds in the remoter reaches of the lake near Kastritza are still frequented by wildfowl, and the magnificent eagles and vultures, which used to attend upon Muchtar's shoots in vast numbers, are still occasionally seen.

After one such shoot, Hughes was invited back to the island by Muchtar for dinner. The village is situated at its northern end, facing towards Mitzikeli, and is reached by an opening through the reeds. Today motor launches come there from their berths under the plane trees by the Ioanniniot *kastro*, a popular service as there is a good restaurant, offering live river trout from a farm on the Louros and freshwater crayfish.

Leake recorded in 1809 that the island contained a house for the Vizier, five small monasteries, in which Hughes later searched in vain for manuscripts, and a village of a hundred houses amidst gardens and plane trees. Hughes thought that the houses displayed 'greater neatness than I ever remember to have seen in any part of the world'. The village today is as neat as in Ali's time, the footpaths paved with stone and the cottages whitewashed. Many of the villagers take in tourists. Some of the older women still wear their traditional costume but the girls prefer contemporary summer dresses.

A footpath, mostly under oak and plane trees, follows the

edge of the island, on three sides of which great banks of reeds stand whispering between the shore and the open lake, enlivened only by the croaking of frogs or the sudden plop as one of them takes shelter in the jade-green water. Inland, the island rises to a low ridge, and on the gently sloping ground to its west stand three of the monasteries, now silent except for the echoing footsteps of the caretaker or an occasional visitor. Even in Ali's day they contained only two or three monks as they were used to house Ali's prisoners, where they wasted away slowly on bread and water. Each of these three monasteries is dedicated to St Nicolas.

The monastery nearest to the village, and also the most interesting, both because of its unusual layout and on account of its frescoes, is that of the Philanthropinos and Spanos families. The Spanos family was a benefactor of this foundation towards the end of the Turkish occupation, but the Philanthropini were distinguished in 'the City', that is to say in Byzantine Constantinople, long before a branch settled in Ioannina after the Fourth Crusade; Demetrius Chomatenos, later to become Archbishop of Okhrid, estimated that at least half, if not more, of the City then sought shelter in Epirus. The monastery was founded in 1292, according to an inscription over the entrance, by Michael Philanthropinos, who was steward of the metropolis of Ioannina. A likeness of him can be seen in a painting on the north wall of the narthex, genuflecting to St Nicolas with descendants of his family, three of whom at later dates became abbots of the foundation.

The original monastic church consisted of a single nave with an apse, which contained the sanctuary, and a narthex at the west end. Then, in the middle of the sixteenth century— during the Turkish ascendancy, let it be noted—the monastery was extended by the erection of an outer narthex on each side of the now central nave, into which neither had direct communication except through the inner narthex. A further outer narthex was added so, as a result, the church in outline now resembles a basilica with nave and two aisles, all of equal length. The monastery church stands complete but the monks' cells to the south of it have largely disappeared. Two monks of this foundation, Komnenos and Proklos, were the authors of the *Chronicle of Epirus*, written about 1400,

which was mainly an account of the rise and fall of Thomas
Preljubovich.

The glory of the church is its wall-paintings which were
created after its extension. There are two series. The first
was carried out by an unknown hand or hands in 1542,
principally in the nave and inner narthex. The second series
was the work of two ecclesiastical painters from Thebes,
Giorgios and Frankos Koutaris, the latter sometimes called
Frankos Katellanos; they are known from their distinctive
style to have worked between 1560 and 1568 at Veltsista as
well as in the monastery of Barlaam at Meteora in the Thessalian foothills of the Pindus. Against the dark blue background, the stylized elongated bodies of the saints in brilliant
colours stare sombrely from the walls. As an indication of the
reviving interest in the ancients, these painters also depicted
seven Hellenic philosophers (sic), including Plato, Solon,
Aristotle, Plutarch and Thucydides; they are to be seen in the
outer narthex. There is also a painting of the baptism of
Christ, very similar to that in the nave of the Monastery of
St Nicolas of the Strategopoulos and Dilios families, a little
to the south.

The Strategopoulos and Dilios monastery is the oldest on
the island, dating from the eleventh century. It has a single
nave and narthex; it is roofed with wood instead of the
original Byzantine tiles. The Dilios family of Ioannina was
responsible for restoring the monastery and its wall-paintings
in the sixteenth century and one of its members, Giorgios
Dilios, sent a valuable collection of books to it from Venice
in 1698. Of the two families, the Strategopoulos was very much
the more important. Like the Philanthropini, it came from
Constantinople soon after 1204. Its most distinguished
member was Alexios Strategopoulos, a general in the Nicaean
army who, after the battle of Pelagonia, captured Arta for
Michael VIII Palaiologos, only to be quickly evicted, and
later defeated and captured by the Despot who afterwards
released him.

By an unexpected stroke of luck, Alexios Strategopoulos
captured Constantinople from the Latins in 1261. Sent to
reconnoitre the City's defences, he found that nearly the
whole garrison was away on an expedition. He accordingly

infiltrated troops through a tunnel under the walls, who opened the gates from the inside. Any thoughts the general may have had of proceeding carefully were swept away by the enthusiasm of his staff. The returning Franks were unable to effect a re-entry and sailed away. Constantinople thus reverted to being the capital of the Eastern Roman Empire. It was to Simon Strategopoulos, a descendant of Alexios, that Sinon Pasha sent his order in 1430 that Ioannina should be delivered into his hands, which it was.

At the time of our visit, the little monastery was in the care of an elderly nun, dressed in a faded blue habit, who moved slowly and heavily. She remembered Elli from childhood and together they agreed that Ioannina was not what it had been. 'It's just an overgrown village these days, full of those villagers who were enriched during the war by all those gold sovereigns which the British threw at them out of their aeroplanes.' Certainly the gold sovereigns, brought in by the Allies and predominantly by Britain to finance the Resistance movements, are still considered the soundest financial holding in Greece today.

The third monastery is dedicated to St Nicolas in the name of the Ghiouma family of Ioannina. The structure probably dates from early in the second half of the sixteenth century with wall paintings of two centuries later. It is universally known as the Monastery of Panaghia i Eleousa or 'the all merciful Virgin Mary' from the miracle-working fifteenth-century icon of that name in the nave. Before the war the monastery possessed a fine icon, painted by Theodore Poulakis, who, born in Crete, later settled in Corfu, having spent some years in Venice; he is considered among the finest post-Byzantine painters of the seventeenth century. This icon has since disappeared. The chapel, which is level with the footpath, was badly shaken by the 1967 earthquake, which did much damage in the Ioannina area, and the roof leaked as a result; the icons and the wall paintings suffered damage, but they were then being restored.

We were invited to see the rest of the monastery by Sister Xenia, the daughter of the elderly nun we had met in the previous monastery. We climbed up stone steps to a little paved garden round which puff balls from the poplars were being swirled by a gentle breeze. Here and up a further flight were the monks' cells and the refectory. Everything was well tended and there was a general feeling of contentment.

The path continued round to the east side of the island, where there were no reedbeds; instead, anglers sat patiently under the low cliffs. Just before reaching the village, we came upon the little monastery of St Panteleimon, standing amid aged plane trees. Built early in the sixteenth century, the church is in simple basilica form, a nave with two aisles and a semi-circular apse; steps at the side lead up to three cells. It was in the middle of these three that Ali Pasha was mortally wounded and died on 24 January 1822 from a bullet fired through the floor from the room below.

We did not visit the fifth monastery, that of St John the Baptist, with its unusual chapel built into a cave in the hillside because by this time we craved ice cold beer and crayfish. The site was originally the refuge of a hermit, named Antonios, who had acquired the gift of prophecy. Hither came two brothers of the distinguished Epirot family of Apsaros, Nektarios and Theophanes, who became monks in 1495. In due course they erected a new church on this site in 1507, dedicated to St John. Later they left the island, which had long been a home of anchorites, to go to Meteora where they founded the All Saints Monastery on the rock of Barlaam.

7

The Nomads

In 1945 and 1946, the road between Igoumenitsa and Ioannina was virtually empty of traffic; its crumbling surface, rutted and potholed, ran like a frayed ribbon up the flanks of the mountains, over the passes and down the river valleys. The wild and rugged grandeur of the scenery, when an eagle floating overhead was sometimes the only sign of life, always made this a memorable journey.

In spring and autumn, however, hazards on the road were to be expected. Travelling westwards at the end of April towards the Ionian in a much battered army truck, we could turn a bend in the road and suddenly find ourselves slamming on the brakes as we became engulfed in vast flocks of dusty sheep, bleating loudly in protest at having to hobble along the stony road. Behind came the bounding officious shepherd dogs, lean, aggressive and contemptuous of all who did not belong to their world, and the patient, much-enduring pack horses, carrying blankets, tent poles, kitchen utensils, provisions and the youngest children of the community. Mules, donkeys and goats made up the rest of the four-footed members of the nomadic group. Among them weaved the shepherds, both old and young, using their distinctive shepherds' crooks to guide the leaders and hasten the laggards. The women and the girls were responsible for the goats—but never the sheep for traditional reasons—and as active as the men; whatever they did, however, never for a moment made them slacken at their task of spinning thread from their sheep's wool and goats' hair from a distaff which they held in the left hand. In late summer, when there was more time available, they would weave this thread on their primitive looms into cloth, from which the family garments were made.

Their clothes were traditional. The men wore trousers or breeches, their feet shod in strong leather slippers, sometimes decorated with large pom-poms. On their heads were soft round pill-box-shaped hats or the universal cloth cap, made from their own material. The women's skirts, of the same navy-blue or black cloth, reached to their ankles. Over skirts and blouses they wore neat, sleeveless coats which fell to their knees while their heads were covered with a scarf, the usual sign of modesty.

These shepherds were a slight but sturdy people with wide cheekbones, blue or grey eyes, fresh complexions and hair varying in colour from brown to fair. They moved at a steady pace when driving their flocks and could keep this up for long distances. The women were attractive when young but aged rapidly on account of their hard outdoor life and the innumerable duties expected of them in addition to rearing the children.

Every year, soon after St George's Day, these shepherds moved from the coastal pastures up to the high meadows of Zagori and Pindus. Here they would spend the summer until signs appeared of winter's approach. Sometime after the middle of October, there would begin the long return journey down to the coast or around the Ambracian Gulf for the winter grazing. Known as transhumant shepherds because of this regular annual cycle of activity, these people had followed this way of life since time immemorial. Travellers along the lowland roads in winter would recognize the cone-shaped huts, built by the women from the boughs of trees. Nearby stood their sheep, huddled together against the drizzling rain which in Epirus can continue in winter for weeks on end, attended by the shepherd enshrouded in his long heavy cloak of goats' hair, topped by a black hood to protect the head.

These shepherd communities were until recently found not only in Epirus but elsewhere in mainland Greece, north of the Gulf of Corinth, in the Peloponnese, Thrace and in parts of the Balkans as well. One of their favourite districts, nevertheless, has been the northern Pindus between Epirus and south-west Macedonia, which is snow-covered in winter, but where in summer the shepherds find their land of heart's content.

A proportion of these shepherds were Vlach, an ancient people, probably deriving from the Dacians who inter-married with the Roman legionaries stationed during the later Roman Empire in what today is Roumania. The Vlachs still call themselves Romans—Arumani in Vlach—but the Greeks have also often referred to themselves as Romoi, thus associating themselves with the Eastern Roman Empire of Byzantium. The Vlachs speak two languages—their own, which is unwritten and clearly akin to Roumanian, and that of the Balkan country in which they raise their flocks. Rennell, later Lord Rennell of Rodd, wrote that the name of Vlach or Wallach appeared to be the same word as that used by the German races to indicate 'foreigners'. The Saxons of England applied it to the inhabitants of Wales, calling them Welsh, which in Belgium becomes Walloon and in Polish Wlach. The Greeks call them Koutzo-Vlach, meaning either limping or little Vlach, depending upon whether the Greek *koutzo* or the Turkish *kutchuk* is the origin of the word, according to Messrs A. J. B. Wace and M. S. Thompson, whose *Nomads in the Balkans*, published in 1914, is still undoubtedly the best account of the Vlachs in the English language.

The Vlach skills are not only those of the shepherd but embrace many crafts including bootmaking, tailoring, milling, the making of pack saddles for mules, and the crafts of the blacksmith, goldsmith, silversmith and watchmaker. The pack saddles were particularly important because, in addition to the raising of sheep, the Vlachs held what was largely a monopoly of transport services in the Balkans until the internal combustion engine became supreme. Vlachs are still largely responsible for bringing down timber from the high Pindus to the sawmills by horse or mule, or to convenient places for onward transmission by lorry. Today they are well established in motor transport. They are known as shrewd businessmen and retailers.

The Vlachs first became prominent in Greece when they founded an independent principality in about 1261 in Thessaly and entered into an alliance with Charles of Anjou, King of Sicily, against Byzantium; this dominion lasted until 1333 when it was overthrown by the Greeks. Benjamin of Tudela, the Jewish traveller who toured the Levant about forty years

before the Latin conquest, came into contact with the Vlachs
and argued both from their names, which he claimed were
Jewish, and from the fact that they called the Jews 'brethren',
that the Vlachs had Jewish connections or blood. 'They
showed, however, their brotherly love', wrote William Miller,
'by contenting themselves with merely robbing the Israelites,
while they both robbed and murdered the Greeks when they
descended from their mountains to pillage the plains. A terror
to all, the Vlachs would submit to no king.' But submit they
eventually did to the Sultan when Byzantium finally crum-
bled and Turkish troops took control of the main centres of
communication.

In the nineteenth century, with the emergence of an
independent Greek state, the Vlachs became once more of
political importance. They had become Christians as early as
the ninth or tenth century but, unlike the Serbs, Bulgarians
and Roumanians, who by the end of the nineteenth century
had obtained their own Orthodox Church and schools, they
continued to look direct to the Greek Patriarchate in Constantinople. A Vlach national movement came into being in
1867, encouraged by the Roumanians, who claimed the
Vlachs as kindred because of language similarities. Roumanian
finance established elementary schools teaching Roumanian
in a number of villages in Macedonia and Pindus together
with higher grade schools in Salonika and Ioannina. In this
way the Roumanians staked a claim to some share in northern
Greece if and when the Turkish Empire collapsed.

The Greek state itself expanded northwards during the
nineteenth century and as it absorbed Thessaly and approached the quicksands of Macedonia, it swept away both the
Roumanian schools it found there and those of the Bulgarians,
who had adopted a similar approach for the same reason.
More and more Vlachs came under Greek administration. In
1905 the Turks recognized the Vlachs as a separate *millet*. The
Greeks for their own nationalist reasons opposed this concept
and argued that the Vlachs were but Vlach-speaking Greeks.

The Vlachs have been known as wanderers throughout the
Balkans and European Turkey for centuries, but their pere-
grinations across frontiers largely came to an end with the
First World War. This was not necessarily a drawback. There

are advantages to be gained in having summer and winter grazing grounds close to each other; the farther the animals travel, the more they lose in weight and therefore in value. Again, under modern marketing conditions, it is important to be able to maintain contact with a major regional marketing centre such as Ioannina.

The Vlachs are not easily distinguishable from the other Greeks of Epirus, either in looks or build, but are perhaps a little more phlegmatic. Wace and Thompson, who spent some time among them just before the outbreak of war in 1914 at Samarina, a great Vlach village just over the Epirot border in Macedonia, wrote thus about them: 'A Vlach has the quieter manner of speech, a comparative absence of gesticulation, and a lack of that excessive curiosity which in financial matters is so typical of the Greeks. He is also less hot-tempered and takes the small inconveniences of life in a more calm and tranquil frame of mind—there is a lack of self assertion, and no race perhaps in the Balkans is more easily absorbed by others.' It may be true of the Vlach that when he settles in great cities like Athens and Salonika, he quickly forgets his origins, but in Epirus, and especially in Metsovo, generally recognized as their capital, they remain Vlachs as well as Greeks.

If most of these nomads were Vlach, there were others who led the same transhumant life but who were different in several important respects. The language of the Arvanito-Vlachs, sometimes called the Karagunidhes on account of their black capes, was primarily Albanian. Until the Greek-Albanian frontier was closed, as it still is, they moved freely between the two countries. Leake met a group of them in Ioannina in 1809 when they were waiting to be admitted to the presence of the Vizier to pay their annual dues. Ali's secretary desired all but the headman to withdraw. ' "We are all equal", they replied. They are Albanians and are here named Karagunidhes, or black coats, as a distinction from the Vlachiots, though elsewhere, and often even in common parlance at Ioannina, it is very customary to call them all Karagunidhes, which is the more natural, as the black or white cloak is no longer a distinction, and they all come from the same great ridge of Pindus.'

The other main group of nomads are the Sarakatsani. They

followed the same pattern of life as the Vlach nomads, but whereas the latter have had their own homes in their summer villages for some two hundred years, the Sarakatsani have until recently lived only in huts or tents. Their main distinguishing feature is that they only speak Greek, from which it is argued that they are pure Greek, perhaps the purest Greeks of them all, because, at least until recently, they practised endogamy. Professor Dakaris has written in *Dodona* that 'the Sarakatsani, who have been going up and down Pindus with their herds for three or four millennia, are unconsciously continuing the oldest and most genuine historical tradition of the Greek nation. Racially pure, with their historical continuation unbroken, they constitute first class material for anthropological, sociological, linguistic and archaeological research. The preservation of this wonderful Hellenism of Pindus is a matter of national significance.'

The Sarakatsani have only in this century achieved recognition as a separate group of nomadic shepherds. The first major work about them, *Les Saracatsanes: un tribe nomadique grecque* by Carsten Hoeg was published in Paris in 1925. They first became known to English readers within the last few years through J. K. Campbell's *Honour, Family and Patronage*, published in 1964, followed in 1966 by Patrick Leigh Fermor's sympathetic bravura description in *Roumeli* of a Sarakatsan wedding. Rennell Rodd wrote in 1892: 'In fact, the word Vlach has come to be synonymous with shepherd in modern Greek and so is even applied to the Greek or Albanian herdsman in the Morea'—and now, it can be added, to the Sarakatsani as well.

I was anxious to find out in 1973 how the nomadic life had been affected by changing economic conditions. On arriving in Ioannina, Elli took me to call on Constantine Frontzos, Chairman of the Society for Epirot Studies. A lawyer and a former member of parliament, he has been deeply involved in saving what could be salvaged of Epirus's traditional culture. Several fine village houses have been acquired for preservation by the Society. On the slopes of St George's Hill above Ioannina, an excellent restaurant with a strong Epirot character has been established together with a small open air theatre close by. The Society's headquarters, close to the

Litharitza, are decorated with fabrics designed and woven locally in traditional patterns. The walls are panelled with wood from the surrounding forests. Frontzos has built up a considerable capital for the Society's work to which Epirots have contributed from all over the world. A fine up-to-date library is part of the Society's facilities.

Frontzos's initiative has been responsible for the layout of the garden in the old Turkish barracks. On one side stands the Litharitza, which was originally the name of a Christian quarter, but was demolished by Ali Pasha and its materials used for building this great edifice, which consisted of a light, airy palace, that reminded Leake of Chinese architecture, erected on top of a solid fortress. Inside, the hammering and sawing were deafening as the main floor was being converted into a restaurant, again under the aegis of the Society for Epirot Studies, which is interested in providing more tourist attractions in order to make Epirus better known. Below, the original layout was being restored, including the dungeons where prisoners were left to be forgotten; they were lowered in cages through an aperture in the main floor to their entombment.

In due course we asked Frontzos where to go to meet the Sarakatsani. 'Sarakatsini?' he queried. 'Haven't you heard anything back there in London? They're no longer shepherds. They've sold their flocks and gone to work in Germany. You'll find very few of them now in Zagori and Pindus.'

This was an answer we were not expecting.

'But', he added, 'I've managed to save something of their heritage. Come and see for yourselves.' With a flourish he led us into a large room whose walls were lined with cupboards. Inside them hung row upon row of folk costumes, each district having its distinctive colours and designs. In addition there were leather and metal belts, pens and inkwells, which were thrust into their owners' belts some two hundred years ago, daggers, swords, pistols and long-barrelled shotguns, embossed with the work of Ioannina's silversmiths, and footwear, leather flasks, pottery and personal jewellery.

'You see, I've been able to save something for posterity of the fine craftsmanship which flourished for centuries in these remote parts. Neither the Vlachs nor the Sarakatsani, nor for that matter anyone else are any longer making these things. To collect anything like this today, you'd have to go to the antique dealers who bought up everything they could for virtually nothing and are now asking the earth. Extraordinary. The Sarakatsani suddenly went mad and threw away their past.'

So another centre of fine craftsmanship has collapsed before the advance of modern standards of uniformity. We were to find the nomads settled in towns and villages, convinced that they had got the better of the bargain. They had gained the townsman's creature comforts, previously denied them, in return for losing an identity which had remained intact for thousands of years. What had been happening all round the Mediterranean had now reached Epirus, one of the last strongholds of the pre-industrial world. The Sarakatsani saw on television, when it reached Epirus in the 1960s, a world they had never imagined and were seduced.

8

Zagori and Tzoumerka

The summer lands of the nomads, both Vlachs and Sarakatsani, lie in the upland mountainous country between Ioannina
and the Pindus with its pastures, forests, gorges and tumultuous rivers. Zagori lies to the north-east of the capital with
Mitzikeli as its westernmost bastion. To the south-east is the
Tzoumerka, its dramatic northern ridge plainly visible from
Ioannina's *plateia*. Between Zagori and Tzoumerka stretches
the long, stony valley, largely bereft of timber or shrub, up
whose northern flank climbs the road, leaving the main branch
of the Arakhthos river far below in the valley, towards the
Zygos Pass, the gateway over the Pindus into Thessaly. Below
the Zygos and still in Epirus is Metsovo, the Vlach capital.

Here in Zagori and Tzoumerka are two of the most out-of-
the-way areas of mainland Greece. Until recently, very few
modern roads existed, and the speed of travel was that of the
mule train. As a result the traditional cultures of these
shepherd groups continued largely unchanged well into the
second half of this century.

In recent years, however, ambitious public works pro-
grammes of successive governments have built new roads,
especially in Zagori, so that today there are good all-weather
roads to most parts of Epirus and passable earth-roads to the
remotest villages. However distant, virtually every village is
in touch with either Ioannina or Arta through public transport. The lesson that isolation can lead to undesirable political
complications was learnt during the guerilla civil war between
1946 and 1949.

These wild, semi-barren areas are not suitable for the
motorcar unless the driver is carrying spare parts and extra
petrol, for there are no garages and few skilled mechanics.

Although Greek resourcefulness will often enable the driver to get back to the nearest town, one cannot depend upon this. The excellent bus service is therefore the almost universal way of travelling.

Ioannina boasts three bus terminals; two serve the principal towns in Epirus and beyond as well, including Athens, Patras and Salonika, and the third the remoter villages, especially in Zagori and Tzoumerka. The 'terminus for the unprofitable bus lines' is tucked away on the town's northern edge among the timberyards, the air fresh with resin from newly sawn pinewood. The buses which depart from here are ancient pre-war vehicles, as battered in appearance as the earth roads they follow. On the trunk roads they are left behind in a swirl of dust by the long sleek coaches on their way to Athens or Agrinion. Once into the mountains, however, they come into their own as they rumble cheerfully, reliably and sometimes, it seems, interminably towards their destination. Nevertheless, they are excellent timekeepers and the crews cheerful and helpful as their customers are almost invariably old friends.

Every driver makes a feature of the wall space around him in his coach. There will usually be an icon of the Panaghia and of his patron saint and photographs of friends and places visited. Today, among the younger drivers, the holy pictures are sometimes replaced by a symbol of a contemporary form of worship, namely a coloured photograph of the Ioannina football team. In a country so proud of its national identity, it was interesting to learn that among the eleven swarthy young men glaring the length of the bus there was not, I was told, a single Epirot, not even one Greek. Ioannina's players in 1973 came from Central and South America. It did not matter that these mercenaries were alien in race and religion so long as Ioannina was victorious. The old Hellenic city states hired their troops in the same way.

So it was by bus that we explored Epirus, spending the night, when necessary, in inns where one hires a bed, not a room. As often as not, the two or three bedrooms, each containing several beds with blankets but not linen, are attached to a grocer's shop as in Tsepelovo or to a restaurant as in Pramanda.

The roads twist and turn up and down the mountain slopes

and there are views over wild, wooded, unworkable country
to further mountain ranges whose soaring grassy slopes are
the sheep's summer pastures. These highland districts are
drained of autumn rains and winter snows by boisterous rivers
and their tributaries. The Aoos and the Voidthomatis (or Ox
Eye) run swiftly north-westwards through Zagori to unite in
the Konitsa plain before hurrying onwards into Albania and
so eventually into the Adriatic near Valona. The Tzoumerka
massif, whose highest point, Mount Stroungoula, rises to over
7,600 feet, is protected to the east and the west by the Arch-
eloos and the Arakhthos rivers respectively. The sources of
these great rivers are the heights above the Zygos Pass on
Pindus, although secondary tributaries of the Arakhthos rise
in Zagori. In both cases, their destination is the Ionian; the
Arakhthos flows into the Ambracian Gulf while the Arch-
eloos reaches the Ionian opposite Ithaka at the entrance to the
Gulf of Corinth. In summer, after the mountain snows have
melted, these rivers are calm and shallow, but are transformed
by the late autumn rains into tumultuous swirling torrents
which have carved their imperious way through the mountain
limestone to form gorges of which the Vikos in western Zagori
is only the most spectacular, especially when seen from Monodendri, perched high above it.

Bridges are few. Until after the 1939–45 war, they were
usually Turkish, high, graceful, airy structures, built to allow
as much water as possible through when the river was in
spate. One of the finest of these Turkish bridges is over the
Aoos below Konitsa, but there are a number elsewhere,
including the Plaka over the Arakhthos joining the barren
Xerovouni range to the Tzoumerka, and a fine three-arched
bridge over the Voidthomatis below Kipos, Zagori's administrative centre. N. G. L. Hammond recounts how before the
Second World War he crossed the Arakhthos 'in a box, slung
on wires and wound across on a windlass by an old crone; she
grew weary and left me hanging midstream in the spray, but
help came and I was wound across.'

In addition to the pastures, there are widespread woods of
coniferous and deciduous trees—oak, plane, hazel and
walnut—whose timber is a mainstay of these rural economies.
Sawmills, which are co-operatively owned by village groups,

have been set up at convenient centres and employ local labour so that not all the villages are half empty. There is little cultivation of cereals as the country is too tangled with shrub and in most places has too little soil. This wilderness is the home of bears, jackals, wolves, wild boar, foxes and deer. Bears are comparatively rare, only occasionally encountered in the forests and left alone; the boar are hunted in winter because they damage the scattered crops. There are trout in the rivers and freshwater crayfish while in the air above hover eagles and other birds of prey.

Scattered about these mountain slopes are villages of fine grey stone houses and impressive churches—Koukouli, Tsepelovo, Skamnelli, Kipos, Monodendri and Flambourari in Zagori and Agnanda, Pramanda and Melissouryi in the Tzoumerka to mention but a few. The forty-six villages of the Zagori in the eighteenth century developed a special relationship with the Ottoman authorities; by forming a confederation, they were allowed to appoint their own administrator whose post was in Ioannina to maintain contact with the Turkish officials. As a result the taxes required were speedily collected and handed over to the Turks without delay, in return for which the villagers were allowed to run their own affairs and maintain their own rural guards. In this way Zagori escaped exploitation by the Turkish tax farmers who paid for the right to extract for their own pockets as much tax as possible from the unfortunate *rayah*.

The mountain peoples of Zagori and Tzoumerka, unlike the plainsmen of Thessaly, who had no safe retreats, were never subdued by the Turkish armies nor their initiative frustrated. Often more important than sheep and timber was commerce which many young men from the Zagori villages pursued in all parts of the Ottoman Empire, especially in Roumania, and beyond in Russia. Each merchant venturer who left his village for this purpose would, if he prospered, return home in due course, first to marry a local girl and then to father children, always departing once more into exile until he had made sufficient to retire to his village in comfort. These villages flourished in the eighteenth and nineteenth centuries on money from the Danube and the Black Sea as many do today from America, Australia and Germany.

The village churches epitomize the sturdy character of these highland communities where the blood of Albanian and Slav has mingled with that of the indigenous Greeks. The building and embellishment of these churches continued throughout the Ottoman ascendancy. Their design is usually in basilica form—a nave and two aisles of equal length—with the apse, containing the sanctuary at the east end, and a narthex at the west end where women, strangers and those not fully members of the Orthodox Church could follow the service. In their construction, the mountaineers proved themselves excellent stonemasons and woodcarvers and, because of this, were employed in the building of the mosques of Constantinople.

In Zagori, especially at Koukouli, Tsepelovo, Negades and Monodendri, the whole of the church interior is painted— walls, ceiling, the pillars between the nave and the aisles and the curved arches connecting them. No space which can be used to tell the Gospel story or the life of a saint has been left unadorned. The basic ground colour is royal blue on which we found the apostles and saints finely represented in a rural but authoritative way. During a great festival of the Church, such as Ascension Day, the occasion on which we visited the church in Koukouli, the golden iconostasis, separating the nave from the sanctuary and hung with icons, each of which has its traditional place, the flickering candles and the thin points of reflected light from the icons and the wall paintings, the elaborate ceremonial robes of the priest and the golden haloes of the saints depicted on the walls in their bright coloured garments gave an impression of infinite richness and immense mystery. The wall paintings and the carved wood of the iconostasis and pulpit are almost invariably the work of local craftsmen from Monodendri, Konitsa, Metsovo or from south-west Macedonia, just east of the Pindus, and the village churches throughout Zagori are glorious with their work. On occasion, as with the little chapel of St Paraskevi, perched above the road into Skamnelli, the exterior has also been painted, although in this case mutilated by carved initials. The churches of Tzoumerka are sometimes of more recent origin and their interiors and exteriors are more often unadorned.

In the rural communities of Greece, the Orthodox Church still has a place of primary importance. The church is where heaven and earth meet. The worshipper, surrounded by the saints on the walls and on the iconostasis, is in the presence of God and His heavenly host. The sanctuary with the altar signifies the eternal world of the spirit, while the nave represents the Ark in which the children of God traverse the sea of life from birth to death. In between the two is the iconostasis, at first built only to a modest height but later raised much higher to take several banks of icons, but never to make the congregation feel separated by it from the priest in the sanctuary. The dome, rising in the centre of the church, represents the union of heaven and earth. From high up in the dome's ceiling, the image of Pantocrator, the Almighty, looks down sternly upon His congregation, as out of reach from them as the dome itself.

The Almighty is remote but can be approached through the intercession of the saints and especially of the Panaghia, Mother of God. The Orthodox liturgy emphasizes that the material body of man can be transfigured by the spiritualization of man's senses, and the saints are those who achieved the ability to see the invisible Kingdom of God through their sanctification. The worshipper asks the saints to intercede on his behalf. The icons that represent the saints are kissed and illuminated by candles placed before them, but they are venerated, not worshipped or adored; no question of idolatry arises. The Seventh Oecumenical Council, held at Nicaea in 787, made this clear: the homage rendered to the image is transferred to the prototype. He who venerates the image venerates in it the reality that it represents.

Many villages, such as Tsepelovo and Kapesovo in Zagori, have Slav names. The district of Ioannina has by far the most. The Slavs and Avars first descended into Greece in the middle of the sixth century A.D., settling as far south as Laconia in the south-east Peloponnese. Before the recent war, General Metaxas, dictator and prime minister, made a great effort to replace these Slav names with Greek. This policy is still being pursued, although many people continue to use the old names.

Most Zagori villages today are largely empty; only the old and the very young remain in the care of their grandparents while their parents work in a Greek city or in Germany.

Koukouli, for example, has about a hundred fine old houses but only about fifty people live there throughout the year. More return in summer when the population can reach two hundred and fifty. Others intend to return but never do, yet they would rather their houses collapsed than sell them to strangers, although I subsequently heard of a Corfiot who had managed to purchase one in Papingo. Many of the houses, as we could see, were disintegrating; balconies had collapsed and creepers fattened on decaying walls. Sometimes an absent family appoints a local inhabitant as caretaker; sometimes the house is therefore used to shelter the caretaker's grain or animals. The houses in occupation had an air of faded charm; the floor and settees were covered with ancient rugs of local design and a little lamp usually glowed before a holy icon, placed at the east end of the room or house, so that in turning to it one was facing towards Jerusalem.

Today the village inhabitants are a mixture of Greeks, Vlachs and a few Sarakatsani, who have been moving into village houses in recent years. Further east in Zagori, the villages are predominantly Vlach.

After the Ascension Day service, Elli and I strolled into the square, the meeting place in villages as well as in towns. The common feature of these squares is the enormous plane tree which inevitably gives them shade. Here we found the men passing the time, while the women were at home about their household duties. Their bearing was a mixture of curiosity and reserve, each one of them intent on maintaining his individual dignity in the midst of associated but not entirely similar groups.

'Where', we asked one elderly man, 'are all the young men?'

'Gone to Germany, Australia, to places throughout the world.'

'But what do you live on if you are without their help?'

'Oh, we have our supplies—a few animals, some vegetables.'

'On fresh air and tightening our belts,' said another.

'Bah,' replied the first speaker, 'when has anyone in Zagori starved?'

Several of the men were Sarakatsani, who are now generally accepted in the villages where they are now householders. This is the result of a law, passed in 1938, which stipulated that nomad shepherds should have their names enrolled in either the nearest winter or summer village, closest to their grazing grounds; this encouraged some Sarakatsani, who had previously always lived in tents or huts, to acquire property in the village where their names were enrolled. This they did with the money acquired by selling their flocks in the mid-1960s.

Tsepelovo, higher up the mountainside, is a larger village than Koukouli, its grey stone houses and whitewashed cottages stretching over a considerable area. There was greater activity here on account of its timber and cheese-making interests. As usual we soon found ourselves in conversation with a group of elderly men as we sipped a cup of coffee.

'Here we sit all day,' said one, 'discussing emigration to America or Australia'—at this making an upward gesture to the heavens above—'from which there is no return.'

'Is it true that people in London live to be a hundred and thirty years and more?'

I told them that the average age at death of Londoners was in the early to middle seventies.

'Gracious,' he replied, 'we live much longer here. All of us you see here are over eighty and there is nothing wrong with any of us.' London's standing in Zagori had obviously slumped.

They asked me about previous visits to Greece and Elli mentioned that I had served with the Allied Military Mission to EDES. Several of the company said that they had been *andartes* (guerillas) with General Zervas, and a younger man in his early seventies added that three of his mules had also seen service with EDES.

Magnificent decaying stone houses stood on the surrounding slopes but the little shops and the inn where we spent the night were single-storeyed; the fragile simplicity of these buildings distantly reflected the domestic architectural styles of the Ottoman domination which had ended only sixty years ago. Close to a grey stone clock tower, built in 1967 in no recognizable style—a gift to the community from a well-wisher—stood the post office, which previously had been a chemist's shop established by one Tsouflis, another benefactor. Everywhere we went we found evidence of generosity by successful individuals to their places of birth—surely a sign of civilization. Tsouflis had left Tsepelovo when this area was Turkish for Bessarabla where intelligence and enterprise had earned their rewards. In his will he left sufficient money for the establishment of a chemist's shop and to support two full-time school teachers, a doctor and a priest. Now this fund is administered by public trustees for use wherever required and not merely for Tsepelovo, for these services, which did not exist under the Turks, are now everywhere provided by the authorities.

Gyftokampos, halfway between Tsepelovo and Laista, was merely a wayside halt, where a log cabin, the only building there, provided refreshments for the traveller. Above to the north stood the great ridge of Timfi whose lower flanks were heavily timbered except where there were outcrops of limestone. The mountain air tingled like iced champagne which enlivened everybody.

'If you want to photograph a spring of really cold water,' said a cheery old hoaxer, beckoning to us, 'then follow me.'

'I know whose photograph will get taken in that case,' chuckled a crony of his.

'It's wonderful water,' continued the first speaker unabashed. 'It helps the digestion remarkably well and, if your stomach is empty, it goes through you like a scythe. Personally I prefer ouzo,' and he went off to the hut in search of some.

'No need to go abroad to make your fortune,' said another man. 'There are always opportunities at home. If only I had planted walnut trees when I was young, I should be a rich man today.'

'Ah,' said his friend, 'but what about the superstition that anyone who plants a walnut tree will die within the year?'

'Absolute nonsense,' replied the first speaker, 'I've planted many walnut trees during a long life and I still flourish.'

'Nobody believes these old superstitions,' added his friend, 'but it's best to be on the safe side. That's why I always ask very old people to plant any walnut trees which I need on my land.' Another variation of this superstition is that he who plants a walnut tree will die when its girth equals his own.

The road ends at Laista, a large scattered village spread out on green Alpine slopes and surrounded by pine and deciduous forests. From the main square there is a magnificent view due west of the Timfi massif with Gameela (the Camel) at its northern end, rising to about 7,500 feet; due north was Smolikas, the tallest mountain in Pindus over 8,600 feet high. The potential for winter sports hereabouts must be considerable and there is a well organized ski-lift at Metsovo. The Greek Alpine Club has several huts in the area and goes to immense trouble to help climbing and walking enthusiasts find their way among these remote ranges.

Today only a few of Laista's houses are occupied, but the village must once have been prosperous as there are nine churches in the neighbourhood. The main church in the square, dedicated to St Michael and St George, was airy and light, but the interior, including the lovely beechwood iconostasis, was not gilded nor were the walls richly painted. Wace and Thompson were here in 1913 but found the village largely empty of able-bodied men, because most had gone abroad. They added that the village, 'if asked would declare itself to be of pure Hellenic stock, but in private all its inhabitants talk Vlach glibly.' Its basic character is unlikely to have changed.

In the bus back to Ioannina we found a Laista family setting out to return to Brisbane, where the father, a carpenter, had had an excellent job. He and his wife, both born in Laista, had returned with their children, two boys and a girl, to see their elderly parents once more and to reassess the prospects for work; if favourable, they had been prepared to settle once more at home and look after their parents in their declining years.

Yet after only twelve days in Laista they had decided to go back to Australia. But first, having bought single air tickets back to Athens, they had to earn enough for their return fares to Australia. The elder of the two boys, an insufferable thirteen-year-old, explained to the other passengers that they were going back to Brisbane because it held a better future for himself, his brother and sister. He did not intend to be a mere carpenter like his father, but had decided to study architecture. When they reached Ioannina they would all find jobs locally—cleaning shoes, acting as waiters, never mind how humble the job—and they expected it would take some six months to save up for the air tickets. One could not but be impressed.

Sitting under the great plane tree in Pramanda, we could see the bare northern shoulder of the Tzoumerka towering above the dark green forests in between. Close by water gushed continuously from the mouth of the village pump, made in the shape of the head of a heavily-moustached, shaven-headed man in middle age. Was he a Turk doomed to vomit forth water eternally because of crimes committed against the village? The village priest, who sat with us, claimed ignorance on the matter. He was far more concerned with magnifying the status of his church, said to house the mortal remains of St Paraskevi, and that of the clergy. He did this by relating accounts of miracles. One was about the prior of the monastery at Vilista during the Turkish occupation. This monastery had attached to it several old women, whose charms had long departed, to carry out the chores. One of them, while gathering wood, tumbled over a precipice. The prior, who was then in his monastery, immediately announced that a cow had fallen down the mountainside and would be found at a spot which he described. Sure enough, there she was, completely unharmed. Similar tales followed.

The priest was more interesting about how the Orthodox Church had in the past helped to cure madmen. These unfortunates would be chained to the exterior of the church to await recovery through divine grace, which was usually given. Chains, he added, were still to be found outside some mountain churches. We did not notice any.

We left him to be taken to Melissouryi by the owner of an ancient bus who wished us to see the local sights. The village, well built like all we had seen, was without electricity and therefore without television. A group of bored men were assembled to see if the bus brought anyone of interest. They settled around us under the plane tree, but there was little life among them. Yet the mountain air was sweet with the sound of running water which flowed deep in the thickly wooded valley below. Opposite were the heavily timbered slopes of Pindus, too high and remote for roads and villages. There is a rough track which leads south from here over Tzoumerka to

Theodoriana and on to Vulgarelli, now known officially as Drosophiyi (or cold stream). It was along this route that the Romans probably marched in 171 B.C. on their way to southern Thessaly to avoid a powerful Macedon army waiting for them on the Zygos Pass.

9

The End of the Nomadic Life

Everywhere outside the towns we found that the rural tradition of hospitality still existed; it had not yet been abused as it has in the more popular tourist areas. Conversation quickly developed. A tiny cup of coffee and a glass of water with a sweet would soon appear, even on occasion a more substantial dish. Visitors are valued for the fresh interest they bring. The main enemy in these outlandish communities is boredom. In return for this hospitality one must be prepared to talk.

On one such occasion in Koukouli, we asked some Sarakatsani women, whose family was now firmly established in a house, about their traditional costumes. A daughter laughed and said that her mother had sold them to dealers from Ioannina; at this, Elli explained how well these dealers were doing as a result. There was surprise and momentary anger.

'Oh dear,' cried the mother in anguish, her voice sharpened by the mountain air, 'they only gave me blankets in exchange. But how was I to know that those old clothes were of value? How was I to know?'

We asked their Vlach neighbours the same question, to receive a very different answer. 'We've long grown out of wearing folk costumes,' said the elderly wife. 'We always wear silk on special occasions like other gentry and so did our grandmothers,' to which her husband added with a wink, 'So you see, God will speak in Vlach on Judgement Day.'

We were often told about the sudden collapse of the traditional Sarakatsani life and how glad they were to be done with it. In the bad old days, everybody by middle-age had either rheumatism or arthritis from exposure in all weathers. Just imagine, they said, being out all day with the sheep in the winter rain or spending the night on the sodden hillside. How could they ignore the better life which work in the towns and in Germany offered them, especially where the future of their children was concerned? An improved breed of sheep had been developed by the Ministry of Agriculture which gave far more meat and milk than their former sheep so fewer were needed to make a living. Instead of being taken down to the coast in winter, they were now kept under cover in what had merely been the summer village but was now their home all the year round. Sheep, when moved today, are taken by truck. With the great increase of motor traffic on the roads, it is now virtually impossible to shepherd two or three thousand sheep, goats and mules on foot round a large town like Ioannina.

We were sitting in the little *plateia* of Koukouli, when a lorry came to a halt close by. A grandmother, her two daughters and a granddaughter stepped down from the driver's cabin. The driver, a son, lowered the tail board and out tumbled puppies, several loudly protesting hens, whose legs had been tied to a mattress spring, and a rather disdainful sheep with a leg in a splint.

'There's a modern Sarakatsani family for you,' said our friends. 'They've a house higher up in the village. Tomorrow three lorries will arrive with the sheep.'

The grandmother was dressed in peasant black, her daughters wore skirts and coloured knitwear—unfashionable but serviceable—while the pretty sixteen-year-old grand-daughter was in a green summer dress, looking very contemporary. She worked as hard as the others carrying bundles up to the house, but, catching the amused smile on the weathered face of a village woman, she said somewhat plaintively: 'It's all very well for you to smile but, unlike my parents, I've never been trained for this sort of work.'

An elegant, well-spoken young schoolmaster, whose work was in Arta, conducted us round Tsepelovo and Skamnelli, a much smaller village higher up the mountainside some two miles further on. He was a Sarakatsan; his father had been a *tséllingas* and an uncle still herded sheep. He had been born into the nomad life, which he hated in retrospect, but which he had now largely forgotten. He was soon to marry a girl from Attica, so the immemorial Sarakatsani tradition of endogamy was obviously something of the past. He invited us to lunch with his family, but there was only his sister, who waited at table but did not sit down in the presence of her brother and of strangers. Leake's remark about the idleness of the village male of Epirus, while the women of all ages were occupied fully in household duties, came to mind. 'The idleness of the Greek, Albanian and Vlachiot mountaineer', he added, 'is not like that of the Turk; he is assiduous and laborious everywhere but in his native mountains.' This is still largely true.

In Metsovo, the Vlach capital, we met M. Evangelos Averof-Tositsas, now the Greek Minister for Defence, but out of office in 1973, because opposed to the 'Colonels' Regime'. M. Averof has had a distinguished public career under General Papagos and during the first premiership of M. Karamanlis when he served as Greek Foreign Minister. He is, in addition, a noted economist and a successful novelist and playwright. He is descended from what are probably the two most distinguished Vlach families, those of Averof and Tositsas; his mother had been Elli's godmother.

'There were', he explained, 'three categories of shepherd. First, there was the *tséllingas* who owned the large flocks; next came the *smichtis* or yeoman shepherd, who owned no more than about fifty sheep and who had no means either of renting grazing ground or producing his own dairy produce, so he threw in his lot with the *tséllingas*; finally there was the hired shepherd who owned no sheep and was paid a small wage by the *tséllingas* who also provided him with his clothes and keep. The *smichtis* and the hired shepherds, who often could not read, were very much dependent upon the honesty of the *tséllingas*.

'The old nomadic way of life lost its attractions for the shepherds as they became increasingly aware of the advantages of city life as a result of improved communications. Then in the late 'fifties came the temptation of work in Western Europe, especially in Germany. Greek Government policy, moreover, then as now, has been to increase the industrial at the expense of rural output. This led to an increasing shortage of hired shepherds and farm workers. *Tséllingates* and farmers

10 Ramparts of Kastritza with Mt. Mitzikeli in background

11. Part of amphitheatre, Dodona, looking south towards Mt. Olytsika

12. General
Napoleon Zervas

13. Ruins of
Cassope facing Mt.
Zalongo, crowned
with concrete
sculpture

14. Paregoritissa church, Arta

15. The bridge of Arta over the river Arakhthos

16. Ruins of mansion of Khamco, Ali Pasha's mother, Konitsa

17. Eighteenth-century monastery church of St. John the Baptist, built on Hellenistic ruins of the Nekromanteion, Fanari Plain

are now offering high wages which inevitably pushes up the cost of living.'

Not long ago there had appeared in a Macedonian newspaper an advertisement offering shepherds television in the *stani* or encampment and individual transistor radios on the grazing grounds.

'The first to give up nomadic life was the hired shepherd with character and initiative; next to go was the *smichtis* whose few sheep gave him a little capital to start afresh. The shepherds who now remain are enjoying higher wages than ever before, but are the least enterprising. As a result, many *tséllingates* have cut the numbers of their sheep from thousands to hundreds, to the number, that is, which one man can control with the minimum of help.

'There is still good reason', M. Averof continued, 'why sheep farming should go on, although on a much reduced scale.' Economically, the high pastures in the mountains and the stony, poor land in the valleys and plains were only suitable for grazing. Some form of migration from one grazing area to another was also likely to continue, if only on a small scale. In the past certain districts had been overgrazed. The pastures around Metsovo could only properly accommodate about twenty thousand sheep, yet in some years there had been as many as thirty-five thousand there. All else considered, he expected that some eighteen thousand would feed there in future.

'Another reason why sheep rearing will go on is that there are some who experience a *meráki* or yearning; this life has been in the blood for so long that a few will feel compelled to continue with it. To regret the decline in nomadic life for its own sake would be sentimental, but economically there is much to be said for reducing the size of the flock and at the same time improving the stock, keeping them under cover in the upland villages instead of driving them great distances every year.'

M. Averof has done much to keep Metsovo alive. He has established a sawmill and a dairy so that many young men have remained in the town for the work. He has also revived the skills of woodworking and plastering, having found at the end of the war, when he returned to restore his properties after four years of neglect, that only two craftsmen were still alive. Now there are apprentices in adequate supply for local demand.

Metsovo, or Amintshu in the Vlach language which is still widely spoken, is divided into two parts. The larger, which is the administrative centre, is called Prosilio in Greek ('towards the sun') and Serinu by the Vlachs (meaning 'sunny' from the Latin word *serenus*) and the smaller part, a scattering of houses far below at the foot of the valley where the Arakhthos flows, is called Anilio (meaning 'sunless') or Nkiare in Vlach (meaning 'sunset'). The houses are finely built of wood and stone. It has nevertheless been said that the tradition of outdoor life was so strong among the Vlachs, that they would only do the woodwork for their houses, leaving the use of stone to Greek masons.

It was in Prosilio that I stayed in a comfortable modern hotel, while the others stayed with friends. Our bus had come the thirty-six miles from Ioannina in two hours. However, it took Henry Holland nearly a day and a half to reach here on horseback, having spent the night in a *khan* (a *caravanserai* or rest house) en route. With him went a Tartar courier, especially sent by Ali Pasha who liked Holland best of all the visiting Englishmen because he was a physician. The courier carried with him the Vizier's mandate and 'when we arrived, we found him examining different houses, to ascertain which was the best. With or against the will of the inhabitants, he opened the doors, entered the different apartments, and was absolute and authoritative in all his actions.'

Metsovo was first mentioned in the *Chronicle of Epirus* in 1380; elsewhere in the same document are many references to the Vlachs of Pindus. We know that by the fifteenth century it was occupied by several Vlach families who wintered their flocks in Thessaly. The settlement gained many privileges through sheltering a Vizier, who in 1656 was forced to flee the displeasure of the Sultan, Mohamed IV. He reached Metsovo where he was concealed by a friendly Vlach, one Steryiu or K'iriu Floka. Later the Vizier was pardoned and allowed to return to Constantinople, but did not omit to ask Floka what privileges he might give Metsovo as a token of gratitude. Floka is said to have asked for tax reductions, special grazing rights and the guardianship of the pass into Thessaly. Certainly Metsovo benefited. It henceforth came directly under the rule of the capital, thus bypassing the additional extortions of the local pashas. Wace and Thompson noted that towns on passes often received preferential treatment, especially when inhabited by muleteers, a class which it was in no one's interest to oppress.

By the end of the seventeenth century, Metsovo had become prosperous and the number of houses steadily increased until by the middle of the nineteenth they had reached a thousand. A French commercial agency was opened here as early as 1719, while Metsovan merchants were active in such diverse cities as Venice, Naples, Moscow, Odessa, Constantinople, Salonika and Alexandria. Their exports included woollen goods, hair capes, pewter plates and dishes, and cheese.

The arrival of Ali Pasha, however, brought an end to both the town's privileges and its prosperity. Worse was to follow. In 1854, after Russia had attacked Turkey at the start of what became known as the Crimean War, Greek irregular bands raided over the frontier into Turkey. A prominent Greek leader, Grivas, seized Metsovo and imposed a levy of 150,000 piastres on the community. Later, on the approach of Turkish irregular troops, he stole the jewellery of the women and burned thirty houses to cover his retreat. The Turks then destroyed a third of the houses and left the remainder in utter misery.

The decay remained until in the last decades of Turkish rule, which ended in 1913, George Averof erected a splendid group of public buildings, including a school. His generosity did not end with Metsovo. Averof, by birth a Vlach, by name a Slav and by education and preference a Greek, therefore considered himself to be Greek as well as a citizen of Metsovo. Having made a vast fortune through the cotton trade, he financed the rebuilding in marble of the Athens stadium. Together with other wealthy citizens of Metsovo, he reconstructed the Historical and Ethnological Museum in Athens. He also presented to the Greek navy a battle cruiser, named after him, the only capital ship the Greek Navy has ever possessed. It was on the *Averof* that the Greek Government returned from exile to Athens in 1944.

Another Metsovo family, the Tositsas, gained distinction when towards the end of the eighteenth century, the head of the family gave his protection to an important Albanian, who was lying ill in a local *khan*. The Albanian was taken to the Tositsas home and nursed back to health. When he finally departed, he left his signet ring with Tositsas and told him to contact him should he ever need help. A few years later, the Albanian was revealed to be Mohamed Ali, then Bey of Kavalla, his birthplace. Tositsas accordingly sent his two sons to Kavalla, together with the ring. Mohamed Ali welcomed them both, then decided that he did not like Constantine but agreed to take the other brother, Michael, into his service. Later, when Mohamed Ali was established in Egypt, Michael joined him there where in due course he became Ali's finance minister. Travelling one day from Cairo to Alexandria, he noted the considerable amount of land lying fallow. He accordingly suggested to Mohamed that it could be made fertile through irrigation. Mohamed granted Michael 20,000 acres to see what he could do with it. Michael, having first obtained confirmation of this in writing, proceeded to bring in agricultural workers from Epirus to work with the Egyptian *fellaheen*, and the result was the vastly successful cotton fields of the Nile Delta, which made Michael exceedingly wealthy. Constantine also did well. He went to Leghorn, set himself up in commerce and banking at which he prospered, and was eventually ennobled by the Grand Duke of Tuscany as Baron Tositsas.

Metsovo is today proud of its distinctive personality. Nearly all the inhabitants wear traditional clothes—the women in long dark skirts, simple blouses and head scarves while the men, especially the shepherds, are dressed in black or navy-blue homespun. In and around the gardens laid out by George Averof are kiosks of pinewood, used as shops and restaurants of a very simple type. We saw examples of fine wood panelling, of pewter work and locally woven fabrics, including rugs, in several private interiors. Fairly stringent restrictions have been placed upon the design of new houses.

The woodcarvers of Metsovo travelled widely in Epirus and beyond because renowned for their skill in carving iconostases for churches. These great screens are at the very heart of the decorative qualities of a church. The walnut iconostasis of St Paraskevi, in the centre of the town, is outstanding; it was carved about 1730 and the upper row of twenty-two icons was then specially ordered for it from nearby Meteora. The ten large icons on the lower row were sent between 1820 and 1840 by benefactors of Metsovan origin then living in Russia. Other examples of fine woodcarving can be seen in the two pulpits. The larger was made at roughly the same time as the iconostasis, the smaller late in the nineteenth century.

In 1959 after careful cleaning there came to light the finely painted ceiling. The ceilings of the Epirot churches are by no means always painted, so the style may have originated in Macedonia, brought here perhaps by painters from one of the great Vlach villages on the eastern slopes of Pindus like Samarina. On the other hand, Messrs Wace and Thompson recorded that the people of Metsovo had a particularly high reputation for the painting of ceilings.

The little Monastery of St Nicolas lies downhill from Prosilio along a neat, winding path. Far below lies the small settlement of Anilio, overshadowed by the surrounding mountain walls. The monastery church, built solidly of stone, is a simple structure. Erected in the fourteenth century, it has a barrel-vaulted ceiling which, together with the Pantocrator painted on it, was damaged in the 1967 earthquake which affected this area as well as Ioannina. The walls are finely painted with the usual scenes from the scriptures and the lives of the saints and were restored by the Tositsaa Foundation. The iconostasis, richly decorated in gold, is imaginatively carved; its base, a part of which had decayed, has been replaced with honest ungilded pinewood. There is a small collection of icons, bequeathed to the chapel by Spiridon Loverdos in memory of his daughter, another good reason for visiting the monastery.

Although we were often told of the existence of *stani* near villages in Zagori, they invariably proved to be three or four hours away on foot. In Metsovo, however, we were told of the existence of a Sarakatsani encampment close to the road about two miles short of Vovoussa, the most easterly village in Zagori and a Vlach centre of importance. After the collapse of the Greek armies in 1941 through the German invasion, the Italians had attempted for propaganda purposes to establish a Vlach Republic of Pindus with its capital in Vovoussa. Few Vlachs took this seriously but a residue of bitterness with regard to those who collaborated still lingers.

Vovoussa has a long history of brigandage and defiance against the Turks. During the eighteenth century three of the best-known captains of irregular bands came from Vovoussa or Baieasa, its Vlach name. They were Yoti Blatshola (1710–50), Nikolak'i Davli (1750–80) and Badzhu Bairaktari (1780–1800); it will be noted that their lives were short. They were men of initiative and courage. Blatshola was on one occasion captured and taken to Ioannina by the Turks, who condemned him to death by immersion in boiling pitch. On reaching the place of execution he suddenly dipped his hands into the tank and flung the burning liquid over his guards and tormenters and managed to escape in the confusion. Towards the end of the nineteenth century, brigandage of the worst sort raged unchecked in eastern Zagori. The threat of burning oil and the practice of toasting women in ovens were among the ways of encouraging the disclosure of hidden wealth.

After four hours in an ancient bus which left Ioannina at 7 a.m. and climbed up through the villages of Greveniti and Flambourari, alive with the sound of running water, we saw the encampment, which consisted of several huts, heaps of firewood and fodder, covered by tarpaulin, and an open hearth for cooking. As we got off the bus, several figures emerged and waved to us to join them. There were three young men in nondescript modern slacks and pullovers, two young women in frocks with scarves round their heads and two elderly women in peasant black. Throughout our visit, the women, both young and old, continued to twist wool and goats' hair into thread, unless specifically asked by one of the men to do something else.

We were invited into the principal hut as it started to rain. It consisted of planks hammered upright into the ground; at each end they were shaped to allow for a sloping roof; the structure was obviously not new but built some years earlier. Heavy ill-fitting sheets of thick plastic material were stretched over these planks and kept in position by the branches of trees placed on top. The floor of beaten earth was covered with a thick goats' hair carpet. Two camp beds, themselves a sign of liberation from the days when everybody slept on rugs on the ground, stood lengthwise, covered with thick rugs, which were needed at night at this height. We as guests were seated on one while the young men sat facing us on the other. The young women stood at one side while the old women crouched on the ground, for there were neither tables nor chairs. Here at least some of the traditions continued. The most coherent of the young men, aged about twenty-five and single, made it clear that here in the mountains the male reigned supreme. He quickly informed us that he expected his sister to marry someone of his father's choice or to produce someone of whom his father would approve. The girls appeared to be in no way embarrassed at this forthright statement.

He then told us something about themselves. The party consisted of two related families owning between them some five hundred sheep which the fathers were at that moment grazing higher up; he and his cousins were about to set up a cheese factory. Here around us were their immemorial summer pastures; the winter was spent near Philippeas on the edge of the Louros plain. But and here a certain tension became apparent—they would not be moving to and fro without proper homes much longer. Why should they put up with this discomfort? He and his kinsfolk intended to move into village houses somewhere in Zagori and keep sheep under cover in winter. There they would have electricity, television and a wider choice of girls to marry. They were being encouraged to seek this better life through government loans and subsidies. He ended by saying with a flourish: 'we are the last generation of Sarakatsani to live in encampments.'

Coffee and *tsipouro* arrived, followed by cheese, fried in butter on bread, which we shared with the young men. The women were excluded from this meal, nor did they once join in the conversation, but their eyes twinkled and there were many nods of approval at what was said.

Two hours later the bus picked us up on its return journey to Ioannina. The front seats were occupied by sturdy men with thick necks and burgeoning waistlines. 'Lawyers,' whispered a far less successful looking man sitting near us at the rear. Suddenly, the lawyers burst into song and kept up a steady flow of Vlach choruses for some time. The previous day, 24 June, had been St John's Day which was always the occasion in Vovoussa for a celebration known as the 'brides' market'. The unmarried girls of the community danced publicly, eyed avidly by the young men who, if they saw someone to whom they felt themselves particularly attracted, began to make enquiries about her background and the size of the *preeka* or dowry. It was a busy and profitable day for the lawyers who were the middlemen in the negotiations.

After about two hours, the singing became more sporadic and heads began to nod. At last the bus emerged from Zagori on to the main Metsovo–Ioannina road. All then became quiet and subdued as in any other country bus approaching the capital, where more Vlachs lived than in the rest of Epirus.

10

Konitsa and District

The north-west of Epirus for some eighteen miles south of the Albanian frontier is a military zone and visitors to Konitsa and neighbourhood in 1973 required passes from the military authorities in Ioannina, which were somewhat sparingly given. It was in this area that Mussolini's attack on Greece in 1940 collapsed. It was later the scene of bitter fighting in 1947–9 when the Greek Communist partisans tried desperately and unsuccessfully to capture Konitsa in order to proclaim a capital on Greek soil. British troops were briefly here in the spring of 1941.

Because of wartime destruction, nearly all the houses in Konitsa are of recent origin. Hughes commented favourably on the quality of building here but in 1973 there was little of architectural interest except for the crumbling ruin of the once stately mansion erected for Khamco, Ali Pasha's mother; it may now no longer exist as its site was then wanted for military purposes. Many of the old families had departed and their places taken over by peasants from the surrounding villages. Some blocks of flats were under construction for local people who considered this the best form of investment for the money they had made working in Germany.

Konitsa, with its population of about three thousand, one hundred and fifty, is superbly sited on the steep, partly wooded slopes of Mount Trapezita which rises to over 6,000 feet. Further back stands the massif of Smolikas with Mount Gameela to the south. Below, the plain spreads north- and south-west. It is large and fertile for Epirus and watered by the Aoos which is here joined by the Voidthomatis. Beyond the north-western edge of the plain, this lovely river is enlarged by the Sarandoporos, swollen with the streams of

Grammos and of the mountains which separate Epirus from Macedonia; for its last few miles of independence, the Sarandoporos forms the frontier with Albania.

To the west and north-west of Konitsa stretch far horizons and distant lines of hills, the most impressive of which is the Nemertsika range, running south-east from Albania between the rivers Drin and Aoos and ending in the dramatic peak of Merope, over 6,500 feet high. On its eastern slope nestles Molyvthoskepasto. This frontier village was our destination, not only on account of its historic churches and its position above the confluence of the Aoos and Sarandoporos rivers, but because there was accommodation for visitors in the Monastery of the Dormition of the Virgin. The monastery was no longer occupied by monks, but the local village priest was glad to offer simple hospitality.

During the two-hour journey the bus, which left Konitsa in the late afternoon, took us through stupendous scenery—distant peaks, sparkling rivers gliding through green valleys, spreading woods and villages with their vines, geraniums, cherry trees laden with fruit, pomegranates and fig trees and their lovely crumbling stone houses. From time to time we were halted at army check points and our passes examined.

The road led on to Melissapetra and other villages along the wooded southern bank of the Sarandoporos. The whole landscape smiled in the golden light which comes before sunset. The Albanian side of the river, as beautiful as the Greek side, was deserted without sign of life except for a large notice which proclaimed in Albanian that 'Anyone landing on this bank without permission will meet with death'. The notice looked dilapidated but our fellow passengers made clear that it should be taken seriously.

After crossing to the left bank of the Aoos, we were within the shadow of Merope and could see the roofs of Molyvthoskepasto shining high up on the mountainside. The name means literally 'shod with lead'. Originally it was the name given locally to the monastery, while the village was called Dipalitsa. Its roofs gleam today in the magic air of this enchanted countryside, but the material used is not lead but corrugated iron. The houses were wrecked by the Germans in 1943 when they damaged the monastery in reprisal for two important bridges destroyed by the guerillas. The people here got off lightly with only two killed; at a nearby village, we were told, forty people were herded into a house by the Germans and burned to death.

We could see the outline of the monastery in the dusk as the bus began its steep climb to our destination. The village was a mile further on and several hundred feet higher. Before we were allowed to descend, our passes were again inspected and warnings given against taking photographs. The Albanian frontier was at the far end of the village.

We moved along the village pathway in search of the priest and a meal as it was after 8 p.m. The first café was occupied by army N.C.O.s so we moved on to the only other café. Here we were cheerfully welcomed by an elderly man with what used to be called an 'Epirot head'—a head which is broad and flat at the back. Some say that this flatness is caused by the newborn infant having its head laid on a wooden pillow. Another explanation was that during the Ottoman Empire a father, on being presented with a son, would strike it firmly on the back of the head, saying 'may you become a baker in the City', meaning Constantinople. Our new friend, Niko, later told us that he had worked as a baker in Cairo, the next best thing, where he had supplied bread to the French Embassy. He had been forced to come home when the Greeks were evicted from Egypt by Nasser and was now living in retirement with his sister and his brother-in-law, who owned the little café-cum-grocer shop. All three were well over sixty.

The electric light was now on and several villagers and soldiers arrived to inspect us. The *tsipouro* bottle soon made its appearance and every fresh arrival ordered a round. The party developed apace and all thoughts of a meal seemed to have been forgotten. It was also certainly too late to go down to the monastery. 'There's nowhere to sleep here,' shouted the innkeeper cheerfully, 'some find the road quite comfortable!'

'That's right,' added Niko, 'we don't like strangers in our houses—they might be Albanian.'

At this moment the *papouli*, the affectionate term for a village priest, who had heard of our arrival, now joined the party to make quite sure that we were being looked after, and quickly decided that we were. He too insisted on standing his round before leaving us with the innkeeper who had by now arranged with his wife for us to stay in his three-roomed bungalow a few yards away. He, his wife and Niko shared one room so that we could each have a room to ourselves. On leaving they refused to accept anything except the promise of a photograph of themselves which we later sent them.

Before retiring for the night, we were taken to see the floodlighting of the Church of the Holy Apostles on a spur at the northern end of the village, facing out over Albania. Here supposedly was a message of hope from Christian Greece to any Greeks in Albania who still cherished the Orthodox faith of their forefathers. In the distance we could just make out the dim lights of Leskovits, the little town from where the village had been administered before 1913, some eight miles inside Albania, but there were no counter-illuminations.

The full splendour of this fine Byzantine church was revealed the following morning. We returned to it in brilliant sunshine along a stone track, passing arches which supported a solid, whitewashed building standing over the path. Under the arches, a spring trickled from the rocks on which the building stood. The spring was said to have curative properties and the building was sanctified for one day a year when a service was held here. Above the spring was a map of northern Epirus on the wall.

From the Church of the Holy Apostles a slope to the north spread down into a broad valley; the first fifty yards were kept clear but for the next two hundred yards there was an impenetrable tangle of bushes. Beyond were fields where men and women were cutting hay. They were in Albania. In the bushes was the barbed wire frontier. We stood on a platform of exposed ground, probably under observation from the Albanian side; from here we could see the junction of the Sarandoporos with the Aoos and away to the north-east the great mountains of Grammos over which a suspicion of thunder clouds was beginning to form. On the Albanian side, a convoy of three lorries trundled along a dirt road to carry away the harvest. Beyond the road rose a green hillside embellished with anti-tank blocks.

Niko remembered that in his boyhood the houses of several

Turkish officials stood on these slopes. He was then always careful to avoid this area because the Turkish children threw stones at the Greek boys and girls, who never dared retaliate. Then, said Niko, at the end of the First Balkan War came revenge. Most of the Turks fled to the comparative safety of the towns, but Greek irregulars slaughtered any they found in this remote countryside.

The Church of the Holy Apostles consists of a nave and two aisles, a five-sided apse and a large narthex where we found a family of bats at exercise. Above the nave rises a twelve-sided, drum-shaped dome, supported inside on four hexagonal columns and capped with a conical tiled roof. There is a covered portico on the south side and a bell-tower, both of which may be later additions. The wall paintings of the interior are exceptionally competent with a fine Pantocrator in the dome, although damp has spoilt much of the surrounding work. From these it appears that the church was decorated in the sixteenth and seventeenth centuries, perhaps by a painter from Mount Athos. Professor Nicol, who has described the churches of Molyvthoskepasto in the 1953 *Annual of the British School of Athens*, thinks that there is little doubt that the structure dates from an earlier period, judging by traces of older wall-painting underneath the Athonite frescoes. According to the diocesan lists of the Archbishopric of Pogoniani, of which the Holy Apostles was undoubtedly the cathedral church, the foundations were laid in 1298.

The importance of Molyvthoskepasto is also shown by the many smaller churches which were built in and around the village during the sixteenth century. Hughes, when he came here, counted nearly twenty churches in ruins; he also experienced more incivility than 'in all the rest of our journey'. We noted only three little churches in addition to that of the Holy Apostles and the monastery church down near the river. One, in the heart of the village, was the little single-naved chapel of St Demetrios, which was in a sad state of disrepair. Scaffolding, however, had been erected prior to its restoration. The Greek Church is preserving its treasures when its means permit. Two others are the tiny chapel of the Trinity (Ayia Triada) perched on a prominence to the north of the path down to the monastery, while lower still is the little chapel of the Dormition, both of them probably of the sixteenth century.

The Monastery of the Dormition of the Virgin is an ancient foundation. According to tradition, the Emperor Constantine IV Pogonatos (668–85) paused here when returning from a successful campaign in Sicily at the beginning of his reign. The monastery was built as a result; its importance grew rapidly and the establishment of the Archbishopric of Pogoniani followed. Its fortunes varied, but by the seventh century, it was known as an important centre of Hellenic culture and the possessor of a good library.

In about 1770, the Albanians destroyed Dipalitsa and the Archbishop retired to Roumania. The Patriarch in 1828 then united Pogoniani, first with the see of Konitsa and later with Vela, but none of these arrangements proved practical. Finally, the Archbishopric of Pogoniani was dissolved in 1863 and the district included in a diocese with Konitsa and Vela. The village never recovered its importance; at the height of its splendour it had supported a population of ten thousand but in 1973 there were barely eighty-five inhabitants.

The monastery stands quietly in its walled enclosure, surrounded by flower beds and trees which shade the stone-flagged walks. There is little sign of the damage done by German troops who in 1943 shelled and looted the monastery church and the conventual buildings, which back on to the slopes up to the village. There have been no monks in residence for many years, but the village *papouli*, a kindly, thoughtful man, has for long devotedly tended the monastery buildings. The outside walls of the building containing the cells are whitewashed and the rooms are spotless. Underneath are the store rooms with fuel for the stove and fodder for the *papouli*'s mule. Flowers grow in whitewashed petrol tins, placed at regular intervals along the paths.

The church itself consists of a small cruciform apse, surmounted by a tall, slender dome, octagonal in shape, capped with a round conical roof of tiles. Joined to the west end of the apse is a single nave, across which rises a barrel-vaulted roof at right angles to the length of the church with two small two-light windows, one at each end. A spacious exonarthex opens on the south side which, with the covered south portico, was built at a later date. Professor Nicol has noted that such porticos were added to many Epirot churches after the Turkish Conquest; they were probably used for storing coffins and bones.

The nave is entered either from the portico or from the exonarthex through a door made from two leaves of dark oak, each divided into three panels; these are finely carved with figures, including the Virgin Mary, St Gabriel and a griffin. The nave is dark and many of the wall paintings have suffered from damp. There are three bands of figures, one above the other: first there is a row of standing saints, above it a row of medallions showing the heads of saints, and finally panels in which scenes from the liturgical cycle are depicted: this pattern is frequently found in the churches of Epirus and Macedonia.

An inscription over the west door gives a brief history of the church—its foundation by the Emperor Pogonatos, its re-establishment by the Emperor Andronikos II Palaiologos (1282–1328) and further restoration and decoration by the faithful of the diocese in 1521, when it is said to have been in ruins. The distinctive architectural features of the church—the design of the apse, the tall octagonal dome and the transverse barrel roof over the nave—are features found in the late Byzantine churches built early in the fourteenth century. This strong Serbian influence, which appears to have coincided with the expansion southwards of the Serbian Empire under Stefan Milutin (1282–1321), lends weight to the evidence that the monastery church that we see today was erected at this later period and not, as tradition has it, in the seventh century.

We paused at Konitsa on our return to visit the Stomion Monastery, some four miles up the Aoos gorge; the monastery is reached by a mule track along the river's south bank, leading towards Mount Papingo. It was a cool, cloudy day, ideal for walking. We had first to descend to the Aoos. In 1973 one could cross either by the elegant Turkish bridge, the only one there in 1945, or by the modern temporary structure then standing next to it. A permanent bridge was being built further on downstream; when completed, the temporary structure will, it is hoped, be removed, so that the old Turkish bridge, sweeping high over the river, can be seen unobscured for what it is—one of the finest bridges of its kind in the Balkans. We were advised to take a guide and so paused at the hamlet to the north of the bridges to acquire one. The inhabitants were originally refugees from Asia Minor, transplanted here after the disastrous Greek defeat in 1922. They are mainly farmers with holdings close by in the Plain of Konitsa. The old men remembered vividly their arrival here from beyond the Aegean and how pleased they were to find that their farming techniques produced better results than those used by the indigenous inhabitants. 'The fact that the Greeks of Asia Minor were refugees', wrote Charles B. Eddy, 'caused it to be forgotten that they were the equals or even the superiors of their western brothers.' D. G. Hogarth has also pointed out in *The Nearer East* that the Asiatic Greeks have always been more highly developed than their European brothers; the growth of communications in Turkey in the second half of the nineteenth century led to the extension of Greek influence inland and there had been a real Greek renaissance in language and ideas, made possible by the peculiar position of the Greek Orthodox Church under the Patriarchate of Constantinople.

The villagers had broad, healthy faces with a touch of gold about their skin which may have been the result of their open air life or could conceivably indicate their affinities with Asia on whose western fringe they had been settled for millennia. Here was another example of the Greeks making a virtue out of necessity. Deprived by the Turks of political power, they had concentrated on maintaining their own prosperity and, like the Jews, had been prepared to go anywhere to earn a living. The Greeks under the Ottomans had not only established trading communities widely in Central Europe and around the Black Sea, but in the eighteenth century had successfully settled as far east as Calcutta and Dacca. They also travelled west and even founded a small colony at Mahon in Minorca under the protection of the British flag, which they rallied to protect in 1756 when French forces at the start of the Seven Years War (1756–63) invaded the island.

The number of refugees from Asia Minor settled in Epirus through the exchange of populations between Greece and Turkey in the 1920s was small when compared with those in

Thessaly and Macedonia. There is a colony in Ioannina, where they are market gardeners; there are the citrus fruit growers around Arta, but there are few others. The reason for this was that Epirus held few settled Turks, being a difficult, mountainous area inhabited by warrior peoples, in contrast to the defenceless plains of Thessaly where the Turks had easily established themselves on land expropriated from the Greeks.

With the arrival of our guide, tall, heavily-moustached and unsmiling, we crossed the Aoos and walked eastwards up the gorge against the direction of the racing, surging, tumultuous river. In June there was still snow on the higher mountain ridges which would have to melt away before the river calmed down.

On the north side of the river, the mountainside soon became too steep for a distance to support vegetation, except in the occasional crevice. The further we went, the more precipitous became the south bank as well; before long we were climbing up and down the slopes high above the hurrying green waters, foam-flecked from rocks in their course. For a time the path became a hard stony track, cut out of the mountainside, the exposed surface moist with trickles of water. Further upstream the slopes became a tangle of trees and bushes, alight with the pale green flames of June. On both sides the cliffs rose to over 2,000 feet with occasional glimpses of snow-capped peaks beyond.

At one point, a long train of horses, all laden with lengths of pine wood from the upper slopes of Timfi, swung past us, each animal delicately and momentarily testing the ground ahead before putting its full weight upon it. Several of their flanks were raw, where a strap had rubbed the skin away, to leave a small, bleeding wound on which flies were trying to settle, but the drivers, sturdy young Vlachs, paid no attention. The authorities have established a sound veterinary service throughout the country, but apparently this is little used. Everyone, man and beast, must endure discomforts from time to time; if the beasts are basically well, as these obviously were, there is no point in wasting time by going to a vet over a few sores.

The Stomion Monastery stood on a spur which jutted out

from the mountain slopes above the mist-veiled river course and forced the Aoos away towards the east. We could see the grey-white buildings, the lower walls of which were obscured by riotous vegetation. Above to the south soared the almost perpendicular slopes of Mount Gameela. We found that the monastery had fairly recently been restored; although the deserted cells, sufficient for some ten monks, were well-kept, the grounds were unkempt. The site is magnificent. The rooms look down on the tumbling river and echo with its muted roar.

The only other person there, standing by the entrance to the monastery church, was a shepherd who had lost several sheep from his flock. He seemed confident that if he stayed here long enough, the missing animals would reveal themselves. When we departed to picnic at a nearby spring, which bubbled sweet water from the rocks, he joined us to share our bread and cheese. Afterwards he accompanied us part of the way back to the end of the gorge.

Suddenly he stopped and, looking up the slopes of Gameela, said in an unconcerned tone of voice to our guide that he was turning back. Was he going to do nothing further about finding his sheep? we asked. Pointing up to the highest ridge, he said: 'There they are.' After some concentration, we could just make out their tiny white specks as they grazed on the summer grass.

'But aren't you going up to them?' we asked again.

'No need, they'll come back down here to the monastery in a day or so.' With a brief farewell, he strode away upstream. This was a mystery to us, but our guide seemed to take the matter for granted.

11

Zitsa, Passaron and Kastritza

The wine of Zitsa has long been renowned. Colonel Leake reported that the village had the reputation of making the best wine in Epirus. He added, however, that while the wine produced by the monks of the Monastery of the Prophet Elias was not unpleasant, the ordinary village wine was pressed from grapes, unripened as well as ripe, then diluted with water to increase the quantity to which much resin was added to give it body. Not unnaturally, Leake found the result to be sour and unpalatable.

We had heard glowing accounts of Zitsa wine long before we reached Ioannina in autumn 1944 and were looking forward to tasting it. Only a year later did the opportunity present itself. A vendor came to the mayor's house, on whose upper floor we had located our office, bringing with him a bottle of wine which he declared was from Zitsa. If we liked it, he said, he could sell us a barrel of it at what seemed a very reasonable price. We tasted the wine from the bottle and found it delicious—a delicate pale pink, slightly effervescent wine—not unlike that from Anti-Paxos in the Ionian. We acquired the barrel with alacrity.

We refrained with admirable restraint from broaching the barrel at once in order to allow the wine to settle after its journey. When later we did so, we found its contents to be a vinegary, bilgewaterish liquor which was quite undrinkable. For the next few weeks, we were all on the lookout for the vendor but never saw him again. If we had then known Leake's experience, we might have been a little more philosophical about our purchase.

A few years later, Zitsa wine of good quality, described by one Hellenic traveller, Robert Liddell, as 'a very tolerable cider', was available in some quantities, but this is no longer the case. More and more vineyards are being left untended because of the flight of labour from the land.

The first recorded visit to Zitsa by an Englishman seems to have been that of Leake in April 1809. He wrote that the village 'commands a beautiful and extensive prospect, the plain of Ioannina, and the fertile hills on which Zitsa stands, furnishing a variety of cultivated scenery, which is admirably contrasted with the great barren summits around.'

In November of the same year, Byron and Hobhouse arrived here after losing their way in a storm, an occasion which the poet celebrated by writing 'Stanzas composed during a Thunderstorm', while his guides were trying to find the road. Byron was in excellent form as shown by his reference to Hobhouse in the following stanza:

> Through sounds of foaming waterfalls
> I hear a voice exclaim—
> My way-worn countryman, who calls
> On distant England's name.

Byron informed his mother in a letter from Preveza, dated 12 November 1809, that he found Zitsa 'in the most beautiful situation (always excepting Cintra in Portugal) I ever beheld.' The village stood on one of the routes northwards to Albania. Byron was on his way to the court of Ali Pasha, then at Tepeleni, a visit described in Canto the Second of *Childe Harold's Pilgrimage*. On his return journey he spent a night in the Monastery of the Prophet Elias. Holland was here in 1813, having read the elegant stanzas from Canto the Second, which begin:

> Monastic Zitsa! from thy shady brow
> Thou small but favour'd spot of holy ground . . .

Holland did not mention the wine, but Hughes did and seems to have drunk well of it in spite of 'a peculiar flavour from the absynthus employed in its preparation'.

In 1848, Edward Lear, like Byron, arrived in a storm, to spend the night in the monastery, 'a place I had looked forward to visiting as much as any in Albania', but it was utterly spoilt for him by the torrential rain, which chilled him to the bone. Fortunately the monks in residence had an excellent luncheon for him (no mention of the wine). Afterwards he was told some anecdotes about Byron, whom the eldest monk remembered staying there, which Lear would not repeat as he refused to 'add to the list of crude absurdities too often tacked to the memory of remarkable men'.

It also poured during our visit to Zitsa except that the rain restrained itself while we entered the monastery. Afterwards, instead of a clearing sky which we had been promised, it returned in greater violence. The taxi had quickly covered the fifteen miles from Ioannina, most of it along the Igoumenitsa road, but the last two miles were up a steep lane past the slopes on which vines once grew in profusion, through the straggling village and up the hill to where, surrounded by oak, fir and some fig trees, the long grey walls of the monastery nestle beneath the brow. On the outside wall is a little plaque, announcing that the Lord Byron stayed here on 12 and 13 October 1809. The monastery is small with accommodation for some five monks; the little chapel is unexceptional and the garden tidy, although there is no one any longer in residence. A faded charm envelops the site. From the hill crest there are splendid views of Mount Kasidiares, whose long ridge sweeps northwards towards Albania. Zitsa, like Karitsa, another wine-growing centre below it, has now only a small population. Its large stone houses and paved streets indicate its former prosperity, but many of the old houses are crumbling. Among them are a few modern bungalows, some roofed with red tiles, others with corrugated iron.

We did not attempt in the rain to visit nearby Radotovi, north-west of Gardhiki, where an important Molossian temple, built at the end of the fourth century B.C., was excavated earlier in this century and identified as that of Zeus Areios, a god of war in the Molossian worship. Instead, we drove up the rough track towards the summit of Gardhiki itself, which dominates the last stretch of the Igoumenitsa–Ioannina road before it descends into the Ioannina plain. It is a long, barren, stony ridge which I had passed many times without noticing the remains of the once encircling wall. Now, as we climbed, we could distinguish more easily the remnants of what is generally accepted as the acropolis of Passaron, an important and well sited Molossian centre. Hammond has written that 'the cities of Hellenistic Epirus were far more handsome than their modern counterparts are today. The massive circuit-walls with their towers and parapets, the finely proportioned gateways . . . and broad roads, built on ramps leading to them, were shown to advantage by their situation on hill-tops or on ridges.' Alas, the rain forced us back to Ioannina.

The Molossians, who perhaps came south-west from Macedonia in the late Bronze Age, were for long, especially under King Pyrrhus, the most powerful tribe in Epirus. There were other tribes, between eleven and fourteen altogether according to Theopompus and Strabo, among which the most powerful were the Threspotians, who occupied western Epirus from the Ambracian Gulf up to the Kalamas river, and the Chaonians, whose territory stretched north from the Kalamas into Illyria. These tribes spoke a form of Greek, but Thucydides referred to them as barbarians, as they were not organized as city-states nor did they enjoy the culture associated with this form of political organization.

The Hellenization of the Molossians began at about the time of the Persian Wars when they established their supremacy over the other Epirot tribes, including the Threspotians, and over the cult at Dodona. This closer contact with the Greeks is illustrated by the claim they then advanced that their kings were descended from Achilles, whose son, Neoptolemus, resided with them for a time on his return from Troy. This descent also implied that the Molossians were Achaeans and as such of older stock than the Dorians who arrived later in Greece. Pindar, Herodotus and Thucydides regarded their monarchs as Greek. By the fourth century their royal pedigree was found to be satisfactory by the stewards of the Olympic Games, thus achieving the hallmark of respectability. Pindar and probably Themistocles as well spent some time at the Molossian court.

Molossian support for Athens in the Peloponnesian Wars brought the tribe under the influence of Attic culture and marked the beginnings of more civilized life in Epirus. This did not mean that the Epirot tribes adopted Athenian institutions, for theirs was a monarchy, carefully counterbalanced by representatives of the various tribes in the Molossian hegemony. The Molossian kings before Pyrrhus were never absolute; they led their people in war and prayer but were expected to note the advice of the elders or councillors which would be given publicly before the assembled tribe.

In the middle of the fourth century Macedon intervened decisively in the development of the Molossians. In 357 B.C., three years after they had joined together in an alliance primarily against the Illyrians, Philip II of Macedon married Olympias, a Molossian princess, who bore him Alexander the Great. In the winter of 343–342 B.C., Philip overthrew Arybbas, the Molossian king, and put Alexander, Olympias's brother, on the Molossian throne; he also reduced the Elean colonies in south-west Epirus, namely Batiai, Bucheteion, Elateia and Pandosia and placed them under the Cassopaians, one of the tribes in the Molossian alliance. By now Molossian Epirus had started to look westwards to Sicily and Italy for increased commerce and greater political power. The Molossian Alexander was killed while campaigning in Magna Graecia. There was also a trend towards urbanization, which developed considerably during the third century, especially under Pyrrhus.

The Epirot Alliance which arose about 330–326 B.C. restricted Molossian expansion at the expense of those tribes which now enjoyed equality of rights as members of the Alliance, but Pyrrhus, whose reign started in 299 B.C., made them again subordinate until his death in 272 B.C. Pyrrhus was brought up in the tumultuous days when the successors of Alexander the Great intrigued and fought for parts of his Empire, and when the power of Rome first expanded southwards down the Italian peninsula. He was fearless and became greatly respected as a general. His martial reputation enabled him to build an absolute Hellenistic monarchy, not only over Epirus and the adjoining territories but also for a time over parts of Sicily and southern Italy.

Early in his reign, Pyrrhus, through judicious meddling in the dynastic quarrels of Macedon, gained the city of Ambracia, today known as Arta, to which he transferred his capital from Dodona. Towards Macedon his policy was consistent; he was determined either to weaken or conquer this kingdom because he regarded a strong Macedon incompatible with a powerful Epirus.

As his power expanded, so Pyrrhus's help was sought against the Carthaginians in Sicily and in Magna Graecia by those states threatened by an expansionist Rome. At first this policy paid off; his alliance with Tarentum helped him regain possession of Corcyra (Corfu) and Levkas, his dowry on his marriage to Lanassa, daughter of the Tyrant of Syracuse. He was not averse to polygamy for diplomatic reasons, but did not always weigh carefully enough the possible results. In this way he lost Lanassa who transferred her marital affections to Demetrius of Macedon, whose ambitions clashed with those of Pyrrhus and led to war between them.

Pyrrhus's campaign in Italy and Sicily, after he had crossed to help Tarentum in 280 B.C. with a force of three thousand cavalry, twenty thousand infantry, two thousand archers, five hundred slingers and twenty Indian elephants, established Epirot troops as the finest in Greece at that time. The Roman legions were more than once defeated, like the Carthaginians in Sicily, and the Epirots on one occasion advanced to within twenty-four miles of Rome. Pyrrhus's dream of a widely flung Empire, however, eluded him as, once victory had been achieved, he had only absolutism to offer; for this reason his allies invariably turned against him. He died in 272, still campaigning against Macedon, during street fighting in Peloponnesian Argos. His death brought about the dismemberment of his kingdom and left only his original state of Epirus to his successors. In the peace which followed, the Molossians still retained considerable influence; trade prospered and walled settlements were built to protect rural populations.

The downfall of the Molossian monarchy in 232 through inexperienced leadership and the replacement of the Epirot Alliance by the Epirot League was followed by a period of confusion on account of Illyrian aggression and the ambitions of the Aetolian League to the south. Illyrian attacks on Roman merchant shipping brought the Roman legions east across the Adriatic and began their involvement with the warring factions of Greece, of which Macedon towards the end of the third century B.C. was the most powerful. Meanwhile the Aetolians marched north and sacked the temples at Passaron

and Dodona in 219, to be avenged in the following year by a
brilliant raid, commanded by Philip V of Macedon, against
the Aetolian capital at Thermon, east of modern Agrinion.

Philip's alliance with Carthage during the Second Punic
War and his building of a fleet to dominate the Adriatic
marked out Macedon as Rome's principal Hellenic adversary.
With the overwhelming defeat of Carthage at Zama in 202,
Rome was able to concentrate her attention east of the Adriatic
and Ionian Seas, and successfully wooed the Epirot coastal
tribes to whom trade with Italy was of growing importance.

The third Macedon War, which erupted in 170, found the
Epirots divided. The Threspotians and Chaonians supported
Rome, but the Molossians stood by Macedon which was
finally crushed by Rome at the battle of Pydna in 168 B.C.
After Pydna, the Molossians were at the mercy of the Romans.
Anicius, the Roman commander, marched into Epirus and
occupied every Molossian city except for Passaron, Tecmon
and two others, which shut their gates against the legions, but
their resistance was short-lived. Once the Molossian leaders
had been killed fighting, these towns surrendered. Revenge
followed and the behaviour of Charops, an influential Epirot
who had supported Rome throughout these difficult days, was
as bestial as that of any Nazi *gaulleiter*.

Aemilius Paullus, the Roman consul, joined Anicius in
camp at Passaron. From here he announced that both the
Epirots and the Macedonians were to enjoy freedom and that
the Roman legions were to be withdrawn. At the same time,
ten men in each Molossian centre were ordered to collect
together all the gold and silver in a public place. Roman
detachments were then sent to the seventy Molossian settlements so that each reached their destination at the same time
with orders to sack them.

The Molossians must have watched the approach up the
hillside of these grim-faced legionaries with mounting alarm
until the full horror of their plight was revealed by the
mounting flames from their homes and the pitiless sword-
slash and spear-thrust as they were driven into slavery. In all
one hundred and fifty thousand Molossians suffered in this
way. Central Epirus was left desolate. This vengeance on a
people whom the Romans considered to be treacherous marked

the end of Epirot power and virtually the end of Greek resistance to Rome.

So Passaron and the other Molossian cities were destroyed. Their ruins lie scattered north and south of the present Greek-Albanian frontier. Some have been identified but by no means all. What therefore of the ruins of an obviously once important settlement on the hillside of Kastritza at the southern end of Ioannina's lake?

The road to Kastritza leads out of the *plateia* of Ioannina and down past the area where the gypsies were allowed to encamp during the reign of Ali Pasha. In return for such squatting rights as he would give them, the gypsies were employed as executioners. Close by were several enormous plane trees on whose branches were hung the miscreants and unfortunates sentenced to death by the Vizier. As many as twenty bodies sometimes dangled from them. The road winds on between humble cottages and past the little square of Sapountzaki, named after a brave Souliot, with its crumbling mosque on the south side, now converted into a café; its blunted minaret is one of the few places where storks still nest in Ioannina.

Before long the road divides into two; the one to the right joins the trunk road to Arta while the left branch follows the lake's shoreline and so to the base of Kastritza after leaving a further branch to the right which continues on southwards into Xerovouni. The steep slope of the hill is overgrown with scrub but there is a road, bulldozed by the army, up which we climbed to the convent dedicated to the Virgin's Birth, which stands high up on a little plateau. From here the hillside drops precipitously to the green fields reclaimed from the lake. The bells of the sheep, idly cropping the grass, sounded distantly in the still air. The lake, a dark opaque sheet of glass, reflected the shadows of the great white clouds floating across the sky.

Professor Hammond tentatively identifies the Kastritza settlement with Eurymenae, but Professor Dakaris, who took us to the site, thinks it may have been Tecmon, which at first resisted the Romans, but which surrendered after the death in battle of Cephalos, the Epirot leader. Cephalos was a man of distinction and a patriot. He had first supported a defensive alliance with Rome, but when he found that Charops was deliberately poisoning the minds of the Romans against him, he had sided with Macedon.

We tried to follow the ancient walls of the settlement through the tangled growth of ilex and *paliuri*, a tightly knotted prickly bush, used to cover church lamps hanging from the ceiling, to prevent the mice running down to drink the oil. The heat of midday drew out the fresh, sweet smell of the herbs. Dry leaves rustled suddenly as a lizard rushed for shelter or, on one occasion, as a grave old tortoise moved ponderously in our direction. Edward Lear was assured by a Greek servant in Epirus that tortoises hatch their eggs by the heat of their eyes, staring fixedly at them until the infant tortoises have grown sufficiently to break out of their shells.

As we came upon traces of ancient construction, Sotiris Dakaris would identify a tower, an entrance gate, a secondary support wall. The walls on the summit of Kastritza stood much higher than those below because it was a longer climb for villagers to despoil them for building material; here they were twelve feet wide, solid blocks of stone on each side with gaps in between for rubble.

Life at Kastritza had probably continued, in spite of damage by the Goths under Totila, into the Middle Ages, as there are signs of medieval walls. In one corner of the topmost wall on the hill crest stood an isolated little Orthodox chapel, whose door was locked. A Neolithic settlement had been discovered along a footpath we could see round the village of Kastritza nestling far below on the south side of the hill.

Eventually, dazed by the sun, we returned to the convent for water and a rest. We were welcomed by a bright-eyed nun in her early thirties, one of the two now caring for the buildings. She led us up wooden steps into the guest room, feminine with the comfort of cushions and embroidered sofa covers. Now, while we toyed with quince in syrup and orangeade, she told us of the vocation she had followed against intense parental opposition, but that she had never regretted her decision. She and her companion had come to the deserted convent only a year ago, since when they had repainted all the walls and built their own kitchen. Now they were installing weaving machinery to earn themselves a living.

12

Dodona

The little village of Dodona sits on a low spur on the north-eastern flank of Mount Olytsika, the ancient Tomaros, which rises to over 6,000 feet and whose continuing ridge runs southwards, after the dip at Varyiadhes, to form the eastern slopes of Lakkasouli. This dramatic peak is snow-covered in winter; even in summer, its head is often wreathed in clouds. On a still, sultry day in late August, distant thunder, reverberating among the mountains, can sound as menacing and the air become as oppressive as if Zeus the Cloud Compeller, the Earth Shaker, the Thunderer was still master of Epirus which he had once ruled from Dodona. Here his oracle, according to Herodotus, had been established under an oak tree by a woman from Egypt. She and a companion in the service of the Theban Zeus had been abducted by the Phoenicians, one to Epirus, the other to Libya, where at Ammon the latter had raised a similar shrine.

I had first visited Dodona in 1945 between the end of the spring rains and the arrival of summer, when the sky was still largely hidden by clouds. Then the road, which branches south-west off the Ioannina–Arta road some three and a half miles south of Ioannina, had been rough and muddy. The area of Dodona had been empty of people and the stone seats of the great amphitheatre tumbled about as if violently shaken by an earthquake. To the south the view was dominated by the great shoulder of Olytsika. A chilly wind emphasized the lonely dereliction of the site.

On my second visit with friends after twenty-eight years, the site had been magnificently transformed. The theatre, the most impressive and complete of the buildings around the oracle, had been restored between 1960 and 1963; the seats were now in order and the retaining wall rebuilt. Above the theatre a gate led into the acropolis whose walls are now less than ten feet high. The remains of the other ancient buildings had been revealed by the tidying away of debris and vegetation and the removal of the top soil. The approach road over a ridge of hills was well made and now used by visitors, nearly all of them Greek.

The site of ancient Dodona was only finally established in 1875, after excavations carried out with the sanction of the Turkish authorities by Constantine Karapanos, an Epirot politician. Here he found various inscriptions and decrees of the Epirot Alliance and the Epirot League which confirmed without doubt that this was the home of the oracle. Prior to that, its whereabouts in Epirus was only guessed at by scholars and travellers, although successfully by Christopher Wordsworth in the late 1830s: having declared 'the former dwelling of the spirit, which once guided half the world, is lost', he then argued the case for the present site, whose extensive ruins were merely known as *Kastro* or *Palaiokastro*. There must have been some unusual reason for this centre to have been set on the edge of a plain with weak defences when Greek cities invariably chose as strong a military position as possible. Here, he argued, was no ordinary settlement. Again, the theatre was much too large for the settlement's few inhabitants and must therefore have been built to attract strangers. For these and additional reasons, including vestiges of a temple with fragments of fourteen columns still standing, when 'there are not, we believe, fourteen other columns remaining in the whole of Epirus', Wordsworth believed that the ruins of Dramasios were those of Dodona; the columns could have been either those of the *stoa* or portico due south of the theatre or of that attached to the *bouleuterion* or council house.

Dramisios is the next village up the valley to the north-west on what was the main route from Ioannina to Paramythia before the road to Igoumenitsa was built. Because of this, both Holland and Hughes saw the ruins and were impressed. Holland, always rather cautious, merely reported that some literary Greeks in Ioannina had assumed that they might be the ruins of Cassopaia, although he thought, and rightly, that the site was too far inland. Hughes talked to the same Greeks and took their word for granted.

Leake had also met the 'learned' of Ioannina, who had referred him to a variety of places in Epirus and Albania for the site. In Volume IV of his *Travels in Northern Greece*, he went to great lengths to try to place the oracle's whereabouts. He took special note of the words of Aeschylus who described the Dodonaean oracle as that of the Threspotian Zeus on Molossian soil, which indicated that Dodona bordered both on Threspotia and Molossia. Another significant clue was, he considered, Hesiod's description of Dodona in a fragment of a lost poem, the *Eoiai*: 'Hellopia was a country of cornfields and meadows, abounding in sheep and oxen, and inhabited by numerous shepherds and keepers of cattle, where on an extremity stood Dodona, beloved by Zeus; here the god established his oracle in a wood of ilex.' Cornfields, meadows, ilex, sheep and cattle are still to be seen in the valley.

Leake was misled by a conclusion he wrongly drew from references in Pindar and Eustathius to a lake in Molossia, that Dodona itself was close to a lake. He therefore inferred that the settlement of Dodona was built on the hill of Kastritza, that Tomaros (now Olytsika) was the ancient name for Mitzikeli and, with the lake in between, that the temple of Zeus and its oracle stood on the site of Ioannina itself, which was also surrounded by cornfields and meadows abounding in sheep and cattle. He supported his theory that Mitzikeli was Tomaros by referring to Theopompus, who described the latter mountain as having a hundred streams issuing from its base. Mitzikeli, as we have seen, has many springs draining into the lake of Ioannina. Leake visited the true site of Dodona, which he called *Palaiokastro*, but did not consider that these were the ruins of an Epirot city, because there were no defences worthy of the name. He supported the theory that here was a public meeting place for sacred festivals and perhaps for civic purposes as well. Nothing he saw there had 'an appearance of remote antiquity', and he concluded that 'the whole perhaps was founded on the site of some renowned temple of the Molossi, with a view of pacifying and civilizing Epirus', much of which was true.

Theopompus gave the clue which Leake was unlucky to

miss. The springs of Olytsika were as numerous as those of
Mitzikeli; the alluvial deposits they brought down covered
within twenty years what Karapanos had excavated. By the
end of the nineteenth century meadows, reflecting Hesiod's
landscape, once more stood around the ruins of the theatre
and the outlines of the buildings had disappeared. Nothing
more could be done, even when the area became Greek in
1913, until the late D. E. Evangelides, the Epirot archaeologist,
resumed work on the site between 1929 and 1933. There
followed a further period of inactivity until after the 1939–45
war, when work started once again under Evangelides. After
his death, his place was taken by Sotiris Dakaris, now Professor of Archaeology at Ioannina University and Director of
Epirot Antiquities for over twenty years.

A settlement at Dodona first came into existence about four
thousand years ago, as the earliest finds belong to the early
Bronze Age from about 2500 to 1100 B.C. These finds, some
of which can be seen in the fine modern Museum of Ioannina,
erected between the Litheritza and the cathedral, consist of
bored celts or stone tools, one or two bowls and a quantity of
sherds of coarse pottery in the Neolithic style, all of which
point to the presence of a very primitive community of
shepherds; for Dodona was situated on two important transhumant routes—one leading west to Paramythia and down to
the Fanari Plain, the other going south through Lakkasouli or
along the Louros valley to the plain beyond. The shapes and
decorative features of some of these finds have a Macedonian
origin from which it would appear that the shepherd community which visited Dodona had cultural links with Macedonia, although some of the design features are of a local
character. This earliest type of pottery discovered at Dodona
goes back, according to Dakaris, to the end of the third or the
beginning of the second millennium B.C. It was the people of
this period who probably developed the original oracle at
Dodona, which was dedicated to the Earth Goddess, a cult
which came from southern Greece and was of eastern origin.

Together with this coarse pottery has been found a small
quantity of better finished vases made of grey or blackish-
brown clay, often burnished, with ribbon handles and angular
outlines, not dissimilar to Minyan ware; this type of pottery,

so-called after the legendary inhabitants of Orchomenos in Boeotia, was brought into Greece by the Hellenes who spoke Greek and were a new wave of invaders of Middle Helladic culture; they came from the north or north-east early during the second millennium B.C. The Threspotians, it seems, were the first of these to settle in Epirus sometime between 1900 and 1600 B.C.; a branch of them, the Helloi—hence the Hellopia of Hesiod—or Selloi occupied the plain of Ioannina and the valley of Dodona. Homer knew of them. In the *Iliad*, just before his account of the death of Patroclus, we find Achilles praying thus to 'thunder-loving Zeus': 'Dodonaean, Pelasgian Zeus, you who live far away and rule over wintry Dodona, surrounded by your prophets, the Helli, who leave the feet unwashed and sleep on the ground' (E. V. Rieu's translation).

The worship of Zeus was associated with the oak tree in which he was said to live. Odysseus, on his return to Ithaka in the Ionian Sea, was, according to Homer, transformed by the goddess Athene into a bedraggled old castaway. In this guise he arrived at the hut of Emmaeus, the swineherd. He then told Emmaeus and a little later his own son, Telemachus, that Odysseus had gone to Dodona to learn the will of Zeus from the great oak tree, which was sacred to the god. From this, it would seem that the will of Zeus was audible from the tree itself; it was not merely an interpretation of the wind soughing through the leaves or the creaking of the branches. Similar evidence is provided by the story of the Argonauts, which was as old, if not older, than that of the *Odyssey*. Here we learn that the goddess Athene took a piece of wood from the Dodonaean oak and fitted it into the keel of the *Argo*, when under construction, to enable the ship itself to speak and to guide the Argonauts at critical moments.

Thus we find two distinct cults associated with the oracle—the oriental Earth Mother and the Indo-European Zeus. Zeus in due course took Gaia, the Earth Mother, as consort; her name was later changed to Dione, the embodiment of fertility and the mother of Aphrodite. Gaia's sacred symbols, the dove, the bull, the double-bladed axe, the tripod and the boar remained at Dodona as part of the cult of Zeus until the end.

There appears to have been no other example of an oak

tree sacred to Zeus in ancient Greece, but such a cult was not uncommon in ancient Rome and was widely known in the Northern European plains, where oaks were worshipped as the homes of supernatural powers. That Dodona had contacts with Central and Northern Europe we shall see in due course.

There are two features to note about the earliest occupants of Dodona. First, there is next to no evidence of dwellings around the sanctuary and only one prehistoric hearth has so far been located here; not all of the site, however, has yet been excavated, especially the acropolis higher up the hillside. It therefore looks on present evidence as if the people who scattered these early pots widely around the sanctuary, were transhumant shepherds. Secondly, the same primitive handmade pottery continued in use not only until the eighth century B.C., when the presence of bronze fragments heralded the arrival of the historic period, but until the ascendancy of the Molossian tribe in Epirus some hundreds of years later.

There have also been Mycenaean finds—vases, weapons and ornaments—at Dodona and elsewhere in Epirus, dating back to the latter half of the second millennium B.C. The presence of these artifacts seems to favour the theory that the traditional Epirot civilization of the transhumant shepherds was already strongly established in these prehistoric days. Here were the direct ancestors of the Sarakatsani. The shepherds sold their sheep and wool to coastal trading settlements, founded by peoples from southern Greece, in return for which they acquired Mycenaean weapons and ornaments.

Dodona was evidently close to a trade route connecting Greece and the Aegean with Northern Europe. We know of this from Herodotus who told of the sacred offerings sent by the Hyperboreans from the Baltic to Delos. These gifts of amber, wrapped up in 'wheat straw', were carried by neighbouring peoples in succession from the Baltic down to Scythia, then west to the head of the Adriatic, then southwards, presumably by sea as far as Valona—and the 'first Greeks to receive them are the Dodonaeans'. These gifts then travelled over the Pindus to Euboea and from there to Delos in the Aegean.

There was also contact with the Urnfield culture of the late

Bronze Age, an important centre of which was Hungary, as shown by the discovery at Dodona and elsewhere in Epirus of typical Urnfield axes. These may have been used in battle and could therefore indicate an invasion from Central Europe sometime between 1250 and 1150 B.C. at the beginning of the Dark Ages which lasted until the eighth century B.C. As there is no sign of changes in or additions to the now traditional Epirot pottery, these invasions were probably transitory. During the four centuries of the Dark Ages, marked according to Thucydides by invasions, piracy and the wholesale destruction of settlements, Epirus appears to have been cut off from contact with the south and there is no evidence of gifts reaching the sanctuary from that direction. By the end of the Dark Ages, when a more settled period reigned in Greece, we find offerings arriving at Dodona once more from southern Greece, such as bronze tripods, weapons and statuettes. The tripods supported bronze cauldrons which encircled the sacred oak. When struck, they vibrated from one cauldron to the next. It was from these vibrations that the priests now interpreted the oracle. Later still in the second half of the fourth century, the encircling cauldrons had been replaced by a wall to protect both the sacred tree and the temple, first erected in about 400 B.C. and several times later rebuilt, each time in a more elaborate manner. A new method of divination had also by now been introduced. A bronze statuette of a boy holding a whip with three lashes stood on a pedestal close to another which supported a cauldron. The whip's thongs, blown by the wind against the cauldron, was now the sound interpreted.

The first settlers in Epirus after the end of the Dark Ages came from Elis in the north-west Peloponnese, to be followed soon after 630 B.C. by the Corinthians who established themselves at Ambracia. The site at Dodona had to wait until the Molossians had gained power before it was expanded; this took place towards the end of the fifth century when they took over the sanctuary from the Threspotians and built the first small temple to Zeus.

The Molossians gained considerable prestige when their princess Olympias was married to Philip II of Macedon. She took a keen interest in Dodona, protested against interference by Athens in the oracle's affairs and later persuaded her son,

Alexander the Great, to contribute handsomely to the sanctuary as well as to others of Pan-Hellenic importance.

Under Pyrrhus the great theatre at Dodona was erected, together with a much more elaborate temple to Zeus, and additional deities were introduced. There were temples to Dione, to Themis, also associated with the great Earth Mother, to Heracles and to Aphrodite. There was also the *bouleuterion* and the ashlar wall which encircled the area occupied by the sanctuary and the other temples.

More troubled times for Dodona followed the collapse of the Molossian monarchy in 232 B.C. In 219 the temple of Zeus was destroyed and the sacred tree uprooted when the Aetolian League raided Dodona, Passaron and no doubt other Molossian centres. Spoils from the Aetolian capital of Thermon, successfully raided by the Epirot League in conjunction with Macedon in the following year, led to the restoration of the sanctuary on a still grander scale. Unhappily the Romans did not spare the oracle in their destruction of the Molossians in 167 B.C. The Epirots were later allowed to revive their centres to a limited extent, including Dodona, only for it to be again pillaged in 86 B.C., this time by the Thracians.

The importance of the oracle was not yet at an end. The ruins left by the Thracians were somewhat clumsily patched up under the Imperial Roman aegis and the theatre converted into an arena for gladiatorial contests and wild beast fights. Augustus and his successors supported the sanctuary. Hadrian visited it in A.D. 132 and Pausanias, the geographer, writing soon afterwards, reported that Dodona was worth a visit. The last Roman Emperor to consult the oracle was Julian the Apostate before the start of his Persian campaign in A.D. 362, but by the end of the fourth century, the oracle had fallen silent forever with the destruction of the theatre and the sacred oak. Instead, Dodona became the seat of a bishop. A basilica church, erected in part over what had once been the Temple of Heracles and was now as desolate as the older temples, endured the invasion of the Goths under Totila in 562 but was abandoned sometime before the ascendancy of the Byzantine Despotate of Epirus.

Ioannina's well-designed modern Museum contains many of the bronze knives, axes and figurines which have been unearthed at Dodona, together with pots, sherds and the strips of lead on which questions for the oracle were inscribed from the sixth century onwards; originally they were oral. The questions asked were personal and about everyday life, not only about the past but for future guidance.

'Am I her children's father?'

'Shall I take another wife?'

'Shall I be successful in my craft if I emigrate?'

'Was it Bostryche, Dorcon's wife, who stole the money lost by Dion during last year's Actia festival?'

The oracle, to judge by the occasional written reply, was at times direct and to the point. Aeschylinus asked if he should travel to Tisates on the Adriatic, to which the response was 'do not sail'. When, however, one Lysias asked if he would be successful in trading by sea and taking a share in the ships, the oracle replied mysteriously, 'you should not offer anything to the earth.'

The glory of Dodona today is Pyrrhus's great theatre and its setting. Here is the same magnificent scenery as at Delphi, the same cool mountain air, the same clarity. Edward Lear would have done justice to the views, but, alas, it was raining so hard when he arrived there on his only visit that the indomitable landscape painter was forced to continue to Ioannina, where the final part of his journey was through wide meadows 'flocked with numberless white storks'.

We wandered among the ruins under the expert guidance of Sotiris Dakaris until the sun began to set behind the western mountain ridge. As we started back for Ioannina we passed four ladies playing bridge in the now setting sun. Instead of watching the magical beginnings of evening over the valley, they sat at their folding bridge table, their heads turned inwards to the omens revealed by their cards. A portable television set stood on a chair close by.

13

Lakkasouli

The wide valley of Lakkasouli lies some twenty miles south of
Ioannina, separated from Dodona by Mount Olytsika. After
the agreement signed with the Allied Military Mission by the
two resistance forces in February at Plaka Bridge on the
Arakhthos, EDES made their headquarters at Derviziana, the
valley's chief village, sited on its eastern slopes. That summer
Ian Scott-Kilvert and I, attached to the Military Mission,
established ourselves in Yeorgani, fifteen minutes on foot
higher up the valley.

The bus from Ioannina to Lakkasouli in summer 1973,
crowded at the start and cheerful because of the presence of
a much liked *papouli*, at first followed the main road to Arta.
Several kilometres beyond the war memorial, commemorating the surrender of the Turkish forces to Crown Prince
Constantine of Greece in spring 1913, we swung off the main
road to the west. Soon we crossed over a stream, the beginnings of the Louros river which rises on the southern flank of
Olytsika and flows between wild laurel and plane trees through
several dramatic gorges before reaching the plains leading to
the Ambracian Gulf. Eastwards there are distant views of the
Tzoumerka range. The pass into Lakkasouli is at Varyiadhes,
a small village where there are traces of Hellenistic stone-
built houses.

The spacious airy valley of Lakkasouli is very different in
character from those in Zagori. It spreads out between two
mountain ranges which, while not high, are each of them
steep and rugged. It is drained by two streams, one on each
side of the valley, which join below Derviziana to become the
Acheron. Between these lively rivulets there is uneven and in
parts heavily wooded ground. On the valley's western side

133

the plain ends abruptly at the foot of the Souli mountains. It is this heroic range which rivets one's attention at first view. Looking out on to this green, peaceful and largely uninhabited valley, one seemed to hear faintly from nearly two centuries ago the crackle of muskets and the shouts of the Souliots battling against the *Shqipetars* of Ali Pasha; then, from much more recent times came the braying of EDES bugles and the echoing rumble of artillery as the invaders of 1941 forced their way back through Epirus with considerable difficulty and under fierce and constant attack by EDES in September 1944, in the hope of rejoining the main German forces before being cut off by the rapidly advancing Russians in the Balkans.

We descended from the bus at Yeorgani close by a wayside café. Here the village houses were not grouped together but scattered behind the road up the hillside. Steep narrow lanes climbed upward between orchards, vegetable beds, tobacco plants and vines, leading to solid farmhouses, where the only sounds were the occasional bark of a dog, the stamping of a mule in its stable and the wind sighing in the trees. The country here is just too high for the olive tree, which grows in abundance to the west beyond the Souli mountains in the valley of Paramythia and the Margariti Plain. During the war a local barter economy developed in this part of Epirus, where the enemy did not penetrate; the villagers on the east side of Lakkasouli exchanged their tobacco for the olive oil of Paramythia and Margariti. For clothing, apart from that made by women from sheep's wool and goats' hair, the peasants were to some extent dependent on panels of fabric from the parachutes which were dropped with supplies for the Military Mission into Lakkasouli; boots, clothing and ammunition arrived in this way. There was a regular tariff of one chicken or five pairs of eggs—eggs always came in pairs— for a panel of the coarse material used for this purpose. Silk or nylon parachutes were used by personnel and were very much scarcer. The hope of obtaining a pair of army boots or part of a British battledress was one incentive to join the *andartes*, in addition to the pay which was in gold sovereigns.

We took coffee with the exclusively male clientèle of the café who sat chatting desultorily, their backs turned to the enchanting and once familiar view towards Souli across the

shining landscape of woods and green meadows, of the
rivulet chuckling far below over its stony bed, and of Derivizi-
ana, a glimpse of which we could catch a little farther to the
south. One of the party was a retired schoolmaster who had
taught Elli in Ioannina. Later he became head, before retirement, of the little school in Yeorgani. As recently as 1967, he
had been responsible with two assistant masters for over a
hundred pupils; by 1973, however, the number had fallen to
thirteen for which only one teacher was now required.

'We are a village of old people,' he explained.

'We certainly don't need to work so hard anymore,' added
a fit, well-built villager. 'I have two sons; one is in Germany
and the other in Athens. Both have good jobs and both send
me money. I've worked for them and it does them no harm
to work now for me.'

The village priest, who had descended from the bus with us,
was somewhat upset that rural life should be declining, that
money was becoming so important.

'But why should we be compelled to go on with the old
drudgery if it is no longer necessary? Everything is changing,'
the villager continued. 'I can do better with twenty of the
improved breed of sheep than with sixty of the old sort we
had in Lakkasouli.'

It was not only the mountain villages of Zagori and Pindus
which were being transformed, but also those nearer the
coast which had no close associations with the Vlach or
Sarakatsani shepherds. Here in Lakkasouli the villagers grew
their own vegetables, tobacco and fruit, raised a few chickens
and sheep, distilled their own *tsipouro*, kept their houses in
repair and spent the summer gossiping with their neighbours
in the sun. Occasionally someone would return to his native
village after many years overseas or in Europe and for a time
there would be fresh subjects for discussion. There were
children but as soon as they grew up they would depart to
Ioannina, to Athens or further afield. Today, these villages are
becoming places for retirement, the interests of the inhabitants
reflecting ever less what was once the rural life of Greece.

'Yes,' Elli was saying, nodding in my direction, 'he came to
Lakkasouli by parachute.'

'Then he would have dropped down there by the river,'

said the schoolmaster, pointing to a wide field below Derviziana. 'In those days, I served with Zervas and was responsible for lighting the flares to guide approaching aircraft. Why,'
looking more closely at me, 'of course I remember you.' It was
a pleasant piece of flattery, but the remark caused some
laughter. In spite of the full moon and the flares, it would have
been difficult to make out individual features. The schoolmaster went on chatting happily to Elli about Ioannina High
School.

While they talked, I looked at that long forgotten field by
the Acheron, remembering the steep climb up to Derviziana,
passing men leading mules for loading and old women in
black who, bent double, carried up almost as much as the
animals. Only male members of the family rode: the females
trudged behind. Conditions in Lakkasouli and in the Greek
countryside differed little from when Edward Lear journeyed
to Souli, savagely bitten by the fleas which were then, and
in 1944, as fierce as their ancestors in their attacks on both the
defiant Souliots and Ali Pasha's *Shqipetars*. Today the neat,
spotless houses of the countryside are vitually free from fleas,
bugs and other afflictions because of insecticides and modern
hygiene.

I sat remembering that blazing hot day in Derviziana
twenty-nine years ago when Ian and I were taken by Colonel
Tom Barnes to meet General Zervas. Colonel Tom was a
New Zealander in command of the Military Mission to EDES;
he had been the sapper in the party of twelve which was
dropped into Greece October 1942 under the command of
Brigadier Myers to blow up the railway bridge over the
Gorgopotamos near Lamia. This task was successfully accomplished with the help of Zervas and of Ares Velouchiotis of
ELAS, the only occasion on which the two guerilla forces
actively co-operated together. Vital German supplies were
thus prevented from reaching North Africa at the time of
Rommel's last offensive against Egypt. Napoleon Zervas was
a professional soldier, brought up in Arta and descended from
the renowned Souliot clan of that name. Before the war he
had been politically involved with such republican figures as
General Plastiras who, in 1944, although an exile in France,
was regarded as the nominal head of EDES, with Generals

Kondylis, Saraphis and Bakirdzis; the last two later joined EAM/ELAS. Zervas is said to have been approached himself by ELAS to become its commander, but his loyalties were not to the extreme left.

Around the General's headquarters there was usually a drifting, aimless throng of *andartes*; some, entwined with bandoliers of cartridges, carried rifles or sten guns, others wore some distinguishing mark on their uniform to denote their regiment—the Agoras regiment, for example, had berets made from parachute material—while others were without weapons, but merely dressed in ill-fitting khaki battledress, nearly all of it supplied by the Allied Military Mission, although the immense smartness of an occasional uniform indicated some contact with the Savile Row of Ioannina or Arta. Beards were widely favoured, but of a style which involved a minimum of trimming. Hair was worn long and unkempt by those who saw themselves as descendants of Klephts or the fabled warriors of Souli, which many of them were. The majority were Epirots, but here and there could be seen the black skull-cap of a Cretan, many of whom remained behind in the mountains when the Greek forces were forced in 1941 to surrender in the face of the overwhelming strength of the *Wehrmacht*. General Zervas's bodyguard and some of his commanders were Cretan. An ear fully attuned to Greek regional accents would easily have singled out the origins of many who came from outside the province, mostly for patriotic reasons but occasionally to escape the Communists.

The *andartes* pressed back to make way for Tom Barnes, a popular figure, so that we could enter. We were then ushered without ceremony into the General's presence. Comfortably thick-set, a little over medium height, a dark olive complexion with black hair turning grey, a formidable beard hiding a strong jaw and shrewd eyes, he was a man of great charm. He could be grave, incisive, severe when circumstances demanded, but he relaxed easily, a broad smile quickly changing into a chuckle. He exercised an easy control over the EDES organization as much by his ability to command loyalty as by his organizing powers. He was brave, humorous and a loyal friend to his Allies. Much was made of his financial greed by EAM/ELAS but, from the British point of view, he carried out what he was asked to do faithfully and usually effectively. There is reason to think from German records that Zervas personally agreed to a secret and temporary truce through intermediaries with the Germans during the winter of 1943–4, which was not even known to his second-in-command, Komninos Pyromaglou. It was at a time when his survival was at stake in the face of outright hostility from EAM/ELAS. It happened when GHQ, Middle East, had in any case banned all guerilla offensive activity in Greece, prior to a final all-out assault on the Germans planned for later in 1944. When orders for this to start came through, EDES attacked with vigour.

After the end of the war in Greece and after the disbandment of EDES at the end of the troubled winter of 1944–5, when EAM/ELAS tried unsuccessfully to seize control of the country, Zervas disappeared for a time from the public stage. Having started as a Republican he re-entered politics in summer 1945, having once sworn to abjure them, as the founder of the right-wing National Party of Greece, which supported the return of the monarchy, and which he then saw as the surest shield against Communism. The National Party was small and was to grow smaller; by 1950 he held only seven seats. Nevertheless he served in the right-wing government of Demetrios Maximos in 1947 as Minister of Public Order, when he was widely criticized for the severity of his methods against political suspects during a time of waxing rebellion by the Communists against the government, and again in the Sophoklis Venizelos government of 1950. This was his last political post. He died not long afterwards.

I was brought back to the present by Elli and the laughter of the others. 'You were miles away. Come, we must go and meet the schoolmaster's family. They have very kindly invited us to lunch before we go down to Derviziana.'

'But there is no point in going to Derviziana,' cried the schoolmaster. 'There is nobody who will recognize you there and there's nothing to see: stay here with us in Yeorgani and you can see your old house.'

The schoolmaster had a sweet wife, dressed in black, and her face, like so many, thin and lined but lively; there were also two sons, their wives and children, who brought us bread, tomatoes, cheese, olives and coffee. 'Come, we must show the Englishman his former home; then he can rest content,' and the schoolmaster led me off. We went to a fine house, with a wide courtyard and overhanging trees, but it was the wrong house. I explained that it had been much higher up.

'Then it's the house of the *proedros* (village headman). There it is—up there.' And so it was. I climbed by myself up the narrow path between the vegetables and vines to the highest house in the village.

The *proedros* kindly showed me round the house. His father, alas, had died but everything was in order as he would have wished. The roof, which had been like a sieve when it rained, had been repaired and our room had a new floor covered with linoleum. The old iron bedstead, which neither Ian nor I had used because of the bugs, was still in the same place; there would be no bugs now. The Souli mountains were blurred in a heat haze, and there was silence everywhere.

Over the years since 1944, memories had returned ever less frequently and ever more faintly of the wonderful view across Lakkasouli. From here, Derviziana was clearly visible. Leake described it as being 'situated amidst fountains, large walnut trees, vineyards and gardens—on the middle descent of the ridge, and enjoying a prospect of the valley below it, which is beautifully diversified with broken ground, streams, woods and cultivated fields.'

Hughes had also admired Derviziana and the prospect across the valley, 'one of the noblest valleys in Epirus'. Here he met a shepherd boy with a pipe fashioned from an eagle's wing. This eagle had carried away several lambs in his care so, armed with a long Albanian knife, he had climbed up the mountain steep, grappled with and killed the marauder on its nest. Hughes's hosts had been at the massacre at Gardhiki in Albania when Ali Pasha had used Greeks to slaughter the Albanian-Muslim villagers, who had raped his tigress of a mother and his sister. Muslim troops, although loyal to the Vizier, had refused to carry out this instruction.

The hospitable schoolmaster on my return was still emphasizing that Derviziana was not worth visiting. I told him that, having travelled some 2,459 kilometres from London to revisit the village, it would be a pity not to go the remaining

one kilometre. At that we were released. We set off along the
way I seemed to remember. I boasted that I knew a short
cut—and so we found ourselves hopelessly lost. I had not
taken into account the immense growth of vegetation over
the past three decades. We were rescued by the schoolmaster's
niece who had watched my mistake with amusement from
above and who then put us on the right track.

There were a number of new houses in Derviziana and a
large school. As usual someone materialized to welcome us.
We were invited by a young couple on to their verandah for
a welcome drink of water after our scramble. 'Ah, here with
the *andartes*, were you?' There followed what we now recognized as the stock joke about the Resistance in Epirus. 'If
you're looking for those gold sovereigns, you are probably
too late. Others have been back before you.'

I asked if they knew the whereabouts of the house which
had been the Military Mission's headquarters. 'There it is,'
was the reply, 'just across the road from us.' The new road
almost touched its walls. On the three other sides it was
almost smothered by trees which certainly had not been there
in 1944. The solid house, probably built shortly before the
war, was now deserted; it was shut up. The owner had
departed and his whereabouts were unknown.

The bus for the return journey arrived punctually. During
the journey back to Ioannina, memories of the many people
who had befriended us kept emerging. There was the elderly
Barba Christo, a Ioanniniot pastrycook who became cook to
the Mission—and a very bad one. He would quote long
extracts from Revelations to anyone who would listen, to
prove that Hitler was the ten-horned beast and that Constantinople would once more become Greek. He put a shirt
which had become stained into a tub of soaking beans as a
sure way of cleaning it—and as a result the smell of beans
was added to the stain. There were various tough regular
officers, some of whom later reached high rank in the Greek
army. There was Komnenos Pyromaglou, an economist of
liberal republican sympathies who had gone up into the
mountains at an early date, to become deputy head of EDES
while remaining a civilian. He had fought with courage and a
cool head at the Gorgopotamos. With considerable foresight

he had attempted to develop a political philosophy for EDES, but this had not been accepted by the many career officers in the movement who said that they had been commissioned by the king and were there purely to fight the enemy. Because EDES, unlike EAM/ELAS, never developed a political basis for its existence, it quickly dissolved at the end of the war.

There were many others. On one journey from Derviziana to a unit some five hours' march away, we had passed a poverty-stricken hamlet. Its occupants, hearing we were foreigners, insisted with much courtesy that we accept a cup of coffee. Ten minutes later, a cup of hot liquid made from acorns arrived; it was all they had. Typical in a different way was the insistence of an elderly but spirited couple that we should arrange for EDES *andartes* to be sent to help occupy Berlin when it fell.

14

Nineteenth- and Twentieth-century Arta

Travellers to the realm of Ali Pasha early in the nineteenth century journeyed by boat from Preveza, the port of entry, to Salaora on the north side of the Ambracian Gulf. Here, where today there are fish hatcheries, horses were procurable for the journey to Arta, twelve miles away. Byron and Hobhouse took this route, and so did Henry Holland, Thomas Hughes and others. Ali Pasha had built a small resthouse here in which two rooms were kept permanently for himself: travellers were welcome to use the others. Here Holland was introduced to the national airs of Albania and its dances, which he likened to 'what might be expected from a Northern American savage'. Salaora fell into disuse after Ali's death and David Urquhart found the little settlement flattened by Greek cannon at the end of the Greek War of Independence. The surrounding marshes are said to swarm with snakes and the only visitors at the beginning of this century were English shooting parties attracted there by the plentiful bags of duck to be found on the green placid waters of the Gulf.

Our first entry into Arta was from Lakkasouli to the northwest. This was a day or so after EDES had moved into the town following the withdrawal of the Germans at the beginning of October 1944. We had spent the night at Threspotiko (formerly Lelovo), a village at the southern end of Lakkasouli, amidst scenery which Edward Lear had found delightful when he spent a night there in May 1849 on his way to Souli. 'It is rare,' he wrote in his journal, 'to find such rich foliage combined with distant lines of landscape, and this, indeed, is a beauty peculiar to the southern parts of Epirus.' Hughes reported that he and his party ate their supper in Lelovo, remarkable for its walnut trees, in the light of the fireflies.

This was not my first visit to Threspotiko. Ian Scott-Kilvert and I had come here a few weeks earlier to interrogate deserters from German garrisons in Preveza and the Louros Plain which guarded the exits from Lakkasouli. These troops were second-rate units, containing many Poles and other European nationalities which the Nazis had impressed into their army. An NCO from Dresden had deserted because he had heard that there were British officers with EDES. Many others would desert, he declared, if they were convinced that this was true.

The local Greek EDES commander and others sat around with us wondering how to exploit the situation. It appeared that we had only to raise the Union Jack for those unhappy conscripts in field-grey uniform to come hurrying to our side. It seemed too easy.

'Why don't you talk to them?' said a senior Greek NCO. 'Their posts near Stefani are only a hundred yards from our nearest point.'

'Yes,' said Alexis, leaving the room, 'I know of the very thing that will make you audible to them.' He returned with the blue flower-painted horn of a pre-First World War 'His Master's Voice' gramophone. Nobody laughed.

Early the next afternoon, having decided what was to be said, we set forth in the heat of the day with a guide, two good marksmen in case our reception was unpleasant, and a mule which carried the gramophone horn. Three hours later after a stiff climb, we reached the EDES forward point, where we were met by a surprised but urbane battalion commander. We were on a dominating mountain spur. About a mile away were lower hills and the Arta Plain with the Ambracian Gulf beyond—a marvellous view. The commander pointed out the various points of interest.

'Where exactly are the Germans?' we asked.

'Down on those hills about a thousand metres away. They can see us here but they never bother us. In any case we are out of range. Now tell me why you have come here and how I can best help.' The difference between a hundred and a thousand metres is not always discernible to the enthusiast!

In 1944 the road penetrated no further into Lakkasouli than Threspotiko; beyond there were only paths and mule tracks.

There was an ancient motor truck at the village which we were told would take us the fourteen miles to Arta. As there was no petrol when we arrived to take advantage of this lift, we had no option but to walk. We emerged into the Plain at Stefani and, having passed the extensive ruins at Rogoi, we cut across country as the main road was unusable owing to the destruction of the bridge over the Louros. Once beyond the river we picked our way along paths, made muddy by the first autumn rains, through villages of refugees from Asia Minor, who clapped us politely as we passed by. Their houses looked like hovels but their orchards of orange and lemon trees, which seemed to stretch on interminably, were beautifully kept.

By dusk we had reached the only bridge over the Arakhthos into Arta, 'a very lofty picturesque bridge', wrote Hughes, 'whose noble Gothic arches, as they vary in their height, form a singular and wavy outline.' There is nothing Gothic about the bridge, and its nine arches, if not exactly curvilinear, are by no means pointed. It is reputed to be seventeenth century, but built on the foundations of a Hellenistic structure. The Arakhthos makes a semi-circular sweep round the north of Arta from east to west, flowing through several channels for most of the way, but here, at the bridge, its waters are concentrated in one bed and are swift and deep. Here was the ancient as well as the modern entry from Epirus into Arta; since the last war, however, an iron bridge has been erected nearby to cope with today's traffic.

The old bridge is well-known for the legend about the unusual circumstances attending its completion. At first, in spite of a large number of enthusiastic labourers, little progress was made because at the end of each day what they had built invariably collapsed. Eventually a little bird arrived with the solution to the problem, which was that the wife of the master-builder should be buried in the foundation. This was accordingly arranged, although with some understandable reluctance by the parties directly involved, and the bridge has stood firmly ever since. Today it is still customary for a cock or hen to have its throat cut over the foundations of a new structure so that the spirit of the place is appeased.

We entered the town, which today has a population of

about twenty thousand, to find the poorly lit streets crowded with EDES *andartes* in their ill-fitting khaki battledress, with peasants wearing their heavy home-spun garments and the townspeople in neat but threadbare dresses and suits. The men sauntered slowly up and down the main street or gathered at such gossip points as the cafés or near the local EDES headquarters where news might be forthcoming. The air was alive with discussions and the acrid smell of home-grown tobacco. Barbers were working late, shaving off the beards and moustaches of those who had returned home from the mountains; no doubt they hoped that this renunciation symbolized the end of war and the return of peace and plenty. Another five years, however, were to elapse before Epirus and the rest of Greece could finally relax from the threat of rebellion and violence.

After three years of enemy occupation, Arta was a drab little town, its lighting inadequate, its roads in poor repair and the walls of the houses badly in need of whitewash both for the sake of tidiness and to eliminate the political slogans with which they were covered. In addition, much damage had been inflicted by Italian bomber aircraft during the ignominious Italian campaign of 1940–1. A number of houses were empty shells, but the rubble had been cleared away, no doubt under Italian supervision during their occupation. Arta in 1973 appeared to have changed little except that small blocks of three- or four-storey apartments had risen on the bomb sites, the roads had been repaired and the walls whitewashed. We got the clear impression that Arta was doing well.

There was a conscious association by many Epirots in the autumn of 1944 between Resistance during the Second World War and the Greek War of Independence, which started in 1821. Several leaders of EDES troops modelled their appearance and manner on the Klephts and captains of Greek irregular bands of the 1820s. One in particular, wearing a red velvet skull cap with a long tassel, boasted continually of his prowess in battle. He had formed his own band early during the Axis Occupation in the Valtos area, east of Arta, with a few relatives, their sons and cousins; in due course he merged his band with EDES on account of Communist hostility. Because there was an element of truth in his bragging, he was indulged by his admiring friends. In any case the tradition of resistance is an ancient one in Arta.

Before the outbreak of the Greek War of Independence, Arta had a population of about six thousand, according to Leake, eighty percent of whom were Greek and the remainder divided more or less equally between Jews and Turks. Arta, then as now, was surrounded by productive plains and higher up by valuable forests on the mountain foothills. Its produce included wheat, maize and considerable quantities of wine, but of indifferent quality; there were also rice, tobacco, cotton, flax, barley, oats and pulses. Holland described the area as one of the most fertile in Albania.

Part of Arta's prosperity in the seventeenth and eighteenth centuries derived from the protection afforded by the Venetians to whom the town paid a subsidy. Venice may for a time have actually ruled the town and the surrounding countryside, but there are conflicting opinions. The Turks, if they nominally remained masters, appear to have been either unwilling or incompetent to protect its inhabitants from robbery and piracy. The association between Arta and Venice was particularly strong after Morosini's capture of Levkas and Preveza in 1684, but not always to the town's advantage. The Venetians won over to their side Liberakis Yerakaris, the Maniot leader and pirate, who changed sides as it pleased him. He had been captured and imprisoned by the Turks, then released on condition that he subdued the ever resilient Maniots. Now, as an ally of the Venetians, he enlivened this new alliance by attacking Arta, which sent a desperate appeal for help to the Doge. Yerakaris was, by the end of his career, the Turkish Prince of the Mani, Venetian Lord of Roumeli and a Knight of St Mark.

Arta was considered a handsome town by all who saw it, with its fine houses, six mosques and twenty-four churches, most of which, especially the mosques, have disappeared. Although under Ali no longer so prosperous, it was still an important commercial centre for the import and export of goods into and out of western Greece, being close to the easiest route over the mountains into Thessaly.

By 1821, when Ottoman forces were besieging Ali Pasha in Ioannina, a Turkish garrison was in turn trapped in the

Byzantine fortress of Arta by the Souliots, for long Ali's deadly enemies; they and certain Greek chieftains had been persuaded by Ali to co-operate with his Albanians against the Sultan's armies. Prince Mavrogordato, a member of the distinguished Phanariot family, who commanded the Greek insurgents in western Greece, then detached Marko Botsaris and his Souliots from Ali, while Omar Vrionis Pasha, sent by the Turkish commander-in-chief to relieve Arta, successfully weaned the Muslim Albanians away from their allegiance to Ali and his Greek supporters by pointing to the destruction of mosques and Muslim villages by the Greeks. As a result the besieging forces melted away and Arta remained in Turkish hands.

After Ali's death, the Turkish troops in western Greece under Omar Vrionis, now Pasha of Ioannina, attempted as a first step in the campaign against the Greek insurgents to subdue the Souliots, but with little success. This encouraged Mavrogordato to send his forces north into Epirus to combine with the intrepid Souliots, although the threat from the Turks in eastern Greece was potentially stronger. His command now included both the strife-torn Battalion of Philhellenes, a heady mixture of idealists and career officers unemployed after the end of the Napoleonic Wars, and the Regiment Tarella, named after the Piedmontese colonel who commanded it, which consisted of European and overseas Greek volunteers who, unlike their native compatriots, knew something of military discipline. There was, in addition, the band of Souliots under Marko Botsaris and a body of Ionian Greeks.

Peta, where Mavrogordato's expedition took up positions, lies three miles east of Arta where the foothills merge into the plain. The heights behind it were held by Gogos Bakolas, a local Greek irregular leader who, according to General Makriyannis, had performed prodigies of valour against the Turks in the previous year. On this occasion, however, he betrayed the expedition, having first persuaded Botsaris and the Ionians to depart to join the main Souliot bands. The Turks then launched a frontal attack from Arta on the Philhellenes and at the same time sent a body to fall unexpectedly upon the insurgents' rear, which Bakolas was supposed to but did not defend. Over two-thirds of the Battalion of

Philhellenes were either killed in battle or subsequently executed by the Turks together with nearly a third of the Regiment Tarella, including its commander.

In Arta, close to the entrance to the great Byzantine fortress, there is a memorial to General Makriyannis (1797–1864), one of the most attractive personalities in the War of Independence. In 1811 he arrived at the age of fourteen in Arta where he prospered in commerce and gained considerable local influence. In 1819 or 1820 he was sworn as a member of the *Philiki Etairia* and was active in trying to protect the Greeks in the area from the overbearing insolence of the Turkish forces gathered to overthrow Ali Pasha. He fought throughout the struggle against the Turks after which he settled in Athens where he became involved in politics during the reign of the Bavarian King Otho.

For the rest of the War of Independence, Arta remained under the Turks with whom the initiative rested until after their capture of Mesolonghi in 1826. But Acarnania and Aetolia were never completely subdued. The main roads and town remained under Ottoman control, but the Greek bands, although sometimes fighting among themselves, were active in the hinterland and from time to time inflicted damage on Turkish convoys and isolated units. From the autumn of 1827 onwards, General Church was campaigning in western Greece to encourage the Greeks of Epirus and Acarnania to rise in support. A professional soldier, born in Ireland, courteous, patient and occasionally overcautious, Richard Church had gained considerable experience of commanding local levies in various parts of the Mediterranean, including the Ionian Islands. In spite of many disappointments, he captured Vonitsa on the Ambracian Gulf in 1829, rallied the Greek bands to his side and forced the Turks at Mesolonghi to capitulate. It was largely due to Church that the frontiers of the new Hellenic Kingdom were drawn as far north as the Ambracian Gulf, from just south of Arta, to the Gulf of Volos, although both Arta and Volos remained in Turkish hands; the earlier intention of the Great Powers was that the Greek state should consist of little more than the Peloponnese.

The years after the War of Independence were not easy for Arta's Greek inhabitants. Not only was there an immense tax to be paid annually to the Turkish governor, but Turkish troops billeted on private households had to be lodged, fed, clothed and even shaved for no return. David Urquhart reported that many Greeks in Arta regretted the passing of Ali Pasha. 'We thought him a tyrant and we rejoiced at his destruction,' they told Urquhart, but added, 'it is not his feet we would kiss but the very dust beneath them, could he be restored to us.' Once an account had been settled with the Vizier, they said, nobody need fear further robbery, oppression, indignity or violence at his behest.

In 1853 Russia and Turkey were at war again. King Otho and Queen Amelia encouraged a national movement to extend Greek territory at the expense of Turkey and in support of the Russians, their co-religionists. Bands of irregulars started raiding into Thessaly and Epirus at the beginning of 1854, Arta was besieged and a Turkish relief column defeated at Pende Pigadhia. The Turks landed at Salaora and relieved Arta, but on 27 January were defeated in their turn at Peta. The 'Great Idea' of recreating the Byzantine Empire with its capital once more at Constantinople was then a fervent dream of most Greeks in the Hellenic Kingdom. They received little support, however, from the Greeks still under Ottoman control who knew what to expect from the Sultan if they launched an uprising which proved unsuccessful.

Then the British and French governments occupied Piraeus, as events drifted towards the Crimean War, and forced Otho to withdraw his support for Russia. In the meanwhile the Greek forces in Epirus and Thessaly were routed. Even Russia gave no encouragement to the Greeks. Tsar Nicolas told the British Ambassador in St Petersburg that he would never permit an attempt to reconstruct the Byzantine Empire, nor 'the breaking up of Turkey into little republican asylums for the Kossuths and Mazzinis and other revolutionaries of Europe'. Ten years later King Otho and his Queen retired into exile to the joy of the majority of Greeks, and a young Danish prince was elected King of the Hellenes. As George I, he reigned successfully until his assassination by a madman in Salonika in 1913 at the end of the First Balkan War.

In 1878 the Congress of Berlin met to sort out the growing

problems between the Sultan and his Christian minorities. The initial findings of the Great Powers were far more favourable to Greece than the eventual settlement made three years later. The Congress offered Greece a large part of Epirus, including Ioannina and Metsovo, but did not take into account the strength of Turkish opposition. In 1881, a convention was signed which gave only Thessaly and the Arta district of Epirus to Greece. The new frontier with Turkey ran along the Arakhthos river at Arta and the Greek *douane* was at the bridge.

15

Ancient and Byzantine Arta

Nineteenth-century travellers covered the forty-two miles between Ioannina and Arta in two days without hurrying, usually spending the night at the *Khan* at Pende Pigadhia, some kilometres to the east of the modern road. Edward Lear made the journey in one day in November 1848, by leaving Ioannina before daybreak. Although he looked anything but athletic with his near-sightedness and his awkward gait, he was able to cover considerable distances in a day during his journeys through Greece and Albania. On this occasion, taking the Turkish causeway, he did not reach his destination until well after dark under a full moon. 'Endless lanes and gardens,' he recorded in his journal, 'seemed to environ Arta and having passed the great bridge over the Arakhthos, we wound through dark and strange places full of mud, among masses of buildings black against bright moonlight,' to arrive exhausted and feverish at the house of the British consular agent. 'I long earnestly to retire at once to sleep,' he added, 'but the hiccuping flutter of a fowl in the death agony, announces, in spite of my entreaties, that a supper is in preparation.' How generous and how kindly meant and, under such circumstances, how unwelcome Greek rural hospitality can be; it is, however, becoming something of the past, especially in tourist areas, because of abuse of this tradition by foreigners.

Today the journey from Ioannina to Arta by bus, much of it alongside the hurrying Louros river, takes little more than ninety minutes. In June, Arta is noticeably warmer than Ioannina, the flowering trees more prolific and more advanced, for Arta enjoys a Mediterranean climate while that of the Epirot capital is Balkan. Pyrrhus (319–272 B.C.), when he acquired Ambracia, must have been impressed by its strategic

position and perhaps even by its charm, for he made it his
capital. Ambracia, when the Romans besieged it in 189 B.C.,
was probably the richest city in western Greece. After its
capitulation, the victors carried away an immense treasure,
including the city's bronze and marble statues.

The main colonizers of the coasts and islands of the
Adriatic and Ionian Seas in pre-classical days were the Dorian
Greeks of Corinth. As early as the eighth century B.C., this
vigorous city-state had established colonies at Corcyra and at
Syracuse in Sicily; further settlements were founded in the
seventh century on Ithaka, Levkas and around the Ambracian
Gulf. Corinth, intent on building a commercial empire, aimed
at retaining political control over her daughter communities
which early led to trouble, at least with Corcyra. A sea battle,
the first on record, took place in about 664 B.C. between
Corinth and Corcyra, because of the latter's objection to
interference by the parent state. Soon afterwards, a tyranny
was established at Corinth which for a time re-asserted its
hold over Corcyra and, about 630 B.C., set up a colony at
Ambracia. It was Corinthian-Corcyraean hostility over who
should control Epidamnus, now Durazzo, that signalled the
start of the Peloponnesian Wars.

Ambracia or Arta stands to the south of the Arakhthos
where it flows from east to west through the gap between the
southernmost ridge of Xerovouni and the northernmost
projection of Mount Valaora. We were rarely conscious, when
walking through the streets, of the slopes rising to the south
because Arta looks away from the sun across the river to the
citrus plantations and the open country beyond. To the
north-east stands distant Tzoumerka, due north is Mount
Xerovouni, bare and stony for most of its length, while the
hills to the north-west guard Lakkasouli; there is a particularly fine view of this wide landscape from the comfortable
Xenia Hotel in the grounds of the Byzantine fortress. From
the bridge of Arta, however, the lower slopes of Mount
Valaora are clearly visible, rising over three hundred feet to
a spur, Mount Perranthes, around which there are still traces
of the ancient walls of Ambracia. From the hill's summit, there
is a view south to the Ambracian Gulf. Much probably still
remains to be revealed about the city's Hellenistic period.

From the Arta bridge, the Arakhthos runs swiftly between tree-lined banks to the Ambracian Gulf. Like the Kalamas and Louros, its course has altered over the centuries. It is still navigable some way upstream towards Arta by small rowing-boat. In the days of Pyrrhus, there was a separate port and stronghold on the Gulf known as Ambracus, which today lies four miles west of the river's present mouth. In 219 B.C., when the Aetolians, who had rampaged through Epirus, were besieged there by Philip V of Macedon, Ambracus stood on the east bank of the river, as did Ambracia, so that there would have been easy communications between them.

If the views are good from the Xenia Hotel, they are even better from Mount Perranthes. Here there are traces of the ancient walls, which descended down its western slope towards the bridge. From the point where it reaches level ground, there spreads northwards and west the area on which Pyrrhus built his extension to the city, known as the Pyrrheum according to Livy who, basing his account on a now fragmentary book of Polybius, described the Roman siege of Ambracia, which was held by the Aetolians in 189 B.C. The erection of the Pyrrheum marked the peak of Ambracia's prosperity, when its population could have been as large as fifty thousand.

The acropolis of Ambracia was not on Mount Perranthes but probably a little to the east on another height above the Arakhthos; it was encircled on the south and east sides by the ancient wall, traces of which have been found running north and then east to the Phaneromene Monastery. A theatre facing east was probably built in the curve of the walls to the south of the monastery, similar in size to that which Pyrrhus had constructed at Dodona. When Christopher Wordsworth came here in the 1830s he described 'the vestiges of the ancient Acropolis' on a craggy hill, more than two miles round and 'surmounted by walls of polygonal style.'

After the Molossian monarchy collapsed in 232 B.C., the citizens of Ambracia smashed open the tomb of Pyrrhus and scattered his ashes. Nine years later the city had become part of the Aetolian League, whose piracy on the high seas aroused almost universal hostility, and which was involved in the raid on Passaron and Dodona in 219 B.C.

During the next thirty years, the political and military

situation was dominated by the antagonism between Rome and Macedon. It was a period of constant intrigue with frequent changes in loyalty. The Aetolian League was for a time allied to Rome, when Philip V, a highly competent commander who ascended the throne when only seventeen, captured the city on one, perhaps two occasions. Peace was patched up for a time, but the restless Philip was soon campaigning again. The situation was further complicated by Antiochus of Syria, who was also at war with Rome and had crossed to Greece in 192 B.C.; he did not, however, heed the advice of Hannibal, who had taken refuge at his court, to invade Italy at once. Instead he remained in Greece and suffered complete defeat by the Romans in 191 B.C. At this time Philip was in alliance with Rome.

The Aetolian League had supported Antiochus and refused to accept the terms offered by the Roman Senate. The Epirot League, with whom the Aetolians were at war, advised Marcus Fulvius, the Roman commander, to capture Ambracia. The siege of 189 was fought bravely and with much ingenuity on both sides. The strength of the defences, formed by the Arakhthos and the city walls, was such that Marcus Fulvius decided to attack from the south, where he would not be cramped by the river and where he could prevent the arrival of reinforcements from Aetolia; in spite of this, two large groups succeeded in joining the defenders before the Romans had completed a rampart and ditch to seal up the town inside the river loop. The Romans employed battering rams, but they found fresh walls behind those they had destroyed. They tunnelled, only to be detected by sheets of bronze whose vibrations revealed their whereabouts to the Aetolians who then used smoke bombs to drive them back. Eventually terms of capitulation were arranged. Although not allowed to be re-fortified, Ambracia became a free, autonomous city and was used as a base by the Romans in their final war against Macedon in 171–168 B.C.

With the foundation of Nikopolis by Augustus Caesar after his victory over Antony and Cleopatra at Acteion, the citizens of Ambracia were forced to take up residence there with Epirots from the ruined Molossian cities and with Roman settlers. A long sleep then descended on Ambracia and much of Epirus. Slowly the monuments and public buildings were dismantled and their materials carried away. Only the transhumant life of the shepherds continued as it had done since time immemorial.

Arta was the only ancient Epirot city to enjoy a renaissance. This was in the thirteenth century when the Despotate of Epirus was established there after the fall of Constantinople to the Fourth Crusade in 1204. Today the town is almost aggressively provincial, but here and there among its unassuming highways and open spaces and in the surrounding countryside as well stand magnificent Byzantine churches, built during the thirteenth and early fourteenth centuries. St Theodora, wife of the Despot Michael II, inspired much of the building either directly or through her husband and her son, Nikephoros. Michael showed some enthusiasm in raising these churches because he wanted to make amends for having temporarily deserted his saintly wife for an aristocratic wanton with the unfortunate but appropriate name of Lady Gangrene.

The largest of Arta's medieval Byzantine churches is the Paregoritissa, our Lady of Consolation, which stands between the bridge and the main square. It is an unusual building. Hughes described it as 'a very curious Greek church of the Lower Empire . . . one of the few remaining monuments of those times, when architecture, without losing all traits of magnificence, became as it were a confused mixture of disordered principles and a combination of distorted proportions'. The red brick building is square and heavy in outward appearance. Its rows of windows are irregularly set in relation to one another. There is a fine octagonal dome at the centre of the roof and four smaller domes, one at each corner, together with an even smaller one over the apse. Work started on it about 1289 under the patronage of Nikephoros and his second wife, Anne, the daughter of the Emperor Michael VIII Palaiologos. The story is told that the original architect became so jealous of his assistant, who in his absence built a far finer church than he himself had conceived, that he took him up on to the roof to discuss some detail and then pushed him off. The assistant in falling managed to grab his master's garments and both crashed to their deaths. According to Anastasios Orlandos, the distinguished Greek scholar of Byzantine architecture, the church could be mistaken for a primitive Florentine palace. There is something institutional about its aspect; there are also traces of Gothic style which reached Arta from its association with Italy through the Italianate dynasties of Orsini and Tocco, established in Cephalonia and Levkas respectively, as well as with the Franks in Sicily.

In 1945, the Paregoritissa was in a sad state. Badly shaken by enemy bombs, there then appeared to be every likelihood that it would collapse. Fortunately it has now been repaired before too late but, although deservedly a national monument, it is no longer a living church but a museum. The interior boasts an unusual device for supporting the central dome in which is depicted in mosaic an impressive but somewhat damaged Pantocrator looking sternly down into the nave. There are some lively stone carvings on the arches high up under the dome but they cannot easily be seen from ground level. Several of the pillars used in the interior are said to have been brought from Nikopolis.

Apart from the first sixty or more years following the start of the Turkish occupation in 1449, when it was used for stabling, the Paregoritissa functioned as a place of worship until the beginning of the Greek War of Independence. Originally intended as a monastic church, it was from its earliest days directly controlled by the Patriarchate of Constantinople. In 1530, the Patriarch Jeremy I celebrated a mass of consecration here and attached it to the monastery of Kato Panaghia. The Paregoritissa was used as a fortress by the Turks between 1821 and 1824, when it was returned to the Christians. By the time Urquhart reached Arta in the 1830s, it was once more occupied by the Turks, one of several occasions when this happened, until it was finally released to the Orthodox Church in 1866.

The Monastery of Kato Panaghia, now a convent, was built by Michael II; it is on the southern outskirts of Arta and its west entrance faces down to the Arakhthos. Entering through its gateway, we found the church and the conventual buildings spread out in the shape of an irregular quadrangle with the west side open and forming part of the garden in which orange, lemon and pomegranate trees flourished. The church, whose exterior is embellished by decorative tiles and bricks to form rich patterns, has three naves, but the transverse vault over the centre one is raised much higher to give the illusion of a dome while sparing the builder the expense of constructing one. The walls of the interior are decorated with eighteenth-century frescoes but much earlier paintings, probably dating from the thirteenth century, have been uncovered in the apse and indicate the date of the monastery's foundation. In the garden we talked with a pleasant, capable nun, the Mother Superior of the community, who told us something of the work being done for the orphans, whose cheery rumpus could be heard in the background.

A taxi took us over the new Arta bridge and then eastwards along a country road amid olive and citrus groves to the Monastery of Vlachernae, which stands a little above the surrounding orchards about a mile north of Arta. The monastic church, perhaps the most impressive of Arta's Byzantine buildings, not only on account of its design but because of its rural setting, was raised during the thirteenth century. It is in the form of a three-naved basilica, of which the middle nave is higher than those on each side, surmounted by an octagonal dome; there are smaller domes on the side naves. In addition to the decorative use of tiles and bricks on the exterior, there are finely carved fragments of marble fitted into the doorframe of the narthex; these were taken from the *templon* or screen, which once stood between the nave and the sanctuary and may have been the work of refugee craftsmen from Constantinople. High up in a niche on the south exterior wall is a marble plaque of the Archangel Michael.

Inside the church, opened for us by an elderly woman who acted as caretaker, the floor was partly boarded over to protect what is left of the original mosaics underfoot. Two square tombs, embellished with much fine carving, stand one on each side of the interior; although badly damaged, they were obviously made with the same loving craftsmanship as the fragmented marble screen. One tomb was probably that of Michael II, while the other may have contained the mortal remains of two of his sons. Both inside and out, the Vlachernae has an elusive charm—the effect partly of the mellowed bricks, tiles and the fragments of once glorious decorations in marble and mosaic, and partly of the silence and the warm sun. To the south of the church are the cells which once housed the nuns, for the monastery was transformed early on into a convent.

St Theodora was not interred here but in the little church originally dedicated to St George Martyr in the centre of Arta, which was subsequently named after her. It was here that she took the veil. The chapel of St Theodora still stands, but the conventual buildings have disappeared, although the ground on which they stood is bare. An old woman, sitting under a tree and cooking herself a meal over an open fire, claimed to be the chapel's guardian and asked for alms, but a passer-by told us to ignore her as the official guardian was inside, where indeed we found him, a poor aged man who was barely able to stir as we entered.

The chapel has three naves, the centre one much taller than the others and whose windows, high up in its walls, give light to the interior. Like the Paregoritissa, some of the material, especially the columns in the sanctuary, is said to come from the early Christian churches at Nikopolis. The exterior is magnificently decorated with bricks and red tiles, an example unparalleled elsewhere in Epirus. Theodora's tomb is situated in the narthex. Its origin is of the thirteenth century but it has been badly damaged and later crudely restored. Of particular interest is the sculptural panel the length of one of its sides which shows St Theodora herself, standing with a smaller figure between the half-length figures of two winged, wary-eyed angels, one at each end. She wears a long gown, boldly and regally patterned, and her head is crowned. The smaller figure probably represents her son, Nikephoros, also in cere-monial dress. It is likely that he was responsible for the erection of this tomb.

Sometime after Pelagonia and certainly by the end of the thirteenth century, the great Byzantine architectural flowering in Arta was beginning to wither. The little church of St Basil with its delightful exterior, decorated with ornamental brick-work and glazed tiles in various colours, which was erected at the beginning of the fourteenth century, marks the end of this period; the interior is without character.

16

Souli

In September during the German retreat we were encamped on the western side of Lakkasouli at Sistrouni, whose little church, its walls enlivened with bright but crumbling paintings, was in use as a military hospital. Below, the swift, sparkling, pellucid stream, not much more than waist-high at its deepest, was ice-cold but invigorating. It took a mental effort to associate these shallow sunlit waters with the Acheron of Hades, yet it was the same river. To the south of Romanon, where a genial, white-bearded patriarch resided in the little whitewashed monastery, then our communications centre, this stream joined its sister branch from the eastern side of the valley; the river then flowed south-west to where, under the heights of the Souli mountains, it swung round to the north-west and, shortly after leaving Trikaston to the south, plunged into a limestone gorge. Professor Hammond, when there, was told by the local priest that this was where the Acheron descended into Hell. From here, the river is largely out of sight until it emerges into sunlight once more under the heights of Kunghi and the other sites of the Souliots, renowned for their heroic defiance of Ali Pasha and for their brave but unreliable role in the Greek War of Independence.

Albania and Ali Pasha became widely known through the publication of Canto the Second of *Childe Harold's Pilgrimage* in 1812. English travellers, instead of doing the Grand Tour, then impossible because of the Napoleonic Wars, came to the Levant, including Greece and Albania. Threspotia was included in their peregrinations not only because of the Acheron, the Cocytus and its other Homeric and Classical associations but because of Souli as well. The wild magnificence of the scenery and the Souliot story made a deep im-

pression. Hughes came to Souli via Paramythia two months
after Holland had arrived here from the direction of Louros
and Trikaston, taking care not to give offence to the fierce
Molossian sheepdogs which had on three occasions torn his
clothes. Like Leake before him and Edward Lear twenty-five
years later, Holland took the steep, arduous route along the
flanks of the Souli mountains, treading dizzy heights above
the dark chasm through which the river plunged. 'This river',
he recorded, 'must assuredly be the real Acheron of the
Ancients.'

Edward Lear felt that Leake's description of the Acheron
Gorge was better than anything he himself could write. Leake
recorded 'a deep ravine, formed by the meeting of the two
great mountains of Souli and Tzikurates—one of the darkest
and deepest glens of Greece: on either side rise perpendicular
rocks, in the midst of which there are little intervals of scanty
soil, bearing holly oaks, ilices and other shrubs, and which
admit occasionally a view of the higher summits of the two
mountains covered with oaks, and at the summit of all with
pines. Here the road is passable only on foot, by a perilous
ledge along the side of the mountain of Souli: the river in the
pass is deep and rapid and is seen at the bottom falling in
many places over the rocks, though at too great a distance to be
heard, and in most places inaccessible to any but the foot of a
goat or a Souliot.'

The Souliots were a tribe or clan of Christian Albanians
who settled among these spectacular but inhospitable mountains during the fourteenth or fifteenth century. Rennell Rodd
reported that during the Despotate, the inhabitants of
southern Illyria and Epirus became generally described as
Albanians. The Turkish conquest of Albania and the Adriatic
coastline was then held up by the daring tactics of the master-
ful George Kastriotes, who was of Christian birth and generally known as Skanderbeg. Supported by alliances with the
Vatican and Venice, he trounced the Turks in a number of
battles and became acknowledged by the Sultan as absolute
monarch of Albania in 1463.

With Skanderbeg's death in 1467, Albania's fortunes went
into a decline. Many clans renounced the Roman Catholic
Church and casually embraced Islam, mainly because they

could then acquire weapons from the Muslim authorities. The story is told of the Christian Albanian inhabitants of several villages around Pogoniani who were unable to withstand attacks from the Muslims of Leskovits through lack of arms. Eventually in about 1760 their leaders solemnly swore in church that they would fast until Easter, three weeks away, and begged the saints in the meanwhile to work a miracle to save them from this persecution; they made it clear that if supernatural aid was not forthcoming by Easter, they would be forced to become Muslim. As no miracle occurred, the villagers converted to Islam and received a plentiful supply of weapons from the authorities with which they proceeded to massacre their enemies.

The Albanian clans were divided into two main groups—the Ghegs in northern and central Albania and the Tosks in southern Albania and as far south as the Ambracian Gulf. Leake divided the Tosks into three divisions: the Tosks proper, who were based on Valona and Berat; the Liapé to the south of the Tosks around Delvino, and the Tzamé who were also known as the Tshamides, Tzamourians or, more recently, the Chams who finally disappeared in 1944. This last group settled along the Kalamas river for some way inland, in such centres as Filiates, Paramythia, Souli and Parga and down to the Ambracian Gulf. Some were Christians. There were also settlements of Greeks in these areas so that there was probably some inter-marriage between the two groups. While the Christian Albanians to the north were Roman Catholic, those to the south belonged to the Orthodox Church.

The Souliots, like other Albanians, were great dandies. They wore red skull caps, fleecy capotes thrown carelessly over their shoulders, embroidered jackets, scarlet buskins, slippers with pointed toes and white kilts. The *fustanella* or kilt, however, had to be soiled as a clean one implied cowardice or sloth. As for their weapons, the scabbard of their *yataghan* or sword with a double-curved blade and the stocks of their pistols, one or more of which were thrust into their broad belts, were usually embossed with silver, their three or four cartridge boxes frequently of gilt and sometimes set with garnets and coral. In addition there would be daggers and a long-barrelled musket. They wore their hair below their shoulders and cultivated moustaches of the fiercest aspect. Their gait was a carefully practised haughty strut.

The heartland of the Souli Republic, for the Souliots recognized no master over them, was in the heights and valleys by the Acheron from its gorge westwards as far as Glyki. Here were their four main villages, in addition to which there were seven others which were considered part of Souli territory as well as a further fifty to sixty villages of mixed Greek and Albanian stock, including those of Lakkasouli, from which they exacted produce and tribute. Government was purely patriarchal with families grouped in clans or *farias*; the head of each *faria* belonged to the Souliot general council. The total Souliot population appears never to have exceeded five thousand, fifteen hundred of which constituted their fighting force, reinforced when necessary by the women who could be as fearsome as their husbands.

The Souliots, originally a pastoral people, were driven from the plains, where they grazed their flocks, into the barren mountainous region of Souli, where they came to depend for sustenance on brigandage and robbery. C. R. Cockerell, who accompanied Hughes and Parker to Epirus, described them as 'nothing but robbers and freebooters and the scourge of the country', who made the area impassable to travellers unless heavily escorted. He, at least, approved of Ali Pasha's eventual success against them.

Before the arrival of Ali Pasha, the Turks had waged eight unsuccessful wars against the Souliots. Ali's determination, however, was greater than that of his predecessors. As the Dervendji Pasha or Guardian of the Passes, he was fully resolved to subdue all troublemakers. Initially he made little progress. Because of their scanty numbers, the Souliots perfected a form of guerilla warfare which took full advantage of the heights among which they lived and of the cover afforded by rocks and shrubbery. Their manner of manoeuvring depended upon the full understanding of each individual's role in his military group; no Souliot was allowed to take part in any action until properly trained. To be wounded through unnecessary exposure was considered disgraceful. Their women often accompanied their husbands into battle, and were highly critical of the men's performance, which was later reflected in the order in which each wife drew water at the well; those whose husbands had least distinguished themselves had to wait to the last. The vendetta, although it existed, was halted whenever possible because of the shortage of warriors.

Ali therefore proceeded with guile. Having announced his intention early in 1792 of attacking Argyrokastro, he invited the Souliots to participate in his campaign and offered them double pay. George Botsaris refused to co-operate but Lambros Tzavellas, another leading chieftain, joined Ali, only to find himself and his seventy followers quickly made prisoner. One Souliot managed to escape and raised the alarm so that by the time Ali's forces reached the Souli area, he found all the passes barred. Tzavellas was then forced by Ali to return home to negotiate terms of submission for Souli, while Ali kept his son, Photos, as hostage. Once back in his native heights, however, Tzavellas defied the Vizier and threatened him with the most terrible revenge if his son was in any way hurt. It is significant that Ali merely interned Photos on the island in the Lake of Ioannina.

Later that year, Ali launched a full-scale attack from Lakkasouli along the track above the Acheron gorge into Souli and, in spite of heavy losses, managed to make progress until suddenly confronted by Moscho, Photos's mother, and a band of Souliot Amazons who wrought such destruction on Ali's forces by musket fire at close range that the latter turned and fled, the women pursuing them with drawn swords as far, according to Hughes, as Varyiadhes. Some three thousand of Ali's Albanians were killed at the cost of seventy-four Souliots dead and a hundred wounded. Ali is said to have become so panic-stricken that he killed two horses galloping back to the safety of his capital. Peace terms followed with the release of Photos Tzavellas and other Souliot prisoners in Ali's jails.

The Vizier's next campaign, again unsuccessful, was in 1800, by which time Lambros Tzavellas had died and George Botsaris and his *faria* had left Souli. Photos, now in command of the Souliots with three members of the Zervas family as lieutenants, fought brilliantly. Ali then decided to try and reduce his enemies by blockading all passes into Souli in order to starve them into surrender. The latter, however, obtained supplies from Parga and, during a lull in the campaign, occasioned by Ali's compliance with an order from Constantinople to march on Adrianople, built a fortress on Kunghi.

The Souliots were now divided in council and Photos was forced to go into exile to Ioannina, where Ali imprisoned him, to be temporarily released only to remind the Souliots of the Vizier's implacable enmity. The Souliots now concentrated their forces at Kakosouli and Kunghi, where they were again joined by Photos Tzavellas who had managed to persuade Ali to allow him to return home once more in order to withdraw his adherents from the defenders, leaving with Ali his wife and children as hostages. Instead, he evacuated the old and infirm to Parga for onward flight to the Ionian Islands and then returned to Kunghi.

The siege by Ali's Albanians under the command of his son, Veli, was eventually successful at the end of 1803, not through force of arms but through the Souliots' lack of water. Although the defenders were guaranteed on oath a peaceful departure by Veli and all his senior officers, Photos Tzavellas and two-thirds of the survivors were treacherously attacked en route for Parga, but managed to reach their destination without heavy losses. A second group of Souliots, making their way to Preveza, rested at Zalongo, which Veli also perfidiously surrounded, and then closed in for the kill. It is here, according to tradition, that some sixty indomitable women of Souli, preferring death to torture and dishonour, danced themselves into a frenzy and then, one by one, leapt off the precipice to their destruction, having first thrown their children before them.

A few survivors from Zalongo made their way to Vulgarelli at the southern end of the Tzoumerka, where other Souliots had settled, hoping that Ali Pasha would now relent, having succeeded in destroying the Republic of Souli. This, unhappily, was not to be. In 1804 Ali sent an army of seven thousand against the thousand Souliot men and women who had taken shelter in a monastery above the Archelaos river. After a siege of three months, the defenders made a desperate sortie, only to be killed or captured and vilely tortured to death, with the exception of a small group which managed to reach Parga.

Two other incidents need to be told about the campaign. Five wounded Souliots were left in the little church on Kunghi in the care of a monk called Samuel and nicknamed 'Last Judgement' Samuel who, towards the end of the fight against Ali, had become, with a Bible in one hand and a sword in the other, the life and soul of the resistance. It was he who built the Kunghi fort for Photos, as well as one at Kakasouli, which in the closing stages of the campaign was lost through treachery. For him there was no question of flight or surrender. Instead, he collected all available gunpowder into the little church on Kunghi, celebrated Communion for the last time with the five wounded Souliots, and flung a flaming torch into the powder barrel just as Albanian despoilers burst into the nave.

The second incident, similar to the first, took place at Riniassa, now called Riza, to the west of Zalongo. Ali, remembering that he had once given twenty Souliot families permission to live there, decided to enslave them to mark the successful conclusion of his campaign. A tower in the village was occupied by a widow, Despo Botzi, who had no intention of surrendering. She armed the other women who were living with her, fired at the intruders for as long as ammunition lasted and then, like 'Last Judgement Samuel', blew up the tower and its occupants.

Today a passable road from Glyki runs north up the eastern slope of the Korillas range, then crosses the Tzingariotiko, a tributary of the Acheron flowing from near Phrosini; the road then climbs southwards up to a ruined village. Here we found a few scattered houses for about a dozen families standing on poor soil and surrounded by largely bare slopes. Several large plane trees and a number of round well-heads proclaimed the presence of water. A few straggling sheep browsed on the inadequate grass. The ruins of other houses were to be seen together with an undamaged whitewashed church which seemed to proclaim that the memories of the slaughtered Christian Souliots would not die. Our taxi-driver from Paramythia said that this was Kakosouli. A map in Leake's *Travels in Northern Greece*, which Christopher Wordsworth also reproduced in his book on Greece, shows Souli or Kakosouli down in the valley to the east, where we could see more ruins. According to Leake we were now in Tzingari. Hughes, however, who published a drawing which he executed with help from Cockerell from Ali Pasha's stronghold of Kiafa, which he built after the end of the Souli Wars on Mount Trypa which we could see ahead of us, showed Kakosouli to be roughly where we stood. The maps obtainable in Epirus were discreetly vague on the subject.

Although little more than 8 a.m., it was already hot in the sun, which was blazing from a cloudless sky. To the south-west we could see through the gap at Glyki the dark green Fanari Plain. The taxi trundled over rough ground close to the little church of St Donatos, where we got out. The solid entrance arch, supporting a smaller arched belfry, bore the date '1966' on its gate.

The highest point was a few hundred yards further on at Kunghi on which were the ruins of St Paraskevi, blown up by 'Last Judgement Samuel'. Close by stood a solid marble slab, erected in 1967 as a memorial to 'the Monk Samuel, National Martyr of Kunghi'. Near it hung a *tsimandron*, which is a large free-hanging bar of metal or wood and struck with a smaller metal or wooden bar. During the Turkish occupation, the Christians, sometimes known as *rayah*, meaning cattle, were rarely permitted the use of bells and so instead used the *tsimandron* to summon the faithful to church. The sound of the *tsimandron* can carry considerable distances. In Metsovo today it is played with infinite variations of rhythm and tempo to announce certain hours during the day. From the top of Kunghi the Skala Tzavellas, a remarkable partly-stepped pathway, descends to Glyki but we were too hot to use it.

To the south of Kunghi the hillside fell steeply away to the foot of the great hill of Trypa, on which Ali Pasha built his great fortress of Kiafa, named after the Souliot village of the same name in the vale below; it is still the most considerable building to be seen hereabouts, although now largely in ruins. Trees grow lower down but the summit of Trypa, largely bare rock, is renowned as a target for lightning. When Holland and Hughes arrived here on separate occasions, they noted with satisfaction the volleys of musket fire, reverberating round the mountains, with which they were greeted by Ali's *Shqipetars*, stationed at Kiafa. Today all is empty and silent.

Ali Pasha was unable to eliminate the Souliots entirely. Sixteen years later he was glad to have them as allies against the Sultan's army. Those who fled to the Ionian Islands, mainly to Corfu, were enlisted by the Russians into six companies of light infantry; Photos Tzavellas was given the rank of captain and his redoubtable mother, Moscho, was made a major. Many of them soon grew tired of the unaccustomed military discipline and, homesick for their native Epirus, left Corfu for Ioannina, where some enrolled in Ali's service. According to one account, Photos was among these. There is, however, a tombstone in the Platytera Monastery on the outskirts of Corfu town commemorating Photos Tzavellas (1774–1811) next to one inscribed with the name of John Capodistrias, the first president of modern Greece.

In the Greek War of Independence, the Souliots made a continuing if uneven contribution to the struggle against the Turks. Nicolas Zervas, a member of the famous Souliot *faria*, some of whom later settled in Arta, fought valiantly in Acarnania between 1827 and 1829 under Church's command. He was in charge of one of two columns which successfully invested Vonitsa and its citadel. Later in the same campaign he was one of the commanders who landed Greek forces on the eastern shore of the Gulf; so successful were they in preventing supplies from around Arta reaching Amphilochia (then known as Karavassara) that its garrison capitulated, leaving only Mesolonghi briefly in Turkish occupation.

The Souliot clans of Botsaris and Tzavellas also featured prominently in the war. Marko Botsaris, who came to prominence when defending Levkas in 1807 under the command of Count John Capodistrias against Ali Pasha, was killed in 1823 during a gallant action by his band of three hundred and fifty Souliots against some four thousand Turks near Karpenisi.

After the Philhellene disaster at Peta in 1822, the Turks agreed to spare the Souliots involved on condition that they went once more into exile like those who escaped Veli's treacherous attacks at the end of the Souli Wars. Byron, impressed by their bravery but blind at first to their insubordination, rallied them to Mesolonghi with offers of pay. His efforts to organize them into a regular body of infantry failed because they were strife-torn: Drako refused to serve under

Constantine Botsaris or Kitsos Tzavellas and each clansman
sided with his own leader against the others. Just before
Byron's attack on Navpaktos the Souliots suddenly demanded
greatly increased pay and innumerable promotions which led
to the attack being abandoned. Their lack of discipline was a
factor which led to Byron's decline and death in 1824. Constantine Botsaris and Kitsos Tzavellas were later engaged
against Ibrahim Pasha and his Egyptians in the Morea in
1825. Tzavellas fought under Church in 1827 at Athens against
the Turks, who had confined a Greek garrison to the Acropolis; the failure of Church to relieve them was largely due to
Tzavellas's disregard of orders. In 1828, Botsaris, now a
general, campaigned with Church at Anatolikon to the north
of Mesolonghi. The martial distinction of the Souliots still
survives today.

17

Paramythia and Filiates

We returned to Paramythia from Souli by the same route that we had come. Although only mid-morning, the late June sun was blindingly strong and the shade of the taxi welcome. We did not stop at Glyki as there is little to see in this dusty little village. Yet Glyki, where tracks from the Souliot villages converge into the plain, had once been the seat of a bishop. His episcopal church, now in ruins by the river bank, had formerly housed the body of Donatos, Bishop of Eurhoea, who had lived towards the end of the fourth century. This holy man, canonized in due course, became the patron of the district. It was St Donatos who, armed with an osier twig, mounted a mule and attacked a monstrous dragon which had befouled a local stream of clear, sweet water. The dragon was about to unseat Donatos when he was banged on the head with the osier twig by the holy man, who at the same time called on the name of the Panaghia, whereupon the dragon collapsed and died. The saint then tasted the water of the stream and declared it to be once more sweet, for which *glyki* is the Greek word. The grateful inhabitants have remembered him ever since in the name of their local churches.

The valley of Paramythia, spread out between the Korillas range to its east and the western hills which border the Margariti Plain, is green and fruitful. Maize, wheat, rice and tobacco have all been grown here. The road passes well cared-for villages, shaded by trees, with Paramythia slowly coming into view to the north, where it climbs up the lower slopes of Mount Korillas itself. Paramythia means 'a pleasant place' or 'place of consolation', and Leake, Holland, Hughes and Christopher Wordsworth all commented on its attractiveness, at least at a distance. In general aspect, it can have changed little since Leake was here. 'Like the generality of Albanian towns', he wrote, 'it covers a large space of ground, and is divided into clusters of houses, occupied by *farias* or family alliances, which often make war upon one another, when in want of an external quarrel.' Leake went on to describe the houses, which were built of the roughly hewn calcareous stone of the mountain and stood amid walled gardens, as they do today, well watered by a multiplicity of streams from Mount Korillas. Scattered about are cypresses and great plane trees which gave shade to Paramythia's mosques and fountains and which still refresh the open spaces and twisting pathways of the town.

Paramythia, once the centre of one of the three *Sanjaks* or administrative areas of Epirus, retains something of an Ottoman flavour. In the early evenings of summer and again during the following mornings the air resounds with the sound of the storks clapping together their long beaks. As in Ioannina of thirty years ago, the storks still nest here each summer in considerable numbers. Most roofs support a great nest of twigs, streaked with the limestone colour of their droppings, which the same family of storks refurbishes each successive year. This clacking is said to denote happiness, the same sort of happiness associated with the song of a lark ascending over an English meadow. Hughes reported that so sacred was the bird held in many parts of Turkey that it was known as the 'bird of Mahomet' and added: 'Nothing can add more to the picturesque appearance of Turkish cities than the frequent occurrence of this majestic bird either standing upon a mosque with all the solemnity of an *imaun*, or seated like a moralist amidst the ruins of antiquity.'

Today, Paramythia with a population of two thousand seven hundred has one or two small hotels, a bank and good bus services. The name of the Hotel Cyprus, in which we stayed, was a reminder of a more recent clash than that between Ali Pasha and Pronio Aga of Paramythia; on the later occasion Pronio, who was already over ninety years old and in secret league with the Souliots, was persuaded to allow ten of Ali's men under the command of a *bolubashee* into the fortress of Paramythia, purely as a means, so Ali explained, of saving his own face after his lack of success against Pronio. These men, once inside, quickly opened the gates to Ali's forces; this enabled the Vizier of Ioannina to seize the aged Pronio's possessions. The hotel had been given this name during the Cypriot troubles in the 1950s, which damaged the genuine and traditional friendship between Greece and Britain.

In 1944, a staunch supporter of Britain was Dorotheos, Bishop of Paramythia, a stocky, sturdily built black-haired man in his early forties, with features which were stern in repose but which relaxed easily into an infectious smile. Bishop Dorotheos was chaplain to the EDES forces. Neatly dressed in breeches, his pectoral cross tucked inside his khaki tunic, a holster containing a revolver on his hip, he was generally known to the Military Mission as the 'pistol-packing Papa'. He spent a considerable time riding a captured German horse to visit his scattered flock.

His popularity was shown in 1944 in Corfu during a victory service at which he officiated with the metropolitan of the island. The service was conducted on the esplanade from the bandstand, built during the British ascendancy in the Ionian Islands; its Victorian design was a reminder of very many similar structures at seaside resorts at home. Instead, however, of preaching a long sermon, he merely slapped his side where a slight bulge could not entirely be hidden by the splendour of his episcopal vestments—*saccos, epitrachilion, amophorion* and *epigonation*—and announced in ringing tones that he was first and foremost an EDES *andarte*. After a momentary hush, the air was rent with waves of *feux de joie* as hundreds of *andartes* fired off their rifles, sten guns and pistols into the air. There were happily no casualties, not even a broken window. Bishop Dorotheos was later translated to Trikkala and eventually to a senior ecclesiastical post in Athens where he died, so I was told, while still comparatively young.

The cathedral of Paramythia is a modern building, erected since Paramythia became Greek in 1913, but there are older churches and monasteries in the neighbourhood; although Paramythia in the nineteenth century was largely Muslim— it had five mosques, according to Holland—there was also a considerable Greek minority with its own bishop. In the graveyard of the Monastery of the Dormition of the Virgin is the well-tended grave of Major David Wallace, who was tragically killed in August 1944 in an attack by EDES on the German troops stationed at Menina where the route from Paramythia joins the main Ioannina–Igoumenitsa road. It was a successful action for EDES who captured one hundred and twenty prisoners and much equipment, including two staff cars, one of which was still in use in Corfu in the mid-sixties. Wallace, who was then only twenty-nine, was Anthony Eden's personal emissary from the Foreign Office on the staff of the Commander of the Allied Military Mission to the Greek guerillas.

Today, Paramythia is peaceful, its fine stone houses in good repair and its churches restored after wartime neglect. Its population is now entirely Greek. One minaret remains. It can be seen, partly in ruins, high up on the slopes of Mount Korillas, close to the remains of a Venetian fort, built on Hellenistic foundations. It has no uses now as the Albanian Muslims, who once lived in this area, have gone. Robert Curzon described them, when there, as 'arrant cut-throats, swaggering about, idle and restless, with their long hair, and guns. . . . The Albanians did not scream and chatter as the Arabs do . . . but they lounged about the bazaar listlessly, ready to pick a quarrel with anyone, and unable to fix themselves down to any occupation; in short, they gave me the idea of being a very poor and proud good-for-nothing set of scamps.'

The Muslim Tsamé or Chams of Threspotia were eternally feuding with their Christian neighbours and, favoured by their Turkish co-religionists, had gained the best lands, while Christians, like the Souliots, had been forced on to less fertile soil. The incorporation of Threspotia into Greece had been unfortunate for the Chams, but they continued to flourish, tending their olive trees for their oil. In 1941–4 the Chams were armed by the Germans and Italians and co-operated with them against the Greek villages controlled by the *andartes*. Many atrocities by them were known. In August 1944, as a prelude to the final battle against the retreating Germans, EDES drove the Chams into Albania as they constituted a threat to Zervas's left flank. Most of them got away but many of those who were not quick enough suffered reprisals in their

172

turn at the hands of the Greek villagers. As Threspotia probably suffered more during those years than most parts of Greece from war, famine and disease, the spirit of vengeance was fierce as seen today by the few remaining ruins of the Cham villages along the lower Kalamas.

There are still many Greek Orthodox villagers in Threspotia who speak Albanian among themselves. They are scattered north from Paramythia to the Kalamas river and beyond, and westwards to the Margariti Plain. Some of the older people can only speak Albanian, nor is the language dying out. As more and more couples in early married life travel away to Athens or Germany for work, their children remain at home to be brought up by their Albanian-speaking grand-parents.

It is still sometimes possible to distinguish between Greek- and Albanian-speaking peasant women. Nearly all of them wear the traditional black clothes with a black scarf round their heads. Greek-speaking women tie their scarves at the back of their necks, while those who speak primarily Albanian wear their scarves in a distinctive style fastened at the side of the head.

The villagers of Threspotia, especially in the Margariti Plain, used to suffer intensely from malaria, partly because of the swamps in the area. Approaching Margariti from Igoumenitsa, one passes an extensive stretch of sinister, still waters, an obvious breeding ground for the mosquito and, according to some, the home of poisonous snakes. Conditions were particularly bad during the last war. An RAMC captain with the Military Mission told us in 1944 that the chief health problems of the Chams were chronic malaria and hereditary syphilis. The medical authorities before the war had planned to eliminate these scourges, but war postponed the attempt. In addition, outbreaks of typhus were not unknown; one out-break in the winter of 1943 accounted for fifty deaths in the Sirrakon district, south-east of Ioannina, then described as the poorest part of Epirus. The cause of typhus was the lice from which most villages suffered.

The listlessness of the rough and simple inhabitants of these sunlit but semi-barren areas was not merely an attitude, often and perhaps rightly blamed on the Ottoman influence, but also due to lack of medical and nutritional care. Syphilitic sores were often to be seen on the faces and arms of children in 1944. Undernourishment was widespread, for in winter these villagers lived almost entirely on a few beans and bread made from maize flour; meat if obtainable was reserved for the major festivals of the Church. Postwar Greece has now very largely, if not entirely, eradicated these cancers of the Epirot countryside in Threspotia.

Filiates, north-west of Paramythia beyond the Kalamas river, was a century ago as Muslim in character as Paramythia. With the Albanian frontier only six miles away, Filiates like Konitsa was in 1973 within the military control area and our passes were demanded before we were allowed to continue with the bus over the river to the town some three miles further on.

The olive trees on the lower slopes near the river were straggly, because unpruned, with many of their leaves black with blight. This, we were told, was because of the flight of labour from the land and of the disappearance some thirty years ago of the Chams who were always far more tied to the land than the Greeks. Apart from agriculture, the only occupations enjoyed by the Muslim Albanians were soldiering and the vendetta. The rulers of Naples and of the Barbary States possessed Albanian regiments. The sacred banner carried annually from Mecca to Constantinople was entrusted to a troop of one hundred and fifty Albanians, armed and dressed, according to Hobhouse, in their distinctive fashion. The vendetta was always alive among these brave yet treacherous people. Certain rules, however, were observed. It was forbidden to kill a man in his own house or with whom salt had been shared or one escorting a woman. Generally a time when killings could be attempted was agreed by the parties concerned such as in the evening when the flocks had been tended; the need while alive to earn a living for one's family was recognized.

Filiates itself is built up and over a hill in the shadow of Mount Farmakovouni, which is over 3,700 feet high. It has a population of some three thousand, now virtually all Greek. It is the market town for a wide area between the river Kalamas, the Albanian frontier and the sea. Here, during the

Ottoman Empire, lived several Muslim landlords of large estates who employed most of the people in the surrounding area. Mr Gladstone, the future Liberal prime minister and then, briefly, the Lord High Commissioner of the Ionian Islands, paid a visit to one of these landowners in 1858. An account of this excursion was written home in a letter by Arthur Gordon, later Lord Stanmore, the great man's secretary, and quoted by John Morley in his *Life of W. E. Gladstone*.

The Lord High Commissioner's party sailed in December from Corfu to Sayiadhes which for the greater part of the Turkish period was one of the principal ports of Epirus, trading mainly with Trieste and Venice. The way usually taken from Ioannina to Sayiadhes went through Filiates and was used by Edward Lear on his way from Thessaly to Corfu in 1849; he described it with much enthusiasm, especially Filiates itself, which he found to be 'a place abounding in exquisite beauty'.

Gladstone and his companions were to stay with an old lady, called the *Valideh*, a great proprietress, who lived in a large ruinous castle in Filiates, 'the greatest personage in these regions'. Gladstone, on reaching Sayiadhes, refused to wait until the train of horses was ready, but strode ahead on the twelve-mile journey, accompanied by a guard of eight white-kilted *palikari* on foot who, to his annoyance, fired off their long guns in all directions.

The whole town turned out to welcome the Liberal statesmen, first the *Valideh*'s retainers, then the elders and the *mullahs* in their great green turbans, followed by the Christian community, and finally at the top of the hill by the old lady's little grandson, attended by his tutor and a number of black slaves. On arriving at the castle, the *Valideh* was there to greet him, dressed in green silk and a fur pelisse, her train held by two female negro slaves. Everything was done in the handsomest way and at dinner eight tall Albanians, each holding a candle, stood like statues behind the guests. Gladstone was shown round the little town, including the bazaar, preceded by a tall black slave in a gorgeous blue velvet jacket who carried a great silver stick. On arriving at the mosque, the *muezzin* was sent, at Gladstone's request, to the top of the minaret to call the faithful to prayer, although it was two hours before the proper time.

Arthur Gordon enjoyed the excursion immensely, even though it rained next morning on the return journey to Corfu. Gladstone's comment in his diary was, however, brief: 'The whole impression is saddening; it is all indolence, decay, stagnation; the image of God seems as if it were nowhere. But there is much of wild and picturesque [sic]'.

Filiates today has none of the picturesque features to which Arthur Gordon referred. Its centre consists of unpretentious houses in pale washes, packed close together along both sides of the main street—shops, cafés, a pleasant little restaurant and private houses. On the outskirts, however, are a number of grander, older mansions built solidly of stone and now largely in ruin, which are no doubt those which once belonged to the great Muslim landlords. We entered one up some stone steps into an entrance hall in which was a well-head with water collected by drainage far below. In one room a single-headed Albanian eagle, in contrast with the two-headed eagle of Byzantium, decorated the wall above the main chimney-piece. The rest of the ground floor would have provided accommodation for one or two horses or mules. On the upper floor were several rooms, one of which, probably the kitchen, had an indoor closet. It was faintly reminiscent because of its stone shape of a small house in the Cotswolds—at least it might have been if surrounded with green lawns in place of the few olive trees growing from the stony ground.

Of the castle where Gladstone spent the night there was no sign. Perhaps, we thought, the local schoolmaster might know something about this. We were directed to his house, a modern cube-shaped villa in a small suburban garden. Behind it, the dappled hillside fell away into a deep valley beyond which rose the long pale brown ridge of Mount Farmako-vouni. The schoolmaster was, at 4.30 p.m., just emerging from his siesta, but took an immediate interest in the subject. He had, however, never heard of Gladstone's visit nor, after consultation with a knowledgeable neighbour, had he any suggestion to make as to the whereabouts of the *Valideh*'s castle. Did we know, he asked, how Gladstone had come into contact with her?

Elli told him what we had learned in Ioannina from the Albanian Muslims whom we had visited there, for they had originated from Filiates. The Démis family, to which they belonged, had been of sufficient importance in the middle of the nineteenth century to receive a sister of the Sultan in marriage. It was an intelligent and well-educated family, and a son of the house, Emin Bey Démis, had served on the staff of the Lord High Commissioner in Corfu. Perhaps it was through him that the invitation had gone to Gladstone. Later, when he had retired from the English service, he was seriously burnt through a gunpowder explosion. In spite of English doctors who came to tend him from Corfu, his burns proved fatal. We could not clarify whether the mishap took place before or after Gladstone's visit, but it may have been his widowed mother, Eminé Hamum of Argyrokastro, who was the hostess on that occasion.

18

Parga

The old road from Igoumenitsa to Parga went immediately inland over the empty hills via Mazaraki and Margariti, a dusty, featureless journey. Today a new road runs round Igoumenitsa Bay and on southwards round the headlands to Plataria, known as Nista in ancient days, where in 1973 a tentative effort to build a little resort was being made. This road was equally dusty, for the coastal hills are also largely bare, but to the west, beyond the calm sea, lay Corfu, faintly enfolded in mist. Before leaving the coast, there was a glimpse of the Syvota Isles, the scene of the two naval battles of 435 and 433 B.C. between the Corinthians and the Corcyraeans at the start of the Peloponnesian Wars.

From Plataria, the road climbs slightly towards the Margariti Plain, leaving Perdhika hidden among the coastal hills; the modern name of this village means 'partridge', but it is still called Arpitsa locally. From Perdhika a rough track runs south-east to Ayia, which is within the boundaries of what was once the little republic of Parga, but the bus has more important centres to visit and a better road on which to travel. Margariti itself was until recently principally Albanian-speaking. Its scattered houses and gardens climb airily up the slopes of the surrounding hills. On an eminence to the south stands a fortress built by the Venetians in the seventeenth century. A damaged mosque and a truncated minaret proclaim the triumph of the Cross over the Crescent, a scene which is repeated in the little village of Eleftherion further down the valley.

At Morfion, our road was joined by one from Paramythia. A wayside café provided a little shade from the late afternoon sun as we waited for a bus connection. Soon we set off again, coasting down towards the Ionian and increasingly under the shadow of the thickly wooded limestone mountain range, which rises to about 2,800 feet behind Parga, to form a protective barrier for the town against attack from the interior and the north wind. The road winds ever lower towards the shore with tantalizing glimpses of the sea with its occasional inlets amid rocks and low cliffs. The coastline of Parga, although facing south instead of west, has many features in common with those of Palaeokastritza in Corfu—the same rocky headlands, the same cypresses and olive groves with their myriad dancing, shiny, grey-green leaves reflecting the light of the sun, the same green and white limestone heights mounting steeply behind the town and the same dark blue Ionian Sea.

The bus pulled into a roughly surfaced street, overhung with trees, at the back of Parga. Apartments and villas were being built on the ground between the town and the mountains, but there was little sign that they were at that time spoiling the character of the place. There were one or two simple hotels, rooms for hire in private homes and several restaurants. Around Parga stretch the olive and citrus groves. De Bosset, the British commander there in 1817, noted that cedrets, a citrus fruit not unlike a lemon, were grown in quantity and exported to the Jews of Trieste or Poland, whichever offered the better price. Admiral Kanaris, now immortal for his bravery in the Greek War of Independence, was born here.

Parga owed its original prosperity to Venice, to which the Parguinots (to use De Bosset's version of their name) remained devoted until the Republic's eclipse in 1797. The little town is built in the shadow of a Venetian fortress, which stands on a rocky, tree-covered headland jutting out to sea between two bays; that to the east contains the town while that of Chrisoyiali to the west has a glorious sandy beach fringed with pine woods. Parga's whitewashed houses, two or three storeys high, often with gently sloping roofs which are distantly reminiscent of the Veneto, climb up and over a conical hill. Stepped, stone-paved alleys meander between the buildings among which broods the occasional open space. Gardens lurk behind whitewashed walls over which rise trees, while flowering plants like bougainvillaea climb along trellises; the balconies are bright with potted geranium and other plants.

On the eastern side of the fortress headland are several cafés built out on stilts over the shallow waters and beyond, a wooden landing jetty to which are tied small boats for hire. The foreshore below the promenade is sandy as is the seabed, which is singularly free of sea urchins, the waters calm and warm. At the far end of the Chrysoyiali beach in 1973 was a camp of the Club Méditerranée and signs of a hotel under construction.

A string of tiny islets, reminiscent of Pontekonisi off Canoni in Corfu, lies out in the eastern bay. The largest is the Panaghia, named after its little whitewashed chapel dedicated to the Virgin; there is another chapel to St Nicolas and a diminutive fort erected by the French in 1808. The Panaghia chapel continues to reflect the evening sun for a while after it has left the town. Out to sea stand Paxos and Anti-Paxos.

When and by whom Parga was established as a centre is not known. There is evidence of Mycenaean settlement in the district but there is little to indicate that there was an important centre here when Octavius, before the battle of Acteion, concentrated his fleet at Toryni, which is generally accepted to have been Parga. Hammond has reported the remains of an ancient mole at the far end of Parga's western bay and there is said to be polygonal walling under the fortress. It was not until the middle of the fourteenth century A.D. that the inhabitants, probably Christian Albanians, from the settlement known as Palaeo-Parga, high up on the mountain behind, descended to the shore and concentrated their population on the fortress promontory, because it was more secure than their former home.

In 1387 Venice, then having the strongest fleet in the Adriatic and the Ionian, accepted control over Corfu at the request of its inhabitants. In 1401, the Parguinots followed suit, having like Corfu suffered from the misrule of the Angevins and the later despots of Epirus. During the fourteenth century, Parga was renowned for its sugar plantations but as these, at the start of the fifteenth century, were no longer profitable, Venice at first hesitated. The Serene Republic suggested that the Parguinots should emigrate either to Anti-Paxos, whose excellent soil still produces a natural, slightly sparkling rosé wine, or to Corfu where land was available for them. The Parguinots, however, insisted on remaining where they were. In *The Latins in the Levant*, William Miller wrote that they 'showed a touching if inconvenient attachment to their ancient home, which was well situated for the purposes of piracy, and they combined devotion to Venice from whom they obtained excellent terms, with the lucrative traffic of selling the weapons sent for their defence to the neighbouring Turks.'

The Venetian ascendancy over Parga brought prosperity and protection to the inhabitants who throughout their history spoke Greek. The Venetians installed a Corfiot governor, but the Parguinots maintained their own council, which appointed the magistrates, and enjoyed exemption from taxes and other privileges. It was agreed that the Parguinots should only be liable for military service in their own territories. The Venetian troops, either Italian or Slav mercenaries, remained under the command of the governor, but his rank did not protect him, if corrupt, from the anger of the inhabitants who on more than one occasion arrested a maladministrator.

The Parguinots several times suffered heavily for their loyalty to Venice. In 1452 and 1475 they were saved from being captured by the Turks by the timely arrival of forces from Corfu. They were again in danger in 1499, but in 1537 the town was captured and burnt to the ground by Kheir-ed-din Barbarossa, after his failure to seize Corfu; the inhabitants were forced to flee into the Epirot mountains until the Turks withdrew, when Venice helped them rebuild their homes. There was peace after this until 1657 when the Turks tried to capture Parga over a three-year period, but in vain. After this, Parga extended its territories to include Sayiadhes, the Fanari Plain to the south, Margariti and Paramythia.

The fortress of Parga was built by the Venetians. Over an inner gate, close to a winged lion of St Mark, is an inscription saying that it had been constructed in 1624 by Paolo Caotorta, Governor of Corfu. Over the castle entrance is another inscription in Italian which reads '1707—carried out by Count Marco Theotocchi, Governor and Captain of Parga'.

Parga changed hands several times after the Treaty of

Campo Formio in 1797, but when Leake was there in 1805, it was controlled by a resident agent of the Porte who, supported by Russian troops, protected the town from the clutches of Ali Pasha, while the inhabitants enjoyed their traditional municipal government unchanged. Sir William Gell, there in 1807, noted that the Turkish magistrate exercised complete control; no doubt he left with the return of the French after Tilsit.

The Parguinots were staunch friends of the Souliots in their wars with Ali, supplying them whenever possible with food and weapons and giving them shelter after their final defeat. Because of this, Ali became more determined than ever to gain control of Parga. He still had many years to wait before he achieved this ambition. General Berthier, the French commander in Corfu after the re-occupation of the Ionian Islands by France in 1807, firmly supported the Parguinots against Ali.

In 1812, Napoleon's retreat from Moscow encouraged Ali to try to seize Ayia, high up in the hills between Parga and Perdhika, as a first step to capturing the town, but he was repulsed with heavy losses. A second attempt also failed. In 1814, with France retreating on all fronts, Ali tried to overwhelm Parga and its French defenders. A considerable army was collected together in February of that year and despatched against the little town but the undertaking was carried out in too confident a mood. Ali's *Shqipetars* took Ayia but on advancing further were thoroughly trounced by well-placed French cannon and by fusillades of French and Parguinot musket fire. The Albanians fled in disorder, leaving many dead behind, including Ali's nephew, Dant Bey, who commanded the attack. They nevertheless managed to hold Ayia, where Ali constructed a fort.

By this time the French were as isolated in Corfu as the German garrisons in Crete and Rhodes in 1945. Paxos was captured in March 1814 by Colonel Church in command of the 2nd Battalion of the Greek Light Infantry, which he had raised. At the same time Foresti, the British representative in Ioannina, alerted General Campbell, who then commanded the British forces in the Ionian Islands, to Ali's designs on Parga, which still contained a small French garrison.

The Parguinots themselves quickly contacted the British on Paxos and asked for the protection of the Union Jack. Campbell agreed on condition that the Parguinots disarmed the French garrison, which had threatened to blow up the fort if attacked. Campbell was much taken with the Parguinots: 'The inhabitants', he reported, 'are Albanian Greeks, extremely tenacious of their freedom, and of the liberty of their small community, and habitually adverse to the domination of the Turks. They are a spirited and independent people, though at the same time docile and easy to command when treated liberally and justly; and all the male population are trained to arms, and expert in the use of them.' It was perhaps unfortunate for the Parguinots that General Campbell was superseded in his Ionian command later in the year by Sir Thomas Maitland, who became the first Lord High Commissioner of the Ionian Islands; this capable, yet unattractive man was known as 'King Tom' to his associates because of his autocratic ways and as 'the Abortion' to the Corfiots because of his vile manners.

Hughes, who was also impressed by the Parguinots, described how they ousted the French: 'An English flag, concealed under the girdle of a boy, was brought into the fortress without exciting suspicion; a signal was given by ringing a bell to the conspirators, who rushed forwards, disarmed the sentinels, seized upon the rest of the garrison, and hoisted the British standard in place of the tri-coloured flag.' The castle Hughes described as weak but its few cannon were thought sufficient 'to keep in awe the savage hordes of Albanian banditti'.

The Parguinots were at first delighted with their new protectors. It was only when the publication of the Treaty of Paris omitted all mention of Parga that disquiet arose. It soon became clear that Turkey was resting on her 1800 agreement with Russia that the mainland possessions of Venice were to be annexed by the Sultan, who now demanded Parga as the price of his acceptance of Britain as the protecting power over the Ionian Islands. Sir Thomas Maitland agreed to this; he seemed in any case to prefer the Turks to the Greeks, an attitude reflected by many of his staff, and sent a young lion as a gift to Ali who, in his letter of thanks, asked permission to loose it upon the Parguinots.

Maitland now selected Lt-Colonel C. P. de Bosset, a Swiss officer of good family who had served honourably under the British crown for over twenty years, to go in March 1817 to Parga to command the British garrison there and to inform the inhabitants of the arrangements between Britain and Turkey. It had been agreed that those Parguinots who refused to remain under the Ottoman administration should be free to emigrate and would be compensated fully for any property they left behind. As the Turkish commissioner from Constantinople had already arrived at Ioannina, it was proposed to effect the transfer of power straightaway. Maitland indicated that de Bosset need only spend a fortnight in Parga before returning to Zakynthos as Resident.

De Bosset, intelligent and conscientious, did his best not to reveal that it was Ali, not the Porte, with whom the British authorities were negotiating, but the Parguinots were not deceived. As this arrangement seemed so out of keeping with the generous character of Britain, and imagining that this measure arose from motives of economy, they even offered to pay the expenses of the British garrison. Because of the uncertainty of the situation, all commerce came to a halt and many were reduced to penury. Ali added to the depression by stopping all food supplies.

Not a single resident Parguinot was prepared to live under Ali, so a valuation of Parguinot property became necessary. This took much longer than originally planned, for Ali, anxious not to pay a penny more than absolutely necessary, insisted on every Parguinot being interrogated at least twice, only to receive the same answer on each occasion. He then attempted to insinuate a body of troops into Parga, but was frustrated by de Bosset. Ali, who had done everything possible to stir up trouble between the British and the Parguinots, was furious and complained about de Bosset to Maitland.

De Bosset was withdrawn from Parga after four months to find himself, instead of returning to Zakynthos, appointed as president of a civil criminal court for the trial of certain Ionians. As this was an appointment for which he had no experience, he tendered his resignation to the Prince Regent, the Commander-in-Chief; this was the accepted procedure in those days for querying the validity or suitability of a posting. Maitland thereupon most improperly published a General Order, announcing that 'the pay of Lieut.-Col. de Bosset as Inspecting Field Officer do cease, his services in that situation having been declared by His Majesty to be inexpedient': only the Commander-in-Chief had the right to make such an announcement, which de Bosset knew.

De Bosset returned to England, disgraced in the eyes of his associates on the Ionian station, to plead his case with the Prince Regent. The flagrancy of Maitland's behaviour was such that His Royal Highness felt compelled to create the misused Swiss a Knight of the Royal Guelphic Order. De Bosset then sued Maitland in the law courts for redress for the very serious injury to his interests and reputation—and won with damages of £100.

In the meanwhile the value of the eight hundred and thirty nine houses and the eighty-one thousand olive trees of Parga were assessed at over £500,000. Ali refused to pay such a price and did everything possible to reduce this valuation; he, refused, for example, to pay for land which was neither built on nor cultivated. Each side then carried out a further valuation; the British agents arrived at a figure of £276,075 but that of the Turkish representative was only £56,756. After further lengthy negotiations, Maitland agreed to accept the sum of £150,000 on behalf of the Parguinots.

Maitland showed no interest in the fears of the inhabitants of Parga about their likely fate if the Pasha's forces were allowed to enter Parga before their departure. When the British-Turkish agreement was almost completed, Ali's troops started massing outside the little town. In spite of Maitland's promises, no transport arrived to carry them away. At last the Parguinots decided that they would have to fend for themselves. Taking the icons from their churches and their ancestors' bones from their tombs, either to be re-interred elsewhere or destroyed, they left their ancient home and sailed away to Corfu. Parga was the last independent Christian stronghold in Epirus to fall to Islam. De Bosset at least saw to it that the shameful treatment of the Parguinots became generally known by the publication of his *Parga and the Ionian Islands* in 1821.

Ali Pasha was so enchanted with Parga that he admitted to understanding the reluctance of the Parguinots to depart. This was his last triumph. Shortly afterwards, the Sultan, having come to realize the full iniquity of Ali's treacherous behaviour, put in hand the expedition against him which led to his death on the island in the Lake of Ioannina in January 1822. A number of Parguinots may have returned to Parga after Ali's death but the icons were not brought back until the Turks finally left Parga at the end of the First Balkan War.

19

The Fanari Plain and Cassopaia

'Set up your sail,' Circe told Odysseus in Book Ten of the *Odyssey*, 'spread the white sail and sit down in the ship. The North Wind will blow her on her way; and when she has brought you across the River of Ocean, you will come to a wild coast and to Persephone's Grove, where the tall poplars grow and the willows. . . . Beach your boat there by Ocean's swirling stream and march on into Hades' Kingdom of Decay. There the River of Flaming Fire and the River of Lamentation, which is a branch of the waters of Styx, unite round a pinnacle of rock to pour their thundering streams into Acheron.'

The Ionian Sea, which fringes the once remote shores of Epirus, can be extremely stormy; the cloud-diffused light of winter can make islands and headlands rise out of the sea while waterspouts stalk the fugitive waves. Once during a winter crossing from Igoumenitsa to Corfu in 1945, a waterspout suddenly emerged from the scudding drifts which veiled the Epirot coast and advanced on our boat, only to collapse when its vacuum, which caused so much water to be sucked into the rain clouds descending ever closer upon us, was punctured by a bullet, fired by a Greek National Guardsman; with a sudden bucketing of water the whole phantom structure disappeared. Inland the rainfall is much heavier than elsewhere in Greece so that deep, navigable rivers, not to be found further south, overflow their banks, and tributaries pour their thundering waters into the main stream.

After the Acheron has surged through its gorge from Lakkasouli, a clear sign to the ancients of its association with the dead, it emerges at Glyki into the more serene, open country of the Fanari Plain. Here it flows westwards, its

187

waters reflecting the green willows which grow on its banks, to reach the Ionian just beyond the hamlet of Ammoudhia, south of the bleached sands of Splantza beach where, in 1944, supplies for the Allied Military Mission were landed on moonless nights by the Royal Navy.

Today, by car, the journey to the Fanari Plain from Ioannina takes little more than two hours; one first goes down the main Arta road as far as Philippeas and on to Louros village, two-thirds of the way towards Preveza, before turning west to join the Preveza–Paramythia road at Arkangelos. We had paused near St George's village, before reaching the hydro-electric dam on the river Louros, to watch the rush of water which emerges from the limestone hills to the east of the road, and to inspect the long tunnel which the Romans bored through the hillside to take the water to the aqueduct beyond and so to Nikopolis, near Preveza, some twenty miles away. The remains of two aqueducts, which once conveyed water over the river to the tunnel, still stand; other stretches of the aqueduct can be seen at intervals marching south-westwards along the foothills which border the Louros Plain. Today, the waters of the spring race foam-flecked into the Louros on whose bank grow vast plane trees. Hughes measured one and found its girth to be twelve feet and afterwards noted even larger ones. On the hills to the west is Kokkinopilos, now declared a national monument because of its wealth of Palaeolithic artifacts. In addition, stratified deposits of Upper and Middle Palaeolithic man were discovered in 1965 close by in the Asprokhaliko Cave.

From Arkangelos we continued north-westwards over the coastal foothills, leaving Mount Zalongo and the site of Cassope to the east, to descend along the Margariti road into Kanalaki, a tree-lined, whitewashed village gleaming in the sun. Nightingales were singing when Leake rode hither from Preveza through beautiful woods of oak and ilex. From here a branch road led down to and over the Acheron where dragonflies hovered by its green waters. We continued to Kastri upon whose rise, separate from the surrounding hills, stands an ancient city and acropolis, which Leake supposed to be Pandosia, founded by colonists from Elis in the north-west Peloponnese, a theory supported by Sotiris Dakaris who came with us on this journey. Poplars of the variety known as Acheronian, brought according to tradition by Herakles to Elis, flourish in the neighbourhood.

We then bumped along a rough road for some three miles over what had in Turkish days been the swampy, malaria-ridden Acherusian Lake, but now drained and under cultivation, to arrive on its far side at the 'pinnacle of rock' where the River of Lamentation, better known as the Cocytos, joins the Acheron. Homer also mentions the River of Flaming Fire. The Cocytos is in fact joined by the Mavros, sometimes known as the Vouvos, a short distance to the north before it combines with the Acheron to flow westwards into the sea.

The 'pinnacle of rock', immediately to the north-west of this confluence of rivers, has since the early eighteenth century been crowned by the Monastery of St John the Baptist, in the centre of which is the chapel, a building more reminiscent of Ionian Island Baroque than the domed and octagonal lanterned churches of Zagori and Tzoumerka. It was a brilliant day, the air alive with the rasping of cicadas and remote from 'where the fog-bound Cimmerians live in the City of Perpetual Mist'. The Cimmerians dwelt near the Black Sea and were unlikely to have been known to Homer; the Cheimerium, however, occupied this corner of Threspotia and the foreland at the northern end of Splantza beach is named after them. Cimmerians, it has been suggested, at some stage by mistake replaced Cheimerians in the story.

Hughes came here after his visit to Souli in search of the Acherusian Lake and from the monastery found the view of the mountains and the sea extremely beautiful. Then, by an inspired guess, having mistaken the ruins at Kastri for those of Bucheteion, he hit the nail on the head: 'Probably this very spot on which we stood was the great Necyomanteum, or place for the evocation of the dead, so celebrated in the early periods of Grecian history.' Herodotus informs us that it stood among the Threspotians on the banks of the Acheron. It remained for Sotiris Dakaris to find the probable Homeric place where Odysseus sacrificed a young ram and a black ewe to raise the shade of Teiresias, the blind Theban prophet, to consult him on the best way of returning to Ithaka. Dakaris directed the excavations carried out by the Greek Archaeo-

189

logical Society between 1958 and 1964. The monastery was found to have been built on a Hellenistic group of buildings, dating from the late fourth and early third century B.C., which comprised the Nekromanteion (or Necyomanteum), the most famous of the Hellenic oracles of the dead.

Walking around the building complex under the eighteenth-century chapel was like going behind the scenes of an empty theatre. Dakaris explained the purposes of the various rooms and corridors of what was basically an enormous deception on man's credulity. The pilgrim, seeking communication with the dead, entered the walled enclosure from the north, then turned left to where, plunged in gloom, were ritual bedrooms and a bathroom. Here the pilgrim underwent purification rites and prepared himself to see visions and dream dreams, aided by the consumption of special foods associated with the dead, such as pork, oysters and beans; these beans were of a type, from traces found of them, which could produce giddiness and hallucinations. This phase could take several days.

When the pilgrim left the north corridor, he threw a pebble on to a heap of stones to avert the evil eye and then entered the final stages of preparation. By now his diet, isolation and the surrounding gloom must have produced a highly dis-ordered mental state; the priest would certainly not confront him with the supposed spirits of the departed until this desired condition had been achieved. The pilgrim then slaughtered a sheep over a trench, just as Odysseus himself had done—the remains of charcoal and animal bones have been found in such a pit—and offered up, among other things, barley flour, lupin seeds and honey which were placed in wide-mouthed vessels, some of which have also been found, as he wandered dizzily through the labyrinthine passage on the south side to reach the central chamber.

Lucian, writing in the second century A.D., satirized the whole procedure when describing a pilgrim being prepared at an oracle between the Tigris and Euphrates for a similar confrontation. The suppliant was led alternatively to one or other river, where he was ceremoniously washed to the accompaniment of long gobbledegook incantations by the priest who finished each session by spitting three times in his face. Lucian may have undergone initiation for the fun of it.

The culmination of the elaborately contrived deception was reached when the pilgrim entered the central chamber, whose immensely thick walls probably concealed passages through which the priests could flit unseen in furtherance of their prestidigitations. Underneath it is another chamber, hollowed out of the rock. Here were discovered a number of blocks and pulleys, now to be seen in the Ioannina Museum, which were used for raising and lowering heavy objects to and from the chamber above. Once the suppliant had poured libations to Aedoneos, King of Hades, and to Persephone, the room would have re-echoed to the barking of Cerberus and the dehumanized voices of the dead, impersonated by a priest, as some object indistinct but awesome, accepted as the shades of the departed, arose out of the floor to confront the pilgrim.

Then, after contact with the dead, came the ritual cleansing in which sulphur, of which clear traces have been found, had its traditional uses; Odysseus burnt sulphur after slaying the suitors on his return to Ithaka. The pilgrim then left the oracle by a completely different route, probably poorer as well as richer by his experience. The thought uppermost in his mind, as he hurried away to the sardonic croakings of frogs in the Acherusian Lake, may well have been the final injunction of the priest not to divulge what he had seen or heard to anyone, or the most terrible retribution would befall him.

Although the Nekromanteion buildings are early Hellenistic, the oracle is very much older. Most traces of previous ages must have been destroyed by the levelling of the rocky platform on which the latest shrine was constructed, but a Mycenaean grave has been unearthed in the sanctuary courtyard and a few Mycenaean sherds of the fourteenth and thirteenth centuries B.C. as well. There are, moreover, traces of an ancient city six hundred yards to the north on the same ridge, which Thucydides mentioned when describing the events which led up to the battle of Syvota between Corinth and Corcyra in 433 B.C. The Corinthian fleet, he wrote, 'sailed from Levkas to the mainland opposite Corcyra and came to anchor at Cheimerium in the territory of Threspotis. There is a harbour here and above it, at some distance from the sea, is the city of Ephyre in the Elean district. Near Ephyre the waters of the Acherusian Lake flow into the sea. It gets its

name from the River Acheron, which flows through Threspotis and falls into the lake' (Rex Warner's translation).

Two thousand years ago, the Bay of Ammoudhia penetrated much further inland than it does today, when the river
mouth is largely silted up. In 433 B.C., there was a safe
anchorage here for the hundred and fifty ships of the Corinthians and their allies. In 31 B.C., the Bay gave shelter to
Octavius's much larger fleet of two hundred and fifty ships,
en route for Acteion. As recently as A.D. 1084, Robert Guiscard
wintered here with his armada during his campaign against
Byzantium and lost ten thousand men through malaria. Now,
only a few shallow fishing boats are tied up to the trees on the
north bank.

Ephyre, perhaps the hill-top at Xylokastro with its three
circuits of ancient walls, where Mycenaean sherds have been
discovered, was legendarily associated with the entrance to
Hades. One of Theseus's exploits was an attempt, with his
companion Pirithous, to abduct Persephone, 'spouse of
Aedoneos, King of Ephyre', but he failed; Pirithous was killed
and Theseus held in chains until rescued by Herakles.
Aedoneos's name was synonymous with Hades and the oracle
of the dead, the Nekromanteion, was only six hundred yards
away from his city.

The Acheron, like the Louros and Arakhthos rivers, was
navigable for some little distance inland, perhaps as far as
Glyki. It was not unexpected that seafaring traders should
establish settlements near their mouths. That of the Acheron
was known as Glykis Limen, or 'sweet harbour', because of
the river's fresh water; later another port was set up to the
south of the river's exit. In addition to trade with the interior,
a pilgrim route started from here for the Nekromanteion and
for more distant Dodona. The earliest known settlers were
probably of Mycenaean culture of the late Helladic period
from Elis in the north-west Peloponnese who came here
during the fourteenth century B.C. Local timber must have
been valuable and there was a shipbuilding yard, where oak
beams for keels have been found, on the southern edge of the
Acherusian Lake, but of an unknown date. The Fanari Plain
was also known to Homer as a source of poison which was
extracted from marsh plants.

During the Dark Ages, from approximately 1100 to 700
B.C., these shores were probably ravaged by raiders—we read
in Book Sixteen of the *Odyssey* of Taphian pirates pillaging
Threspotia—which by making Ephyre unsafe, caused its
inhabitants to move further inland. The original colonists
were reinforced by fresh arrivals from Elis sometime after
700 B.C. and new colonies were established at Pandosia,
Bucheteion, Batiai and Elateia. Through their trading these
colonists came to dominate the economy of south-western
Epirus.

The Eleans were followed by the more powerful Corinthians
who founded Ambracia and other colonies along the shores of
the Ionian. This ended Elean expansion but there is no
evidence that they were enemies, for Thucydides reported ten
Elean warships with the Corinthians at Syvota. The Corinthians lost their ascendancy towards the end of the fifth
century through Athenian victories and the rise to power in
Epirus of the pro-Athenian Molossians. The Eleans seemed
largely unaffected at first, except that they erected defences
round their cities, a sign either of heightened tension during
that period or of increasing affluence or both.

The Eleans may have differed little from the other inhabitants of south-west Epirus because, before settling several
centuries earlier in Elis, they perhaps originated on the
western mainland and might still have spoken a north-west
dialect not dissimilar to that, for example, of the Cassopaians.
The Eleans were primarily concerned with agriculture but
they had also acquired in the Peloponnese the more sophisticated skills of Mycenae. They were thus able to offer the
Epirot shepherds such handicraft products as jewellery, pottery and weapons in exchange for timber, skins, wool, oil and
other local products from the interior. Assuming that
Pandosia, the colonists' capital, was at Kastri, Sotiris Dakaris
has estimated its population in the middle of the fourth
century B.C. at four thousand. The other Elean settlements
were smaller.

In 343–342 B.C., the Eleans lost their independence through
Philip II of Macedon's campaign in Threspotia and were
made subjects of the Cassopaians, whose capital, Cassope,
enjoys a remarkable site on Mount Zalongo above the sea.

The road thither took us back to Kastri, where it runs briefly inside the city's outer defences, and from there, via Kanalaki, back to Mount Zalongo, up which our taxi climbed eastwards to the enchanting village of Kriopiyi (cold spring). The village, which faces south-west towards the sea, nestles under plane trees, the air refreshed by the many ice-cold streams—as the name of the village implies—which tumble down the mountainside. Cassope stands well above Kriopiyi on a southward facing plateau some 1,600–1,700 feet high on Zalongo's slopes which rise to over 2,400 feet immediately to the north of the site. Below lies the dark blue Ionian with the greener waters of the Ambracian Gulf to its east. Beyond the great inland Gulf, the hills of Acarnania fade into the distance towards Aetolia. The square mountainous island of Levkas, its slopes dark green with olive and cypress trees, stands high to the west of the Gulf's narrow exit at Preveza, with Ithaka and Cephalonia in the hazier distance beyond.

Due east of Cassope can be seen the little Monastery of Kozyle, below the legendary Zalongo cliff. Above, on the crown of the hill, is a line of vast, flat, cement figures, dancing with hands linked together towards the precipice, thus commemorating the most dramatic of the many memorable incidents of the Souli Wars. The monument, sculptured by Zongolopoulos and erected in 1954, is unexpected, quite out of place and, when seen from a distance, surprisingly successful.

A little to the west of the monastery, now dedicated to St Demetrios, are the foundations of a temple, the only one so far discovered at Cassope. It probably belonged to Aphrodite, the principal deity of the Cassopaians; her cult may have descended to them via Gaia, the earth mother to whom the oracle at Dodona was first consecrated.

Beyond Cassope, the road descends back on to that leading to Preveza after passing Kamarina, where Edward Lear spent a night in May 1849, on his way to visit the ruins above. So heavy was the rain that 'the Painter of Poetical Topography' had to content himself with sketching the scenery from the doorway of the cottage. Lear, like Hughes who also passed a night here, was captivated by the view of the Ambracian Gulf and the Ionian spread out below, 'nor', he added, 'can I remember a village more deliciously placed as a summer's retreat; the rain has made the herbs and spring flowers around full of fresh odour, and multitudes of nightingales are singing on all sides.'

Cassope had other advantages in addition to the beauty of its situation. It is protected from the north, is away from the malarial mosquito which once lurked around the Gulf, and has copious supplies of fresh water; cisterns were built high up close to the northern defences in case the city should be besieged. Cassope is also near the main routes of south-west Epirus and has easy access to two ports, one at Kastrosikia, due south on the Ionian, and the other at Mikhalitsi on the Gulf; Dakaris considers the latter to have been Berenice, founded by Pyrrhus and named after his mother-in-law, but Hammond favours Kastrosikia as its site.

Cassope, which developed into a city-state in the fourth and third centuries B.C., was originally a centre for the gatherings of a tribe, officially known as the Cassopaians, but probably called the Amymnoi locally, whose settlements were scattered about the area. As the isolation of Epirus was broken through the Peloponnesian Wars and later through contact with Sicily and Magna Graecia, so these outlandish tribes adopted the standards and trappings of the older, more sophisticated Hellenic states. Cassope gained considerable wealth, judging by what must have been the splendour of its public buildings. In addition to the walls, probably erected early in the fourth century B.C., and the acropolis near Zalongo's mountain crest in the north-west corner, there are well laid-out remains of a fine *prytaneion* or guest house, of an *agora* or market place, together with a *stoa* or covered walk on its west and north sides and, due east, a small theatre or council place on raised ground. There is another, much larger theatre high up to the north-west above the gentle incline of the plateau on which the city centre, built on the grid system, once stood. The seats of the larger theatre, which look like those of Dodona before restoration, were still scattered in disorder in 1973.

The walls of the city, whose peak population was about nine thousand, were enlarged at least once, but the Roman vengeance of 167 B.C. on the Molossian cities included Cassope and those of the Elean colonists. Even the Nekromanteion is said to have suffered.

Rome allowed a revival of the old Cassopaian federation, based this time on Pandosia, which issued its own coinage from about 167 to 148 B.C. and repaired some of its defences, but by the latter date, the federation had moved either to Dodona or to Cassope, where the *prytaneion* was partly restored and used perhaps as a town hall. In any case, the life of these cities did not long survive. Octavius's victory at Acteion in 31 B.C. allowed him to establish the new city of Nikopolis, where Roman interests could best be served. Those still living in patched-up accommodation in Cassope and the cities of the Elean colonies were rounded up and made to live in this city of victory, together with Roman settlers, many of them retired servicemen. There was also some Roman settlement in the countryside. The remains of a Roman bath and of floor mosaics have been discovered both in the Louros Plain at Strongyli and at Sistrouni in Lakkasouli. These may have been built by Roman farmers who supplied Nikopolis with provisions, but none of these estates survived the arrival of the barbarians who destroyed the Roman settlements as the Romans had previously razed to the ground those of the Molossians.

20

The Louros Plain and Nikopolis

South of the foothills which guard the entrances to Lakka-souli spreads the broad plain of the Louros, swelled by its tributaries including the springs of St George. The plain opens out after passing untidy, bucolic Philippeas whose belfry is crowned by a stork's nest. A bridge takes the main road to Arta south-east across the river into endless orchards of orange and lemon trees. The Louros Plain itself, however, has remained marshy in parts, especially towards the Gulf, and the rest provides pasturage for cattle, sheep and goats.

The Louros is an inconstant river, for it has changed its course more than once. Originally it flowed south into the eastern fringes of the Tsoukalio Lagoon, where there was once a natural harbour, facing towards the Ambracian Gulf. It then carved out another course which swung further west into the heart of the marshland, reaching the Lagoon at a point much further inland near Strongyli. The present channel leaves the earlier ones to the east, just beyond the southern end of the hill on which Rogoi stands, some three miles south of Philippeas, and curves, first west and then south, to reach the Gulf close to the Preveza peninsula beyond the Tsoukalio Lagoon and close to Mikhalitsi.

Rogous or Rogoi is the name given to the ruins of the Byzantine castle which was constructed on the foundations of one of the Elean settlements which developed into the stronghold of Bucheteion. From the Ioannina–Preveza road its walls are clearly and impressively seen, but it appears to be rarely visited. The only other occupants, when we arrived there one Sunday morning, were flocks of sheep and some goats in the charge of a shepherd, drowsing in the shade of a wall.

More attention was paid to the site by English travellers in the nineteenth century. Edward Lear was one. 'This fortress,' he wrote, 'standing on an ancient site, forms a part of one of those beautiful Greek scenes which a painter is never tired of contemplating. Rising on its mound above the thick woods which here embellish the plain, it is the key of the landscape; the waters of a clear fountain are surrounded by huge flocks of goats reposing. The clumps of hanging plane and spreading oak, vary the marshy plain, extending to the shores of the Gulf; while the distant blue mountains rise beyond, and the rock of Zalongo shuts in the northern end of the prospect.'

Both Leake and Hughes supposed that here was probably the site of Charadra, although Professor Hammond places this stronghold further north in the Louros Gorge. Leake was scholarly and factual in his descriptions, but Hughes had a good eye for colour and obviously derived much pleasure from the behaviour of the Albanian *palikars* escorting his party, as they moved with incredible agility on the look-out for *banditti*, who were said to haunt this area, letting off their muskets and pistols at intervals. Their arrival at Rogoi found the ruins deserted, except for two or three huge snakes with which the plain is said to be plentifully supplied. We saw no snakes during our visit but once, when walking close to the Kalamas with Kenneth Johnstone from Menina, where our vehicle had broken down, to Igoumenitsa, I saw such a reptile, a species of grass snake nearly five feet long, hissing stridently as it moved across our path.

From the Preveza road, we walked down past a line of cypresses and then more steeply uphill towards Rogoi under the inadequate shade of an ancient olive grove. On arrival at the brow of the hill we faced the oldest of the walls. Alone of the Elean colonies, its history did not end with the foundation of Nikopolis.

Bucheteion, the original name of the settlement—for *bous* is Greek for bull—is traditionally derived from the arrival here of a bull, bearing on its back either Leto or Thetis, after the flood of Deucalion; a suitable name to find in a cattle-raising area. The site was already occupied in the sixth century B.C., as shown by the discovery of south Hellenic sherds of that period in the oldest part of the settlement. The most ancient of the walls, that on the crest of the hill, was built in ashlar style probably towards the end of the fifth century. Well-cut rectangular blocks of stone rise to about twelve feet, to which extensive repairs and additions were probably made during the Byzantine period.

Between the end of the first building development and 343–2 B.C., when the Elean colonies became subject to the Cassopaians, there was a second expansion, due west of the original site. The structure of the walls both of this second period and of the third, when an area in size of the first two settlements together was extended north of them, was polygonal in style. Towers were built at intervals along these walls, the larger ones by the Cassopaians.

Bucheteion, like the other Elean settlements, suffered from the Roman devastation of 167 B.C. The walls of the first two sites were, however, repaired between then and the foundation of Nikopolis, and the ancient stones used again in conjunction with bricks of the Hellenistic and Roman periods laid in mortar. The Roman authorities allowed some refortification at a time when, in spite of raids from Thrace during the first century B.C., Roman settlers were apparently arriving in this part of Epirus. The creation of Nikopolis put an end to the revival of Buchoteion.

After Nikopolis, little is known of the history of this stronghold until the Byzantine era. By the ninth century A.D., there is mention of a bishopric of Kozyle and Rogoi, its Byzantine name, which indicates that a sizable township had grown up here, one which then outranked Arta, probably because its harbour was the most important on the Ambracian Gulf; for the Louros was then navigable at least as far as this point. Later it became a key defence point during the Despotate of Epirus. Repairs were carried out as late as the fourteenth century; these can be distinguished from earlier efforts by the use of small bricks and stones laid horizontally in rows.

A wonderful peacefulness today surrounds Rogoi. As we looked south-westwards through the faint heat mist which hovered over the plain, where the dark green Louros meandered towards the Gulf, we saw a little flurry of wind rustle and bend the grass with its scatterings of wild flowers, so that for an instant it seemed that the waters of the Gulf were lapping at the foot of the hill on which we stood. Here anchored the Frankish ship whose captain had stolen the sacred remains of St Luke when the Crusaders brutally sacked Constantinople in 1204. He sold them to the Duke of Cephalonia, who placed them in a shrine in the town. They were still there in 1448 when, on St Luke's Day, Cyriacus of Ancona came here from Arta to worship at the Saint's reliquary. With the advance of the Turks, the Apostolic remains were taken to Smederovo on the Danube, east of Belgrade, and Rogoi became largely deserted.

But not entirely. Here in the area on which the earliest part of Bucheteion was built, we came upon the little church of the Panaghia, its nave and its lower standing narthex both whitewashed; a monastery once stood beside it. The interior, although obviously used from time to time, judging by the burnt-out candles, was little cared for. But reminders of past importance were there—a Byzantine decorated marble slab, perhaps from a tomb or screen, was now used as a step from the narthex into the single nave of the church. Outside, on the wall of the narthex, was a finely carved cross, also in white marble. The only sound was the buzzing of a fly inside the church and the distant muffled bells of the sheep. Below, to the northwest, a ploughed field lay like a ruffled fawn carpet between the tower-dominated Hellenistic north-west wall and the Louros, moving secretly behind the trees on its bank which here protected it from view.

Cyriacus of Ancona ventured down the river to reach the Ambracian Gulf east of Nikopolis, where he was shown the supposed shrine of Dodonaean Jupiter, and marvelled at the extent of the ancient walls and ruins. My first view of this vast and once populous city was in 1944 from an army truck, driving along the pot-holed road from Philippeas to Preveza just after the German withdrawal. The road follows the course of the Louros at a safe distance and swings south-west under the hill of Mikhalitsi to avoid the Mazoma Lagoon, an inlet of the Gulf, before continuing south for the remaining three miles into Preveza. Even in the torrential rain of that autumn afternoon, the vastness of the site impressed.

The brick-built ruins of Nikopolis were obviously of Roman construction and in Preveza we heard something of the fine mosaics which had been discovered there as recently as 1915. The huts, which had been erected to protect what has been described as the finest group of mosaics in the Balkans, had, we were told, been used as shelter by Italian troops during the Occupation. Parts of these pavements are badly damaged, but not necessarily for this reason.

Nikopolis, built by Octavius, later Augustus Caesar, to celebrate his naval victory over Antony and Cleopatra at nearby Acteion in 31 B.C., became the Roman headquarters for Epirus, Acarnania and Aetolia down to the Gulf of Corinth. It was an ideal staging post for merchantmen sailing between Italy and the Levant. The gently sloping Ionian shores both north and south of the entrance to the Gulf were suitable for beaching the sea-going craft of that time. In addition to the Greeks from the surrounding area, many Roman ex-servicemen were settled here. Nikopolis was also sufficiently prosperous to attract a Jewish colony with whom St Paul probably spent the winter of A.D. 64, as mentioned in his Epistle to Titus. Epictetus, a celebrated Stoic philosopher, came here to teach when banished from Rome by Domitius.

Nikopolis was built spaciously where the Roman army had encamped before the battle. Embellished with many fine palaces and temples, the question of defence was largely ignored. City walls were built but on the west side they also served to support the aqueduct from the springs of St George on the Louros. Now that Augustus Caesar bestrode the Mediterranean world like a colossus, what forces, Greek or otherwise, could possibly endanger the Roman Empire, let alone Nikopolis?

Unlike Rome, however, Nikopolis was not to be eternal. Mamertinus, according to Christopher Wordsworth, informed the Emperor Julian in the middle of the fourth century that the city had fallen into lamentable decay; the houses of the nobility were in ruin, the public buildings roofless, the aqueduct crumbling and dust and rubbish everywhere. Malaria from the Gulf of Ambracia must have been prevalent, but could this have been sufficient to humble Augustus's city? There must have been a revival under Byzantium in the fifth century to make its sacking attractive to Genseric and his Vandals in 475. The city must have recovered once more for it was plundered again in 551, this time by Totila and the Huns.

Later in the sixth century, the Emperor Justinian (527–65) restored part of the city and built the great wall which runs parallel and a little to the west of the modern road; for material he used the remains of earlier Roman buildings. The Byzantine citadel, protected by this wall, covered only about a third of the original city, for the area to the west was left in ruins. Yet it is here that the most impressive single building among the ruins, the Roman Odeion, still stands and is used on occasion for summer theatre. Its solid construction of bricks and mortar rises on its own foundation, instead of being cut for support into the side of a hill as was more usually the case.

It was late afternoon when we passed through the arch of the west gate of the Byzantine wall, once guarded by strong points on both sides, and shadows were climbing up the golden-pink semi-circular auditorium of the Odeion, which faces north towards Mikhalitsi. In between, bushes, scrub and the occasional tree stood on the uneven ground which still conceals much of the Roman city. The general scene cannot have changed all that much since John Sibthorp's visit in 1795. Sibthorp, who was Sherrardian Professor of Botany at Oxford University and spent some five years in Greece to collect plants, was interested in the past and observant about the present; it was here that he was taken ill and returned to England only to die at Bath. In his Journal, reproduced in part in R. Walpole's *Travels in the East*, 1820, he wrote: 'Arriving in Nikopolis, we were shown an oak tree, which is in this place the boundary mark. The ruins are very considerable and extensive, and the broken walls, built of brick, encompass a large circuit. . . . The situation of Nikopolis on a gentle rise approaching the mountains, commanding Actium and the Gulf of Arta, is beautiful and striking, and the extent of the remains are evidence of its former magnificence. The plough is continually turning up ancient ornaments or memorials. I saw several gems, and large collections of coins have been made within its ruins.'

In 1801, soon after Sibthorp, when the Rev. Philip Hunt toured Greece on behalf of Lord Elgin to warn the Pashas against the machinations of France—and to keep a weather eye open for antiquities—Ali Pasha promised to send to the British Ambassador in Constantinople anything of interest, adding, tantalizingly, that he but recently destroyed several statues which 'only seemed to want breath'. Ali Pasha was always hopeful of finding treasure. Holland found him eighteen years after Sibthorp's visit sitting on a crimson velvet couch near one of the walls, close to where excavations were being made. Perhaps his most important find was a bust of Trajan which was later to be seen in his *serai* in Preveza.

The largest building, the great brick theatre, capable of seating some twenty thousand, is cut into the sides of Mikhalitsi and towers above the modern road. It was originally built early in the life of the city and later restored, perhaps by Justinian. Much of the auditorium is today covered with verdure and the stage buildings, like those of the Odeion, are somewhat battered. It was at the top of this hill, beyond the little village of Smyrtoula, that Octavius pitched his camp before his victory; after it, he erected a temple here in gratitude to Apollo, remains of which are still to be seen. Later the bronze statues, which embellished this edifice, were taken to Constantinople, only to be melted down with many other relics by the Crusaders in 1204. Two of these effigies represented a peasant and his mule. Octavius met them while reconnoitring the position of Antony's fleet; on asking their names, he was told that the peasant was called *Eutyches* (or fortunate) and the mule *Nikon* (or victor), an incident which Octavius regarded as a highly favourable omen and afterwards placed their figures in his temple. Close to this site, Ali Pasha built himself a small *serai* so that he could watch in comfort and safety Muchtar's attack on Preveza in 1798.

To the west of the theatre, a large sports stadium was raised over a long narrow depression. Today it is almost completely overgrown, but the few visible remains leave no doubt as to its use. The Acteion games, which had originally been celebrated on the southern shore of the Gulf opposite Preveza, were transferred here. The modern road passes close to its rounded eastern end; a little further on, close to where it is joined by the road from Paramythia, there are the ruins of the public baths.

In due course, as Christianity replaced the pagan gods, churches were built here; the ruins of three basilicas are to be found within the Byzantine periphery, one of which, that built close to the northern Byzantine wall, is only just discernible today. The remains of the other two are sufficient to give a clear picture of their design and something of their history as revealed by their mosaics and the accompanying inscriptions.

What is left of the church, dedicated to St Demetrios, stands close to the modern museum and is known as the Dometios basilica after the name of its founder who lived at the end of the fifth and well into the sixth century. The other basilica is named the Alkyson after its founding bishop and lies just to the east of the main road, where it runs parallel to the Byzantine wall. Although there is no list of bishops of Nikopolis until the end of the sixth century, it is probable that Dometios succeeded rather than preceded Alkyson, who died in 516, and that the church of St Demetrios with its fine mosaics was erected in the second quarter of the sixth century, during the earlier years of Justinian's reign. A second Dometios was responsible for the mosaics in the atrium of the church, the quality of which is cruder than those of his predecessor; these may have been executed after the city was sacked by the Huns in 551.

The two mosaics from the transept wings of St Demetrios are in the museum. That from the north transept portrays an island on which grow fruit trees, flanked by a cypress at each side; the fruit is depicted in red and yellow hues against a background of dark green. Birds stand in front of the trees or fly above them. Around this central panel is a decorative band, beyond which there is water in which fish abound. Below the central picture there is a bold inscription which makes clear that the mosaic represents the universe in which the earth is seen surrounded by the boundless ocean; it concludes by saying that the church is 'the foundation of Dometios, the great-hearted archpriest'.

The meaning of the mosaic from the south transept is not so clear, because the inscription has been badly damaged. The central panel is filled by two full-length figures of armed men in between whom a large tree grows. Around this panel is a broad band in which hunting scenes are depicted. This mosaic is pagan in feeling but could be a symbolic rendering of paradise, according to Ernst Kitzinger's essay on the 'Mosaics of Nikopolis', published in *Dumbarton Oaks Papers* No. 6 (1951). The two central gladiatorial figures could represent martyrs who had triumphed in moral strife. The basilica of Bishop Alkyson also contains mosaics but they are in much poorer condition; this church also contains a circular pedestal with a Hellenistic relief of a battle.

As a result of Justinian's restoration, the city flourished for a time. Early in the eighth century, Leo the Isaurian made it the capital of the *theme* for Western Greece. Later, with the Slav invasions, its position became untenable and the administration was accordingly moved to Navpaktos. How soon Nikopolis became completely deserted is not known. The Bulgarians were here in 1040 and doubtlessly did further damage as did the occasional earthquake, for the city stands on an earthquake zone which runs south through Ioannina along the Louros river and continues through Levkas to the southern Ionian Islands. It is likely that life continued for some time further. Cyriacus of Ancona found one Turnus celebrating his daughter's marriage here some four centuries later. By the time that Ali Pasha started probing among the ruins, the city must have been completely abandoned. Hughes dreamt of it rising again in terms of an early nineteenth-century revival with churches built on the sites of the temples, the gymnasium converted into a tennis court and the stadium into a riding school!

21

Preveza

Preveza at the south-west tip of Epirus stands at the entrance to the Ambracian Gulf. Between it and Nikopolis stretch what were once magnificent olive groves, planted under the Venetians. It is the main cargo port for Epirus. Byron and Hobhouse, Holland, Hughes and other travellers first set foot here on Epirot soil. A few years earlier, the Hon. Frederick North, later the fifth Earl of Guilford, gave five hundred piastres, according to Leake, 'towards the establishment of a school, by means of which and other donations a small house was built at the gate of the principal church. It has since been converted into a court of justice but there is a school in which writing is taught, with a sufficiency of ancient Greek to read the Testament.' This gift was probably made between 1788 and 1791, when North made his first prolonged stay in Greece and was baptized into the Greek Orthodox Church in Corfu.

Until 1797 the town had long been a dependency of Venice. After the Peace of Campo Formio, the French installed a garrison of a thousand here under General La Salsette. News, however, of Napoleon's absence in Egypt and the consequent outbreak of war between Turkey and France gave Ali an opportunity of achieving his ambition of seizing both Preveza and Vonitsa, which is on the southern shore of the Ambracian Gulf. On 12 November 1798, some six thousand Albanians under Muchtar took up positions around Preveza's neglected defences. Then, enflamed by the *mullahs*, they worked themselves into a frenzy and their charge swept away all resistance. The severed heads of the French were piled up like cannon balls, to be carried by those still living in a ghastly march over the Pindus to Constantinople at the beginning of winter. The Greeks of Preveza also suffered. As many as possible were slaughtered by the Albanians, so that they could take over their possessions; their heads, after their moustaches had been shaved off, were also sent to the Bosphorus with the pretence that they too were French. Before 1798, Preveza's population was said to have been between ten and sixteen thousand; Hughes in 1813 estimated the number at no more than three thousand.

Yet Preveza, at least at a distance, had immense charm. Hughes, sailing from Levkas, wrote: 'At length a prospect truly oriental rose to view. This was Preveza, with its gorgeously painted seraglio, forts and minarets, surrounding that fine inlet of the Ambracian Gulf where a cold-blooded tyrant and a hot-brained debauchee contended for the empire of the world.' The seraglio was burnt down by Ali's son, Veli, when besieged by the Sultan's troops in 1820, but Hughes's remarks referred to the battle of Acteion in 31 B.C., fought between Octavius and Antony off the entrance to the Gulf.

Acteion is the name of the little promontory opposite Preveza, where once stood a temple to Apollo. It was here, late in 32 B.C., that Antony had brought his fleet and army from Egypt, having, under the complete domination of Cleopatra of Egypt, thrown down a challenge to Octavius for the mastery of the Roman world. He did this by supporting the declaration that Caesarion, Cleopatra's natural son by Julius Caesar, and not Octavius, was the true heir to Julius. If he had struck quickly against Italy, Antony might have succeeded. Instead, he preferred to winter in Athens with Cleopatra in 33–32 B.C. Having established his navy in the Ambracian Gulf, and his army to the south of Actcion, he again turned back for the winter, this time to Patras.

These delays gave Octavius his opportunity of deploying his smaller forces; his army camped where Nikopolis was later to rise and his fleet was stationed in the Ionian outside the entrance to the Gulf, thus bottling up Antony's armada and preventing a further advance towards Italy. When Antony returned to Acteion in the spring of 31, he found himself completely trapped. Should he retreat with his larger army from the Gulf to more favourable ground in the hope that Octavius would follow him, or should he try to break through the blockading fleet? An important consideration was the large number of warships, belonging to his Asiatic allies, which would have to be abandoned if he followed the first course. Time dragged on through the spring and summer of 31. Eventually at the beginning of September, under pressure because of sickness, desertion among his troops and supply difficulties he decided upon the second course.

His mixed fleet advanced in close order upon the Romans. In front were his enormous galleys with from six to ten banks of oars, their decks crammed with troops. In the rear was Cleopatra's own squadron of fast sailing ships. Antony had calculated that Octavius's fleet, under the command of Agrippa, would advance into the Straits and be crushed, but this Agrippa was resolved to avoid.

A freshening wind helped decide the issue. Antony was forced to extend his fleet into more open water, which gave Agrippa his opportunity to attack. Antony's unwieldy ships were fighting resolutely against the swift, lighter, more elusive craft of the Romans when, at the height of the action, Cleopatra's squadron was suddenly seen with its sails fully spread in flight, making for the open sea and the south. Antony, blind to the consequences, quickly followed, leaving his now unco-ordinated armada to fend for itself. His fleet fought on, but his great galleys fell easy victims to the fire balls which the Romans catapulted into them. By nightfall Octavius was completely victorious, joined by Antony's army. He speedily regained control over the vassal Roman states in Asia Minor, which Cleopatra had claimed for herself, and then annexed Egypt as a Roman province. In the meanwhile, Antony and Cleopatra had committed suicide.

Another sea battle was fought in these waters over fifteen centuries later. In 1537, during the long drawn-out struggle between Christendom and Islam for mastery of the Mediterranean, Kheir-ed-din Barbarossa, the Turkish admiral, had sailed up the Ionian as far as Apulia, while Andrea Doria, the only Christian admiral thought capable of opposing him, lay becalmed in the Messina roads. Barbarossa, frustrated at not achieving a battle, ravaged the Ionian Islands, including Corfu, as his great slave-driven galleys turned back towards the Levant.

A year later, Andrea Doria was in a much better position.

In Corfu harbour he marshalled under his command the combined fleets of Genoa, Venice and the Papacy. Anchors were then weighed and the great armada swept out in search of the enemy. Barbarossa, informed of what was happening, hastened northwards from Crete, but was glad to slip through the Preveza channel into the Ambracian Gulf when he discovered that the Christian fleet was so much larger than his own. If Doria had seized the forts at Preveza, he could have bottled up Barbarossa with his guns. Alternatively, he could have followed the Turks into the Gulf, confident that his greatly superior fleet would give him victory.

Doria did neither; instead, he sailed away to the south, followed by a warily exultant Barbarossa, who sensed that there was something here to his advantage. Doria, it appeared, was primarily concerned for the safety of his fifty large Venetian galleons, the most up-to-date naval craft then in service in the Mediterranean. When Barbarossa caught up with the largest of these, there was a short sharp action in which the latter's well-aimed guns wrought havoc among the Turks. Doria was therefore urged by his commanders to attack. This Doria refused to do and instead sailed away back to Corfu, leaving the smaller Turkish fleet in command of the sea.

The Venetians, who already had trading rights in the area, first occupied Preveza in 1499. Afterwards the town changed hands several times. It is unlikely that the Venetians were in occupation when Barbarossa fled into the Gulf in 1538. Morosini took the town in 1684, after capturing Levkas from the Turks, but the port was returned to the latter by the Treaty of Carlowitz in 1699. In 1715 the commander of the Venetian defences of Corfu, Count von der Schulenburg, a tough professional soldier who had fought with distinction under Marlborough in Flanders, hustled the Turks out of Corfu and out of Levkas, Preveza and Vonitsa as well. From then until 1797 the town remained under the Lion of St Mark during a period when internal law and order were breaking down as La Serenissima had no longer the means of maintaining them. Everybody was allowed to carry arms in self-protection at a time when open robbery and murder were common events.

The Russo-Turkish agreement of 1800 forced Ali Pasha
to surrender Preveza and Vonitsa to the Sultan, who appointed
a bey to collect the taxes and a garrison commander with
thirty-six men. When Leake went there in 1805, he recorded
that most of the best houses, many of them Venetian, together
with several churches, were in ruin as a result of Ali's assault,
and that the greater part of the dwellings were but wretched
huts made of wattle branches, plastered with mud. Yet he
was able to say that Preveza was still a very agreeable town
because of the abundance of gardens and olive groves beyond
them. Venetian courts of law were still administered by Greek
magistrates who gave directions to the garrison commander.
There was still a Maggior Consiglio, composed of forty noble-
men who elected the magistrates. The Russian consul made
sure that neither Ali Pasha nor the garrison commander
encroached on the privileges of the townspeople.

The Turks grew tired of the expense of administering this
remote little port. This and the withdrawal of the Russians
after the Peace of Tilsit in 1807 gave Ali the free hand he
desired. He therefore took over Preveza and set about
destroying the Greeks financially in order to make way for his
Albanians. The one source of prosperity which the Vizier of
Ioannina did not seize were the fisheries, because it was the
sort of work which did not appeal to Muslims. The Ambracian
Gulf was then, as now, teeming with fish, including shrimps,
and the fishing rights were retained by a group of Greek
families of Preveza.

The only new houses, built after Ali's assumption of power,
were, according to Hughes, the few erected for 'their Turkish
despoilers, and', he added, 'with the melancholy dejection of
the fallen Greeks is contrasted the stately dignity of the
turbaned Osmanlee or the haughty strut of the Albanian
mountaineer with his flowing hair and white capote thrown
loosely over his shoulders.' Hughes also remarked upon the
new mosque, erected by Ali 'contrary to the solemn faith of
treaties, for the service of those who were now fattening on the
spoils of unfortunate Preveza.'

But if the town's Greek inhabitants were too exhausted and
poverty-stricken to rebuild their own homes, Ali was quick to
make them strengthen the town's defences. In Venetian days,

two forts, now dilapidated, had been built; the Pantocrator still
faces the Ionian and the St George the channel into the Gulf.
To these Ali added two more—the New Fortress, sometimes
called St Andrew's and just to the north of St George's,
close to the town, and the Punta on the opposite side of the
Preveza channel, a ramshackle structure which was occupied
by EAM/ELAS in the autumn of 1944. Ali also caused a
deep ditch to be built across the isthmus and strengthened
the defences with artillery, which consisted, according to
Cockerell, of ancient English cannon of all sorts and sizes 'in
the worst possible order and rotten as well'. Here also was the
one vessel of Ali's navy, a Hydriot merchantman which he had
seized and converted into a frigate; it had a Turkish captain
for the Turkish members of the crew and a Greek captain
for the Greeks.

Ali's downfall was often attributed to his meanness; the
Preveza cannon would have been useless against professional
troops. Yet he had the sense to improve communications in
Epirus. A road was built from Salaora to Arta and most of the
way onwards to Ioannina. Ali also constructed a canal between
Arta and Preveza, according to Cockerell who, like others
who had no dealings with him, found him an agreeable old
blackguard.

The Turks reoccupied Preveza during their campaign
against Ali and held it continuously until 1912. During these
nine decades, it remained a sleepy little port facing eastwards,
its back to the open sea. In 1890 there was a stirring of life
when the Turks made it the chief port of entry into Epirus
by opening up the Ioannina–Preveza road. As a result Salaora
fell into decay. The later incorporation of Preveza and Ioannina into Greece at the same time ensured that the two centres
continued to work together.

Preveza finally became Greek in 1912. The First Balkan
War started in mid-October that year with Serbia, Bulgaria
and Montenegro in alliance against Turkey. The Greeks
joined this alliance three days later, with many volunteers
returning home from as far away as Egypt, Odessa and New
York to serve under the blue and white flag. The Greeks at
once crossed the bridge of Arta into Ottoman Epirus and
some two weeks later attacked and pushed back into Preveza

the Turkish garrison encamped at Nikopolis. On 3 November, the Greek attack on Preveza started at first light and lasted until sundown when the Turks capitulated.

In 1944 Preveza was again liberated, first from the Germans in mid-September, and again towards the end of the month from EAM/ELAS. Preveza, together with Ioannina and Arta, was in 1944 regarded as an EDES stronghold; this was a few days later confirmed at Caserta, where Zervas of EDES and Sarafis of ELAS were taken to confer with General Maitland Wilson, the Supreme Allied Commander, and given their instructions about their role, now that a British force was going into Greece to expedite the withdrawal of the Germans, and the Greek Government in exile was returning to Athens. Before this had taken place, General Mandakas of ELAS had infiltrated troops into Preveza and had seized the forts to the south of the town. EDES reached the town shortly afterwards but this did not deter some EAM supporters in Preveza from demonstrating against EDES and the Greek authorities. The ELAS forces withdrew on instructions from Caserta, but not before there had been some fierce fighting between the opposing guerillas and not before some EAM enthusiasts had suffered at the hands of EDES extremists. For the next two months under the greying skies of approaching winter, a great effort was made by the Allies to supply Epirus with badly needed food, clothing and equipment and some progress was made towards a return to normality.

The outbreak of fighting between EAM/ELAS and the Greek government in Athens quickly involved British troops. It also became clear that EDES forces in Epirus would be attacked. Zervas had weakened his own position by loyally carrying out Allied instructions to hand over EDES's small-arms ammunition to ELAS. It was argued that since Epirus was free of Germans, EDES had no further need for this ammunition. Enemy troops were still in Macedonia, whose departure ELAS, said to be short of ammunition, could expedite if Zervas would co-operate in this way. This ammunition was soon to be used against the Greek authorities, Allied troops and EDES.

ELAS began to attack EDES in Epirus on 18 December and Preveza soon became filled with refugees from Ioannina and elsewhere in search of transport to the Ionian Islands and beyond. EDES personnel retired in good order under Zervas to Preveza and were transported to Corfu by the British and Greek navies together with all the refugees they could carry. Christmas Day, 1944, was spent in loading what could be carried away by ship and on the following day a long line of naval craft sailed up the Epirot coast towards Corfu under a green enamel sky while a thick black oily column of smoke rose straight up into the still air from the destruction of stores at Preveza which could not be carried away.

Today, Preveza is inhabited by a quiet, comparatively prosperous community. The roads are in good repair as are the colour-washed houses which add a haphazard picturesqueness to the Eastern Mediterranean scene. The population, which before the war was a little under nine thousand, has now grown to nearly twelve thousand, their interests mainly commercial. Every evening from about six onwards, the inhabitants, like those of Ioannina and Arta, stroll up and down the waterfront facing on to the Gulf, where two or three merchantmen are usually tied up. Here also are the usual cafés and an open-air cinema in summer but, in spite of the proximity of Nikopolis, there is little catering for tourists, although a coastal resort is coming to life on the western shores of the Preveza peninsula. Preveza is the hottest town in Epirus in summer so the atmosphere becomes sultry and the inhabitants are inclined to emerge from their homes only in the evening when it becomes a fraction cooler.

There are now few signs of antiquity, of Venice or of Ali Pasha in the town. The architecture though tidy is undistinguished, the churches well-kept but unpretentious. The principal church is that of St Nicolas in the centre of the town; although of Byzantine origin, the present structure was erected under the Turks and shows a strong Ionian Island influence. There are flowering shrubs everywhere.

Preveza, facing the Gulf's tepid waters, is provincial and mundane, without the blessings of Arta's Byzantine churches or of the invigorating air of Ioannina. There is no escape from here except by bus back to Arta or Ioannina or an occasional caique to Levkas. But nearly every Greek town has some jewel to offer and Preveza is no exception. Holland wrote that from here 'the dark mountains of Souli and the snow-capt summits of the more distant Pindus form one of the most magnificent backgrounds the imagination can offer.' Holland was absolutely right. The view is there to be seen from the quay, a beckoning promise of stupendous scenery, of lingering traditions older than history, of ancient sanctuaries, of ruined monuments raised by oppressors who have since passed away, of highland stone villages and glorious painted churches, of the presence of a sturdy independent people for whom danger and suffering have rarely been far away, a people who in spite of the infusion of fresh blood from time to time have remained endowed, in part by their physical surroundings, with the qualities needed to survive triumphantly. This view across Epirus to 'one of the most magnificent backgrounds the imagination can offer' will continue to beckon as long as memory lasts.

Bibliography

Anderson, Patrick, *Over the Alps*, London, 1969
Auty, P. and Clogg, R. (eds), *British Policy Towards Wartime Resistance in Yugoslavia and Greece*, London, 1975
Blake, Robert, *Disraeli*, London, 1966
Boardman, John, *The Greeks Overseas*, London, 1964
Bosset, Lt-Colonel C. P. de, *Parga and the Ionian Islands*, London, 1821
Braudel, Fernand, *The Mediterranean*, London, 1972
Broughton, Lord (John Cam Hobhouse), *Travels in Albania and other provinces of Turkey in 1809 and 1810*, London, 1855
Campbell, J. K., *Honour, Family and Patronage*, Oxford, 1964
Cervi, Mario, *The Hollow Legions*, London, 1972
Chirol, Valentine, *Twixt Greece and Turkey*, Edinburgh, 1881
Clogg, Richard (ed.), *The Struggle for Greek Independence*, London, 1973
Cockerell, C. R. (ed. Cockerell, S. P.), *Travels in Southern Europe and the Levant*, London, 1903
Comnena, Anna, *The Alexiad*, trans. Elizabeth A. S. Dawes, London, 1928
Cross, G. N., *Epirus: a Study in Greek Constitutional Development*, Cambridge, 1932
Curzon, Robert, *Visits to the Monasteries in the Levant*, London, 1849
Dakaris, S. I., *Cassopaia and the Elean Colonies*, Athens, 1971
—, *The Island of Ioannina* (in Greek), Athens, 1971
—, *Dodona*, trans. Elli Kirk-Deftereou, Ioannina, 1971
Dakin, Douglas, *Greek Struggle for Independence*, London, 1973
Davenport, R. A., *The Life of Ali Pasha*, London, 1837
Dupré, L., *Voyages à Athènes*, Paris, 1825

Bibliography

Eddy, Charles B., *Greece and the Greek Refugees*, London, 1931

Eliot, Sir C. (Odysseus), *Turkey in Europe*, London, 1900

Forster, Edward S., *A Short History of Modern Greece*, London, 1941

Foss, Arthur, *Ibiza and Minorca*, London, 1975

—, *The Ionian Islands*, London, 1969

Gibbon, Edward, *The Decline and Fall of the Roman Empire* (ed. Low, D. M.), London, 1960

Hammond, N. G. L., *Epirus*, Oxford, 1967

Hoeg, C., *Les Saracatsanes: un tribe nomadique grecque*, Paris, 1925

Hogarth, D. G., *The Nearer East*, London, 1902

Holland, Henry, *Travels in the Ionian Islands, Albania, Thessaly, Macedonia, etc.*, London, 1815

Hughes, the Rev. Thomas Smart, *Travels in Sicily, Greece and Albania*, London, 1820

Johnstone, Pauline, *Byzantine Tradition in Church Embroidery*, London, 1967

Kitzinger, E., 'The Mosaics of Nikopolis', in *Dumbarton Oaks Papers*, No. 6, 1951

Lancaster, Osbert, *Sailing to Byzantium*, London, 1969

Leake, William Martin, *Travels in Northern Greece*, London, 1835

Lear, Edward, *Travels of a Landscape Painter in Greece and Albania*, London, 1851

Leigh Fermor, Patrick, *Mani*, London, 1958

—, *Roumeli*, London, 1966

Liddell, Robert, *Mainland Greece*, London, 1965

Makriyannis, General (ed. Lidderdale, H. A.), *The Memoirs*, Oxford, 1966

Melas, Evi (ed.), *Temples and Sanctuaries of Ancient Greece*, London, 1973

Miller, William, *The Latins in the Levant*, Cambridge, 1908

—, *The Ottoman Empire and its Successors, 1801–1927*, Cambridge, 1936

Morley, John, *The Life of W. E. Gladstone*, London, 1903

Myers, E. C. W., *Greek Entanglement*, London, 1955

Nicol, D. M., *The Despotate of Epiros*, Oxford, 1957

—, *Meteora*, London, 1963

Bibliography

Nicolson, Harold, *Byron: the Last Journey*, London, 1924

O'Balance, Edgar, *The Greek Civil War*, London, 1966

Pallis, A. A., *Greek Miscellany*, Athens, 1964

Plomer, William, *Ali the Lion*, London, 1936

Pouqueville, F., *Voyages dans la Grèce*, Paris, 1820

Rodd, Rennell, *The Customs and Lore of Modern Greece*, London, 1892

Runciman, Sir Steven, *The Sicilian Vespers*, Cambridge, 1958

St Clair, William, *That Greece Might Still Be Free*, Oxford, 1972

Sweet-Escott, Bickham, *Greece: a Political and Economic Survey*, London, 1954

Urquhart, D., *The Spirit of the East*, London, 1838

Wace, A. J. B. and Thompson, M. S., *The Nomads of the Balkans*, London, 1914

Walpole, the Rev. Robert, *Travels in Various Countries of the East*, London, 1820

Ware, Timothy, *The Orthodox Church*, London, 1963

Wheler, Sir George, and Spon, Dr, *Journey through Italy, Dalmatia, Greece and the Levant*, London, 1678

Woodhouse, C. M., *Apple of Discord*, London, 1948

—, *The Philhellenes*, London, 1969

—, *The Story of Modern Greece*, London, 1968

—, *The Struggle for Greece, 1941–1949*, London, 1976

Wordsworth, Christopher, *Greece: Pictorial, Descriptive and Historical*, London, 1839

CLASSICAL WORKS

Herodotus, *The Histories*, trans. Aubrey de Selincourt, London, 1954

Homer, *The Iliad*, trans. E. V. Rieu, London, 1950

—, *The Odyssey*, trans. E. V. Rieu, London, 1946

Polybius, *Histories* (6 vols), trans. W. R. Paton, London, 1922–7

Strabo, *Geography* (8 vols), trans. H. I. Jones, London, 1923–32

Thucydides, *The Peloponnesian War*, trans. Rex Warner, London, 1954

Index

218

Index

Index

Index

Index

Index

Index